M000286250

Praise for *Beyond Emotional Intelligence*

"Michele Nevarez has done it! Her years of study and personal experience have come together in a beautiful way to deliver *Beyond Emotional Intelligence*. This is a book that melds intellect with humanity and provides a framework for truly understanding mind-based habits facilitating an existence with life's most valuable riches."

—Kim Ades
President and Founder of Frame of Mind Coaching and
The Journal That Talks Back

"Finally, a book that focuses on developing the inner landscape and habits that have profound impact on the quality of our life experience. Brilliant, insightful and actionable practices to take living to the next level through leveraging the power of your mind and the abilities you hold within to shape your everyday experience."

—Carla Reeves
Mindset Coach and Host of the podcast, Differently

"*Beyond Emotional Intelligence* takes the imperative yet intellectual subject of emotional intelligence and makes it as accessible as having a conversation about your most favorite ideas. This book creates a pathway for a generation of thinkers, doers and dreamers from all walks of life to understand themselves and those around them better. To me, it is a must-read."

—Deepak Ramola
Founder and Artistic Director of Project FUEL

BEYOND
EMOTIONAL
INTELLIGENCE

BEYOND EMOTIONAL INTELLIGENCE

A GUIDE TO ACCESSING YOUR
FULL POTENTIAL

S. MICHELE NEVAREZ

WILEY

Published by John Wiley & Sons, Inc., Hoboken, New Jersey.
Published simultaneously in Canada.

For general information on our other products and services or for technical support, please contact our Customer Care Department within the United States at (800) 762-2974, outside the United States at (317) 572-3993 or fax (317) 572-4002.

Wiley also publishes its books in a variety of electronic formats. Some content that appears in print may not be available in electronic formats. For more information about Wiley products, visit our web site at www.wiley.com.

Library of Congress Cataloging-in-Publication Data

Names: Nevarez, S. Michele, author.
Title: Beyond Emotional Intelligence : a guide to accessing your full potential / S. Michele Nevarez.
Description: Hoboken, New Jersey : Wiley, [2022] | Includes index.
Identifiers: LCCN 2021036639 (print) | LCCN 2021036640 (ebook) | ISBN 9781119800200 (hardback) | ISBN 9781119800224 (adobe pdf) | ISBN 9781119800217 (epub)
Subjects: LCSH: Self-actualization (Psychology) | Emotional intelligence.
Classification: LCC BF637.S4 N466 2022 (print) | LCC BF637.S4 (ebook) | DDC 158.1—dc23
LC record available at https://lccn.loc.gov/2021036639
LC ebook record available at https://lccn.loc.gov/2021036640

Cover Image: Barn Swallow: © Andrew Howe/Getty Images
Picture Frame: © amtitus/Getty Images
Cover Design: Wiley

SKY10030217_100121

To my father, Robert Carrizales: may the profound sense of love, gratitude, and loss I feel from our paths having but narrowly crossed—you departing as I was arriving—dissolve within the Dharmakaya level of aware emptiness. Let us meet where there is no coming and going or meeting and parting. Let us all meet in the open field of our own awareness.

Contents

x Contents

Preface

We all have habits, but we often don't take much, if any, time to consider the many kinds of habits we have, the purpose they each serve, or their impact on our lives and the lives of those around us. Take my grandma Harriett, for example, whose mental habits had steep consequences yet ultimately served as coping mechanisms as she attempted to organize her environment to deal with the unwieldy responsibilities placed upon her. She was born a twin in the 1920s, weighing in at three pounds. Not expected to live, the nurse attending her and her twin brother's birth took them both home, where she fed them goat's milk and kept them snuggled in cotton next to one another inside a cigar box, which she kept warm inside a propped-open oven—a story that no doubt bears the marks of a proper fairy tale. Over the course of her life, Harriett suffered from a series of "mental breakdowns"—a word that when uttered was always in hushed tones or guarded whispers. One of these said mental fallings out occurred following the birth of her fifth child—my mom. Each time Harriett suffered what was deemed a mental collapse, she was sent away to Warm Springs, which only later did I come to learn wasn't a resort where guests went to enjoy the salubrious effects of soaking in natural hot springs but was in fact the Wyoming state mental institution, where guests received generously dosed cocktails of medicine before, during, and after shock treatment. For all we know, Harriett was just experiencing postpartum depression each time she had a child or was having a difficult time coping as she attempted to raise her five children in a four-room shack without running water. Sadly, we'll never really know which came first, her "mental illness" or the "remedies" she received to treat it.

While we each have a unique constellation of circumstances and contexts in which we find ourselves, we must each ultimately make our way in this world. ***Our visible habits are born from the sum total of our life circumstances and experiences. But it is from our invisible habits of mind, our perceptions and how we make sense of them, that we set everything into motion.*** Though our brain mostly curates our experiences for us, it's up to each of us to figure out what we have at our own disposal to intervene. Not unlike attempting to juggle a set of Cutco knives, we often find ourselves facing a juxtaposition of unexpected and ever-evolving circumstances as we grapple with the intricacies of our own lives and those of the people around us. Yet we don't receive any formal training to navigate life's mysterious bits, which nonetheless represent the vast majority of what we wake up to and have to face each day. Instead, we don habits like armor as we go through life, making the best of it, crossing our fingers, hoping today isn't the day we'll come apart at the seams. Each habit we have serves one if not many purposes, one of which is as a coping mechanism we unconsciously craft and come to rely upon, often well past its expiration date. We continue to pull from the bank of experiences we've had up to this point as we attempt to make sense of and adapt to our surroundings. We are each the beneficiaries of the belief structures, the artifacts of meaning, passed down to us through the respective contexts influencing us since birth—our shared and unique lineages of sense-making.

As is the case with most of us at various points in our lives, Harriett's life circumstances exceeded her ability to cope with life's devastatingly precise blows. Harriett wound up getting married right out of high school and was immediately catapulted into a life of abject poverty, hard work, and the stress of dealing with situations she'd not encountered up to that point. As the story goes, she and her twin had supposedly been coddled as they were growing up, no doubt in response to the thread upon which they precariously glided into this life and upon which they remained delicately balanced thereafter. Harriett had many children in close succession following her husband's—my grandfather's—return from World War II during a time he was meant to have attended Dartmouth College, just as his own father had. Instead, he found himself responsible for the care of a growing family and a wife struggling to keep all of the remnants of their lives stitched together. Directly upon his return from the war, he was put in charge of the daily operations of the family farm. It was a situation in which no one was set up for success, yet everyone had to carry on the best they could anyway—no doubt a familiar refrain that plays at times softly and at other times more loudly against the backdrop of everyone's lives. Each suffers the collateral damage life doles out. Like spoonful of ipecac, we swallow what is placed at our lips with the faith that it will help more than it harms, knowing full well that there will be consequences.

For Harriett, these life challenges yielded erratic and unstable states of mind, not to mention an array of notably unconventional habits. While surely not an intentional strategy, her unusual habits served the function of getting her through life's extraordinary circumstances. They also happen to be what we fondly remember her by now. If her novel and unexpected combination of words didn't have the effect of keeping you teetering on the edge of your seat, then her quirky collection of habits certainly would. Upon entering her house, guests might be greeted by a rotting chicken carcass sitting atop the washing machine in the mudroom, where the anticipation of what lay in store would dissuade them from taking off their shoes. Harriett would stow away freshly baked chocolate cake in the filing cabinet, possibly with the logic no one would find it in there, although everyone eventually did. She cultivated a spectacular garden of colorful molds and crystals she kept inside the refrigerator—juxtaposed with the food that would be served each day. Growing up, my mom had to fish her clothes out of the deep freezer where Harriet conveniently placed any freshly washed laundry in twisted heaps parked next to packages of frozen meat wrapped in butcher paper. Each morning my mom would have to excavate, thaw, dry, and iron the frozen clothing if there were to be any hope of reanimating and donning pieces of her wardrobe again. Imagine what those kinds of experiences prepares a human for.

Harriett also had a number of pithy sayings we now lovingly refer to as *Harriettisms*. After the untimely death of my cousin, my grandma Harriett offered up the following words of wisdom when the discussion among family turned to the topic of the upcoming birth of my daughter Sonya: "You only have so much potential, and that's it." She then made a clicking noise with her tongue against the roof of her palette as if she were suddenly atop a horse signaling it to giddy up and move on out before throwing her head back in unbridled laughter. While everyone else exchanged nervous and furtive glances around the table, someone thankfully broke the uneasy silence with a suggestion that we have the choice combination of words embroidered on a baby blanket. It was a toss-up between that and another of Harriett's favorite sayings, "You don't have the sense God gave a soda cracker!"—a phrase, if you were the recipient of, you could be sure wasn't a compliment.

As is the case with many people we interact with in our lives, dialogue with Harriett was more like a one-way conversation, from her to you, interspersed with rhetorical questions she mostly didn't want you to answer, although nodding was tolerated. She would often go on and on telling stories about the Emblem Bench. As a child I thought she was referring to some kind of home base, a place where people go to rest and take refuge from being chased as they do in the game of tag, which in this case ironically it kind of was. The Emblem Bench was how she referred to the small farming community in the middle of nowhere, Wyoming—population 23—where she and her family lived on the Edwards family ranch. Other times, she would become engrossed in telling stories about *Werbelows*, a reference many mistook for mythical creatures or a species of marmots when, in fact, she was referring to the neighbors whose surname was *Werbelow*. Yet despite all Harriett came up against over the course of her life, she managed to keep emerging and prevailing. She outlived my grandfather by a decade and passed away at the age of 88 on Thanksgiving Day.

Like Harriett, we are all dealt a seemingly random and at times brutal hand from a deck that seems hopelessly stacked against us. While we do our best to keep everything straight, we often find ourselves dropping what we can no longer hold or adding to an ever-evolving inventory of mismatched sets and runs as we attempt to discern which cards to retain, discard, or simply play. Similarly, it's up to each of us to figure out which aspects of ourselves and our largely unexplored habits of mind will go unchecked as they predispose and set into motion our actions that define our outcomes— stark reminders of the choices we've made in an ongoing tally of our wins and losses.

We each have habits; although yours are likely different than Harriett's, they also serve some purpose in your life. Whether they bear the mark of tediousness and routine or take the form of stories and beliefs intended to help us cope, we each have them in spades. We come to rely upon a repertoire of habits—an entourage at the beck and call of our mind. Yet among the variety of purposes our habits serve, the one our brain and body is by design the most preoccupied with is the conservation and efficient use of our body's resources. As our brain perpetually predicts and anticipates what's coming next, it adjusts the balance in our allostatic reserve. Anything it perceives will require a greater metabolic lift, such as applying conscious thought or attention, carries a heftier price tag. Habits partially solve for that by bypassing the need or permission for our conscious involvement.

Typically, we think of habits relative to our daily living patterns, like whether we managed to make it to the gym at least once before our membership expired, or whether we binge-watched yet another British detective series while polishing off our last bottle of wine and peanut M&M's. Others of us might have the aspiration to dial back how many hits of caffeine we imbibe every hour on the hour, or the number of times we consult our pocket oracles—otherwise known as our social media apps—to satisfy our uncontrollable urge to see who liked, loved, or ignored our last post. Who among us isn't waiting on the edge of our seats to check out this week's latest amateur TikTok videos, or to put to bed once and for all the question keeping millions of us up at night and dutifully checking our LinkedIn feeds each day to discover what in fact makes a good leader? A topic that has certainly kept us rolling in a seemingly endless mashup of articles and books on the matter.

Similarly, much of merit has already been written on habit change, mainly from the perspective of tactics and strategies we can take incrementally to shift our rather predictable responses to our outer context and environment. Yet, it is the internal landscape of our own minds that offers the richest set of clues about the constellation of mental habits giving rise to our outer or visible habits. What this book attempts to unravel is how our habits of perception and interpretation shape and inform how we make sense of what we perceive, and, in turn, how we act on them. As the reader, you will learn how what you think, say, and do is largely a habitual expression of how the brain is designed to make sense of each of these dynamic components relative to its own experience; how your habits of mind are the default, the source of how you habitually experience yourself, others, and the world around you. You'll learn to relate to your own awareness and its various qualities as the primary vehicle you have to shift your vantage point in the present moment and your perspective and interpretation of what follows. By developing your own capacity for conscious awareness, you begin to see yourself as an agent capable of discerning when your mental habits governing your interpretative narratives may be getting in the way. You'll learn where in the soup of perception you can have greater conscious involvement and say in what we otherwise experience as a seamless unconscious process. When we learn how to relate to our own cognitive and sensory processes with greater mental acuity, a.k.a. conscious awareness, we welcome the possibility for greater parity between our desired actions and outcomes and the ones we're setting ourselves up to get. At a minimum, we can act with a more informed knowledge of what we do and do not have the capacity to influence within ourselves, and how we can act with greater clarity of being, if not unencumbered then at least less encumbered by our interpretative overlay. Not once and for all, of course, but in each new moment our perceptions call upon us to do so.

You'll be introduced to a number of frameworks and methods throughout the book, each meant to provide you with practical strategies to remind you what you have influence over within yourself and how best to access it in the present moment. Both the MindBody Map and the 12 Self-Discoveries are designed to help you surface and work with the mental models informing the interpretative overlays you use to make sense of your perceptions, and, in turn, the influences that give rise to your self-identity and your social identity, the source and expression of how you move through the world and are in relationship with yourself and others. You'll explore how each of these components of who you are feeds your overall sense of purpose, agency, and wellbeing—a blueprint of what you rely upon to make sense of your experience. As you learn to practice new ways of *minding*[1] and paying attention, you'll gain perspective and insight into how you are the common denominator, the creator of your own experience. You'll learn how enacting various aspects of your own awareness better positions you to evaluate whether the mental models you regularly employ to organize and make sense of your life are reflective of what you want to prioritize and elevate—and if they aren't, how you can start accessing your own awareness to shift your perspective and develop new ways of parsing the meaning you choose to make.

Upon embarking on this inner journey, you'll have a much better sense of whether the mental constructs you employ again and again are yielding the ideal outcomes and relationships you want to have, and how you can become more cognizant of and intentional about how you habitually make sense of life. In the same way you can be strategic about creating the external conditions to be conducive to the behaviors and habits you want to reinforce and promote in yourself, so too will you learn how to do this on an internal basis. By becoming familiar with and learning to notice the qualities and expressions of your own awareness, you'll increase what you're capable of influencing by virtue of your own agency of mind, the primary gateway to accessing your full potential. In short, we will investigate how the meaning we habitually attribute to our perceptions sets us on a trajectory that takes on a momentum and life of its own—for better or worse—and where you have the opportunity to intervene on your own behalf.

Despite our best-laid intentions, the frequency with which we often succumb to indifference or quickly lose interest in anything requiring ongoing effort requires we have enough interest to reinvigorate our aims once we've noticed they've petered out. This dynamic we face within ourselves is not dissimilar to the low-stakes attitude pervasively taken towards the global climate crisis or the various socioeconomic and political divides that run deep in almost every community across the globe. Maybe this is because we don't fully grasp the import our habits have on the individual and collective quality of our lives on this planet, or because the consequences of our habits aren't within close enough reach for our brain, whose primary job it is to assess and prioritize our body's most immediate needs, to have a natural inclination to do so. In other words, we don't immediately spot the causal relationships between perception and interpretation and the outcomes we are repeatedly getting on an individual and societal level. It is owing to a similar disconnect that our divisive and uncharitable narratives about ourselves and each other go unchecked and are at the root of a much deeper and more profound rift we perpetuate not only with other people but with ourselves.

If what I'm writing about has any hope of reaching the level of benefit and positive effect it has the potential to have, then it must also have the capacity to serve as a starting point for us each to unpack, reframe, and rewrite the mental models responsible for the inner state of affairs giving rise to the outer state of affairs. Although I have no background—literally none—in the arena of politics or social justice, the mechanisms for addressing the societal and collective narratives at the heart of any societal divide are not different than what is needed to address the personal narratives and habits of mind that hold us back as individuals in our own lives. After all, it is the stories we tell ourselves and the sense we habitually make of our perceptions that are at the heart of what gives rise to the patterns and themes that keep us complicit and comfortably opaque. Our mental models carry with them the seeds that separate and divide us from ourselves and each other. What plays out at a societal level is basically the same impasse happening inside each one of us on a much broader scope and scale. Anything we do to arrange the outer conditions with the intent to reform, such as much-needed policy and structural changes, will continue to be met with obstacles and resistance unless and until we attempt to dismantle the confusion at the level of individual perception. It's a "both and" value proposition—it's not one or the other. Both have to happen in tandem.

Given the incredibly complex and nuanced nature of perception both from a physiological and psychological perspective, I've taken the liberty of putting together a working model that attempts to capture the perceptual process along with its outcomes. I refer to this as the *value stream map of perception (VSM)*. In case you are wondering what a value stream map is, it's a methodology derived from the discipline of Lean process management and is meant to visually map a process from beginning to end. It is a clever mechanism that allows us to see the big picture and pertinent details in a single visual snapshot. It's an ingenious way to conceptualize and study the elements of any given process and to be able to visualize the otherwise invisible relationship between each step, obstacles to flow, efficiencies to be gained, redundancies, and opportunities for optimization. It enables us to conceptualize what has been right before us all along but has been both too close and too distant for us to see and aptly relate to. By depicting what is otherwise inaccessible to us, we can start to see patterns, themes, and nuances—pointing us toward the inner workings and potential of any given system. With perception and our habits of mind at the center of our inquiry, we can start to uncover where we may consistently be getting hung up or derailed and, in turn, where we have direct and indirect influence on the process.

What could be more important than our ability to influence our own outcomes? I can't think of anything more relevant or important than exercising whatever measure of influence we have over what we think, say, or do in response to our perceptions. Can you? In this book, I introduce you to the mechanisms underlying your patterns of perception and how you habitually make sense of what you perceive. By becoming both an observer and witness to what is operative underneath the results you're consistently getting in your life and in your relationships, you'll practice paying attention to the meaning you attribute to your own experiences. In so doing, you'll learn where the potential exists to influence your own behaviors and habits that might otherwise remain unconsciously ingrained, including those aspects of perception that are preconscious. As you're able to spot and exercise what you have influence over relative to your own experience, you'll be in a better position to act in accordance with what matters to you most. Assuming having influence and efficacy in your own life are important to you, you're in luck because that's exactly what this book will give you—practices that allow you to regain the stronghold of your own mind.

With those objectives in mind, you'll have a chance to investigate where your interpretative overlay may be more of a stumbling block than it is helpful. You'll see where you have the wherewithal to act upon each inflection point, those discrete moments of possibility between what your brain curates for you by way of your perceptions and what you, in turn, make of each of its clues. We have the choice of whether to continue reenacting habitual ways of navigating the vicissitudes of life or to take a step in the direction of what may serve us and those around us better. With each step, the invitation will be to sharpen your own powers of observation, to unearth and piece together your habits of mind, and to engage the introspective and observational capacities of your own awareness. Through rigorous self-discovery, you'll practice employing the internal wisdom you have at your own disposal while exposing the deleterious effects of how you habitually make sense of your experience and learning to cultivate more conducive ones. As you gain insight into how to uncover and work with unhelpful mental patterns, you'll experiment with new ways of producing better responses and outcomes, ones that bring more benefit than they do harm and help more than they hinder.

Introduction: Out of Sight, Out of Mind

In the same way scientists discovered an entire ecosystem of microorganisms living within a single drop of water, we can each discover the universe of possibilities percolating within us, a dynamic display just ready to express itself in any number of ways and combinations. As Leonard Mlodinow writes in his book *Elastic*, the magnificence of the human brain lies in its ability for "bottom-up" or elastic thinking (Mlodinow, 2018). This is the kind of novel and creative thought process that has at its beck and call a seemingly infinite number of possible connections it can draw from, resulting in unique ideas and unexpected creations. The brain's capacity for free and nonlinear association is still more of a mystery than not and hasn't yet been successfully replicated outside of the stomping grounds of the human skull. In the same way the brain's capacity for elastic thinking has given rise to humanity's greatest inventions, our brain has the unique and unparalleled capacity to simulate its own reality, casting predictions that piece together the fundamental ingredients of perception itself. *While we each have the experience of leading our lives out in the world, in fact we live our entire lives from the cockpit of our own minds.*

Despite the fact that it seems we're strictly responding to stimuli on a reactive basis, contrary to how we experience our own perceptions and emotions, the brain is thought to proactively simulate its own version of reality. According to the latest neuroscience research, the brain draws on its prior experiences to predict what will happen next, anticipating how we will need to respond. Our brain makes real-time adjustments to its estimations to account for its own prediction errors and metabolic requirements by factoring in input from our senses as well as our interoceptive sensations. Words and concepts are the brain's currency for making sense of its own perceptions relative to what it anticipates will happen next and how we will need to respond in a context-appropriate manner. Lisa Feldman Barrett has written extensively about the brain's functioning relative to each of these topics in her book *How Emotions Are Made* (Barrett, 2017). It's a book I highly recommend to those interested in delving into the latest research on the neuroscience of emotion. In the following chapters, we explore the practical implications of what all of this may mean, and how this relatively new way of understanding perception and emotion as constructed experiences invites us to rethink and reenvision what it means to be emotionally intelligent. As we navigate the territory of our own mind, we will surface what's at stake and where we have wherewithal and agency within the context of perception itself.

Beyond Emotional Intelligence approaches the topic of habit change from an intrinsic perspective, introducing you to cognitive and contemplative practices for identifying and working with your own habits of mind. This is a fancy way of saying you'll learn how to use thought to change thought and awareness to change everything, starting with your perspective. The focus of this book is to help readers connect with what they have available within themselves as their primary means—qualities they don't have to go somewhere else to find, starting with their own awareness and capacity to perceive. By developing your inner coach, the source of wisdom from within, you access the aspect of your own mind that is inexhaustible and always present for you to connect with. Only through awareness do we have the possibility for our actions to be consciously derived and our intentions purposefully acted upon. Our ability to shift our perspective and relate to our circumstances in the moment is dependent on our capacity to activate the rudder of our own minds.

Without a doubt, emotional intelligence and the broader mindfulness movement have done much to bring the value of self-awareness and contemplative practice into the mainstream, while demonstrating the generative effects of empathy and compassion. However, I believe we've only touched the surface of what we each have available to us to access the inherent qualities of our own awareness. There is far more to explore by way of the mind's expression of awareness and how we can familiarize ourselves with something that is always with us but we are rarely cognizant of. With this goal in mind, you'll be introduced to the Awareness Matrix, a framework that gives you a bird's-eye view of what you do and do not have the capacity to be consciously aware of relative to your MindBody functions—at least from a scientific point of view. You'll learn how self-awareness is simply one stance, one way of being aware among many invaluable ways in which we are already aware and can become even more so. The intrinsic qualities of our own minds are present whether our attention or awareness of them is or not. This is the jumping-off point for this book.

We will orient ourselves to the topic of habit change from a very personal and practical vantage point. The book addresses the importance of cultivating and training our attention to notice its own habitual patterns and to optimize and select for choices that contemplate and account for the interplay between our inner and outer habits and the conditions that give rise to them. You'll be asked to look at specific themes and clues within your own repertoire of mental habits, noticing how you consistently make sense of your own experience and the actions you take in response. Typically, we perceive disturbances to our peace of mind and sense of wellbeing occurring as a result of external events or circumstances. Even though we may perceive our emotions to be discrete, universal responses triggered in response to stimuli, we will learn from recent findings in neuroscience that this is only how things appear—likely owing to what we've been taught up to this point about what gives rise to our emotions and how we behave in response. It is more accurate to say that our brain proactively curates our perceptions and our emotions for us. However, becoming consciously aware of how we interpret and act on them relative to what our brain has predicted is where we have a say in the matter.

Irrespective of whether we perceive ourselves or our emotions as being triggered, or whether we operate on a more precise understanding of how we come to feel the way we do, we are each at the mercy of our brain's ongoing display and constantly evolving simulation of reality. When the salience or valence of our interoceptive sensations rise to a level at which we become cognizant of them, and our brain decides that they are important enough to assign them meaning, the output is our affect, which may or may not materialize into an instance of emotion we are consciously aware of. Despite what it may seem, we aren't at the whim of outside circumstances nearly as much as we are at the mercy of our own perception of these circumstances. As we'll learn more about relative to one of the 12 Self-Discoveries in particular, we are, in a very real sense, the common denominator of our own experience. Ultimately, we are the beneficiaries of what we think and how we feel, as are those whose lives we directly or inadvertently impact by how we make sense of and respond to what we think and how we feel. Therefore, it's up to us to find practical ways to work with our own perception of reality along with the mental models that shape and inform how we make sense of our experience.

La Chispa: The Spark to Our Affect

Throughout this book, you'll be invited to identify and reflect upon your own mental models and belief structures that influence how your brain subconsciously anticipates what you perceive as well as how you then make sense of its perceptions. What you then do with that information on a conscious basis makes all the difference. We'll use the MindBody Map and the 12 Self-Discoveries to unearth and discover the mental models we habitually use to create meaning. You'll be invited to notice what motivates and drives you, not only physiologically but psychologically. I refer to this pull or valence that magically draws us toward what holds salience and interest for us as "la chispa," which is Spanish for *spark* or *flame*. La chispa speaks not only to what we need to function optimally at a physical level, but to what we need to thrive psychologically. In my own experience and in coaching people over the years, I've observed that we never have just one why. We're more complex than that. We tend to have many whys that evolve and morph over time and vary depending on which area of our lives we are focused on. In fact, our whys emerge relative to the context in which we find ourselves and as a result of what we expect and hope to have happen. But unless we do intentional work to uncover what's at stake for us in each of the key areas of our lives, we remain mostly unconscious of the role la chispa and our mental models play in the process. La chispa continues crackling and smoldering within us even when we ignore its presence; its flames rise up with a force we can no longer ignore in response to the messages our bodies are constantly sending us. La chispa does the picking for us as we move through our lives. So, until we make a point of uncovering its path and inner workings, it remains alive within us without us necessarily being aware of its influence.

La chispa gives us accessible language, a metaphor, to reference what we'd otherwise refer to in scientific terms as our affect and on a psychological level our motivators and drivers. Affect is thought to be a by-product or consequence of our interoceptive sensations. It is our experience of feeling, a precursor to an instance of emotion as well as the source of valence, either drawing us toward what we like and are attracted to or repelling us away from whatever we dislike and subsequently reject. Our affect acts as a kind of homeostatic oracle, taking a first pass at registering our interoceptive sensations and plotting what and how we feel somewhere along the spectrum of pleasant, neutral, or unpleasant, which our brain then acts upon. While not all affect registers at a level at which we are consciously aware of its presence, it guides our brain in its primary job of managing our "body budget," a term Lisa Feldman Barrett uses in her work to describe the brain's primary job of regulating the body's metabolic resources, or source of energy—what I refer to in my work as our MindBody Map, or physiological and psychological wellbeing.

Affect and Ego: A Tale of Two Good Buddies

What neuroscience has not yet connected the dots on in this equation, as far as I have been able to discern, is the role of affect's sidekick "ego," defined in this context as our pervasive and enduring sense of self, the psychological lynchpin of our fundamental drive for self-preservation and search for meaning. We each move through the world with a primal and mostly unconscious reliance upon our sense of self as the "owner" of this body and mind. It is thanks at least in part to the continual manifestation of affect that we have the impression of being a self in a body in which we have the capacity to feel and to make conscious and volitional choices. Moreover, it is owing to our capacity to be aware that our experience manifests and registers to begin with. Irrespective of whether our awareness is inseparable from consciousness, the capacity and continuity of which may persist or cease the moment our lease on this body is up, or whether consciousness is independent of or dependent on our physical form, we each have the undeniable experience of being aware and existing as a self in a body. I've not met a person yet who doesn't have the distinct impression they exist. From this perception of agency comes our instinct to find personal purpose and meaning, offering a psychological rationale and counterpart to our physical existence while at the same time playing the role of an inbuilt cheerleader, an ebullient advocate who knows just when to break out the pompoms and *Let's Go Bananas* routine when the wattage of our chispa for life wanes. Whether a construct or not, our sense of self is a pervasive feature of our experience. While we may very well have ego to thank for the ongoing sequel of embodied existence, experientially it seems to serve the purpose of being the functional "owner" of this body in which our capacity for awareness has made all perception possible. Part and parcel of our physicality is a psychological imperative, albeit both temporary. Meanwhile, our affect and awareness serve as both the map and navigation system. We'll look at what recent neuroscience research does and does not have to say about each in the chapters that follow.

For the purposes of this book, we'll mostly approach things from the level of what is practical, acknowledging that how things appear may not be as they actually are. The fact we have the perception we exist as a self, moving through the world in a body we call our own, is what we have to work with. It would be silly to ignore it. Instead, we need to embrace it, learning to work with our habits of mind and internal navigation system in which our affect surfaces emotion while our awareness becomes a natural first choice for navigating its own perceptions. By investigating what moves you—the psychological momentum behind all that you do—you'll begin to discern how you're habitually organizing and prioritizing what you pay attention to and act upon. With each self-discovery comes a clue, an additional piece to the complex puzzle of how your brain ascribes meaning to what it perceives. In turn, you'll learn to spot and work with the mental models and interpretations that may or may not be conducive to your overall aims, and when they aren't, what you can do about it.

Creating Optimal Internal Conditions

You'll have an opportunity to experiment with what it looks and feels like to create the necessary conditions within yourself to be able to exercise awareness. It turns out there is great opportunity to dial in our understanding of the mind's role as well as that of perception itself in the formation and evolution of our mental habits and the vital role each plays in absolutely everything we do. Then, and only then, will we be in a position to know where in the value chain of conscious perception and interpretation we can take an active role in shaping our habits and outcomes. Once we understand how the brain simulates our perceptions and proactively shapes our experience from our prior experiences and beliefs, we can start to address the interpretative mechanisms at play within our day-to-day lives and decisions.

Turning our attention toward the otherwise invisible inner workings of our minds, we will become aware of its go-to habits. To not do so would mean that our internal habits would remain hidden to our attention and conscious awareness, obscuring an entire realm of our experience. In order to maximize the wisdom inherent in our own perceptual capacity, we will practice increasing the dexterity of our own awareness to detect what is underlying our assumptions, biases, and mental models. We'll also pay particular attention to how our narratives reflect back to us the logic and meaning of our own perceptions, behaviors, and choices. Finally, we will investigate how the storylines we create not only serve the purpose of helping us make sense of our current perceptions but predispose our future ones along with our responses and actions.

The Value Stream Map of Perception

As you've likely already begun to glean, our awareness, conscious action, and habits of mind play a far greater and more central role than we typically give them credit for relative to what we habitually think, say, and do. They are the variables we have most readily available and at our disposal to work with. Our goal will be to operationalize our insights about each and the profound implications they hold for the quality of our lives, our relationships, and our outcomes. To this end, the value stream map of perception (VSM) is meant to orient us, to provide both a framework and an anchor for our inquiry into our own habits of mind and where we have options for conscious choice within it. It is by no means meant to be an anatomically correct depiction of all that is presently known or studied about the brain, the body, or the human mind. It's simply meant to be a highly accessible, understandable, and practical working model that gives us a starting point. Since I've not yet met a model or framework that has this as its scope or aim, while not perfect, the VSM just needs to serve its intended purpose as a visual representation of perception and the cognitive and sensory processes that accompany it.

You'll be introduced to each of the 12 Self-Discoveries, which serve as both a diagnostic and tool for you to examine the paradigms of thought either hindering or helping you, along with the practices you'll need to reappraise and shift your outlook and mental approach. As we look at each segment of the VSM that sketches out the primary ingredients of perception, we will see where we have the least and greatest possibility for direct influence. We will train in observing where within our own habits of mind we have the opportunity to influence our own beliefs and concepts, if not directly then indirectly. In fact, you are expanding your knowledge base and conceptual frameworks available to you simply by reading this book, or anything else capable of conveying knowledge, and even more so when you apply what's in it. We'll find out what happens at the stage of conscious interpretation, which is where our opportunity is the greatest to work with our mental models using the 12 Self-Discoveries and awareness practices. You'll be invited to notice your patterns of response, to examine what you think, say, or do again and again, and the implications each has for your own life and those around you. With each segment of the VSM and each of the 12 Self-Discoveries we'll see where we have the best chances to impact our own outcomes and how we can go about cultivating the optimal conditions within ourselves to do so. Finally, we'll explore our natural tendencies and where we have a higher propensity to derail or flourish depending on our present relationship with our own habits of mind.

The 12 Self-Discoveries

Now, a bit of background with respect to the 12 Self-Discoveries. Each of the 12 Self-Discoveries captures habitual tendencies we have relative to how we perceive and make sense of our own experience. They are interwoven habits of mind that can either help or hinder, depending on how conscious we are of their influence on us. Through identifying how we invest our time and energy, achieve a desired outcome or purpose, improve our relationships, develop a new skill, establish a new habit, or live in alignment with what we value most, each of the 12 Self-Discoveries reveals how we may be getting in our own way as well as how we can work with the mental patterns that are keeping us stuck. Each serves to focus our attention on the patterns of thinking and beliefs largely hidden to us, yet often apparent to others, highlighting where we may be getting led astray by the very functions we use to make sense of our moment-to-moment experience. Each of the 12 Self-Discoveries offers unique clues and insight into what may be holding us back or where we may not be operating at our best. They function as an internal barometer for when our expectations aren't met and our beliefs about what should have happened fall short. Ultimately, they provide us with a clear path to uncover and work with our mental models and patterns of response, giving us the possibility to exercise our agency at key moments. While not an exhaustive list of potential mental traps or pitfalls, or their antidotes, the 12 Self-Discoveries provide us with an empowering narrative of agency in which we each come equipped with the wherewithal to bring about the changes in our lives we deem most important. They are reminders for how we can choose to move through the world more intentionally while working at the level of what is within our conscious awareness and ability to choose.

1

The Evolution of Emotional Intelligence

Each generation rides on the invisible wings of the great thinkers and doers who came before them but from whose departure in substance, style, and approach we often stand to gain. What if we hadn't moved beyond the insights of Aristotle or Newton, for example? Without even knowing it, we are constantly iterating upon the uptake of residual knowledge of those who have come before us, be it our teachers, our contemporaries, or the collective wisdom (or lack thereof) of the context in which we find ourselves. In writing this book, I've often pondered where the world might be if the big thinkers in the various fields of science or quantum mechanics had as their primary object of inquiry the mind and had rigorously applied their fancy-pants formulas and analysis to its movement and behavior. Or what if the most skilled meditation masters had applied their wisdom and direct experience of the mind to the study and behavior of the physical universe? And how amazing would it be if there were a clearer path between the two, a practical crosswalk between them?

The Business Context from Which Emotional Intelligence Emerged

Thanks to the collective wisdom of the younger generations and those who are demanding a new model of leadership and ways of doing business, the leadership paradigms of yesterday are starting to budge—maybe not as much in practice or as quickly as we'd like, but they are shifting. A senior leader I worked with in the investment management industry once told me he thought emotional intelligence was a bunch of hooey. Instead, he wanted us all to read *Good to Great*. Needless to say, he didn't have an overabundance of the skills and competencies we've come to think about as being foundational to emotional intelligence (EI). The popularization of EI has been gaining momentum over the past 25 years since Daniel Goleman published his first book on the concept. His work has been a beacon beckoning and guiding leaders whose ships are lost at sea.

Like many other disciplines of scholarship and study that have historically placed a higher value on the ideas and voices of a select few, the field of emotional intelligence is no exception. It isn't that there aren't subject matter experts of diverse perspectives and backgrounds doing important and interesting work in this space; it's just that their voices are still comparatively muted and their presence largely overlooked. It's really important we change that. Part of what this entails is looking at how the models we're using now were derived and evaluating whether they adequately reflect what we understand both from a neuroscience standpoint as well as what we ideally want leadership to look like, not to mention EI itself. Are there EI competencies, for example, that when practiced and developed explicitly articulate a vision of inclusive leadership and result in leadership that doesn't destroy the planet and acts in service of world benefit? Equally important, we need to ask ourselves what EI looks like outside of the business domain from which its most popular iteration and framework emerged. What would a model based on what we understand about the brain and its bidirectional relationship to the body look like, for instance?

To the extent we iterate or improve upon existing models of EI, we need to make sure that what we feel is valuable to democratize is reflected and is fully considered from the variety of contexts in which these models are being taught and practiced, like education, government, or medicine, for example. What we have come to value in leaders has most definitely shifted since the early competency studies used to inform and shape the EI model Daniel Goleman made famous. Essentially, the current EI framework is itself a leadership or behavioral competency model whose later iterations were inspired by studying the competency models of 188 large global companies at the time (Goleman, 1998). The fact that its credibility has been strengthened by virtue of a mostly self-referential process means it still resonates, and any analyses done since support its perceived efficacy; although, candidly speaking, I'm not sure how, given that EI doesn't consist of just one or two things. It consists of many behaviors and skills among a sea of intervening factors—like context—which is what makes measuring it relative to its current definition, apart from anecdotally or qualitatively, a difficult if not impossible undertaking. Moreover, if we were to poll companies now, 25 years later, to find out what their leadership competency models consist of and what sets apart leaders who succeed in those distinct environments from those who don't, we could expect to find out what those individual organizations we polled value, promote, and reward in their own cultures. We may also spot values of a more aspirational nature than a true depiction of the qualities the leaders in those companies embody. Finally, to the extent commonalities can be found among successful leaders inside those companies or the competency models meant to describe and guide them, instead of concluding these are indicative of good or excellent leadership, it would be more accurate to say that any trends we see are reflective of what prevailing models of leadership elevate and deem as important in the context of doing business today or that their similarities reflect the values they have in common from an aspirational standpoint—which often means very little unless they are also backed up by effective systems of learning, application, evaluation, and reward. Otherwise, they remain just that, aspirational.

Like anything that is contextually constructed or derived, leadership competency models are artifacts of what is presently valued and prioritized—either in real terms or aspirational ones—within the respective contexts we find them. If we aspire to change the value proposition of business, which I happen to believe the fate of our planet is balanced upon, then instead of working solely from current competency models and norms of doing business in which increasing shareholder value is still the primary objective, we also need to work from the point of view of what we want to have happen. I don't know about you, but I would like a world populated with leaders who shape themselves and the businesses they run as agents of world benefit versus agents of world greed. In this regard, we would do well to channel the ever-increasing innovation and drive toward continuous improvement toward benefiting beings and the planet instead of toward how much wealth and power we can acquire and amass.

Because the most popular of the current models of EI evolved from and within the realm of leadership and business, we also need to decide whether we care enough about EI as a paradigm to see what it might look like in other contexts and whether it holds enough weight outside of the one it was derived from and largely created for. If the answer is yes, which is what my guess would be, then we need to be explicit about which of its elements can be backed up by science and defined in a way that we can apply it and not just talk and write about it. We explore in the last chapter of the book what EI might look like with these objectives in mind and in practical terms.

Democratizing Emotional Intelligence

When I began my work in 2016 to democratize emotional intelligence, it was with the express goal of broadening access to make its practical wisdom available to all, not only to the upper echelon of leaders. My second aim was to translate the theory of EI into an applied methodology and set of practices people could apply in their own lives with the intent to close the knowing-doing-being gap, by which I mean attempting to bridge the chasm between what we have the capacity to know intellectually, what we have the capacity to apply relative to what we think we know, and finally, the degree to which we embody each. Early on in this endeavor, I remember looking at the Goleman-Boyatzis model of EI, consisting of four domains (Self-Awareness, Self-Management, Social Awareness, and Relationship Management) and 12 underlying competencies, and thinking, "Where on earth does one begin?"[1] Certainly, we can aspire to be proficient in each, but if I felt the undertaking was daunting and overwhelming as someone trying to help people acquire these skills, I could only imagine how it might feel to be on the receiving end of this training. I knew a simplified approach would be necessary.

I asked myself what I thought was the next logical question: "Which, if any, of the domains and competencies are prerequisites to perform the others?" Put another way, "Which, if any, of the domains and competencies when applied result in the demonstration or skillful application of the others?" From there I set out to find whether there were any necessary and sufficient causes to perform the various EI domains and competencies. While I started my inquiry intending to pinpoint the prerequisites of EI, I quickly found myself asking a bigger question: "What makes developing anything in ourselves possible?" This is a question I've been asking in slightly different ways since as early as I can remember, and one that is perfectly logical to ask given the task at hand—to create a methodology that bridges our conceptual knowledge of EI with our ability to develop, apply, and embody it. Asking and attempting to find answers to questions, like what enables us each to be able to shift, change, and grow, and what are the causes and conditions that allow us to be the most authentic versions of ourselves as much of the time as possible, led me to where I am at now, writing a book on a topic that is much broader than that of EI. I realized then, as I do now, that the methods and frameworks we use for this or any other purpose need to serve us and not the other way around.

However, bound to the parameters of my aims at the time, I found myself gravitating back to the work I had done as an adjunct faculty member of *Cultivating Well-Being*, a program developed as a joint initiative between Dr. Richard Davidson's foundation, Center for Healthy Minds, and the University of Wisconsin School of Business's Center for Professional & Executive Development. The program was aimed at a corporate audience and was based on the insights, methodologies, and neuroscience research Dr. Richard Davidson has written about along with Sharon Begley in their 2012 *New York Times* bestseller, *The Emotional Life of Your Brain* (Davidson & Begley, 2012).[2] During this same period of time, I was also in the process of obtaining my master's degree in Positive Organizational Development and Change from the Weatherhead School of Management at Case Western Reserve University. I was taking courses with Dr. Richard Boyatzis, who, along with Daniel Goleman, developed one of the first behavioral models of emotional intelligence, which is still in broad use across the globe today. I had made mental note at the time of a synergy I spotted between what Richie Davidson refers to in his research as the six emotional styles (outlook, resilience, social intuition, self-awareness, sensitivity to context, and awareness) and several of the domains and competencies of EI. I gravitated toward Richie Davidson's work, however, because his research not only establishes a brain basis for the six emotional styles but identifies specific contemplative and cognitive-based practices that when applied consistently can move the needle on our brain basis to develop them.[3] I remember feeling both excited and hopeful that his research had established a scientific basis upon which EI could be practiced and developed, something I felt had been notably missing from all of the then-existing EI models. Granted, I don't believe this was in any way his motivation or intent—rather, he was most fascinated by the topic of resilience and how it is that some people are better equipped at dealing with life's slings and arrows, as he eloquently puts it.

The fact that the concept of EI is thriving 25 years after its debut in Daniel Goleman's writings on the topic is clearly because there is something about EI that resonates deeply with people's experience. When I accompanied him to Europe to hear him speak about EI, many people told me reading his book changed their lives and, in some cases, literally saved their lives. While not everyone would attribute EI or Goleman's work as the reason they decided to stick around on the planet, most of us if given the choice would prefer to spend time with someone who demonstrates EI than with someone who doesn't. Though when pressed to say why that is or to articulate exactly what it is about someone who exhibits or embodies EI that causes them to respond this way, I'd venture a guess that while we might hear similar themes, we wouldn't hear a common response as to why they feel this is so. Emotional intelligence still mostly eludes simple explanation, as would seem to be the case based on the countless articles and books written about it—although that may be equally indicative of EI fast becoming a lucrative industry in its own right.

Despite people having a lot to say about emotional intelligence, we still don't have a common or agreed-upon definition pointing to its definitive meaning or scientific basis. Thus, it isn't surprising we've collectively struggled to articulate what exactly it is or how we definitively measure and develop it in ourselves. After all, our ability to understand and apply something relies on our ability to define what we mean by it. Only at that point can we reliably determine how to approach developing it and training others to do the same. Emotional intelligence is no exception. It relies on our ability to extrapolate the many behaviors and skills from the model—consisting of four domains and 12 competencies—and formulate them into specific practices that when applied result in our becoming more emotionally intelligent—again, once we've defined and agree on what that means.

The Prerequisites of Emotional Intelligence

When I began working with Daniel Goleman and the team at the time to formulate the wisdom of EI into practical applications people could learn and apply, I determined we needed to isolate the prerequisites for developing what his model asserts differentiates top leaders from mediocre ones. My first instinct was to do a crosswalk between his work and Richie Davidson's, knowing it would provide a compelling scientific basis for the prerequisite skills of EI. Daniel Goleman and Richie Davidson had just published *Altered Traits* at the time, which was largely aimed at sorting science from bunk on the topic of mindfulness as well as sharing their personal stories that had inspired them to do work in their respective fields (Goleman & Davidson, 2017).

What began as an intentional strategy on my part to create a methodology to train and coach people wanting to develop EI led to me reorganizing the domains and competencies on the basis of three factors: (1) whether it stood the test of being a prerequisite to develop other EI competencies; (2) whether it had a direct tie to one of Richie's six emotional styles, which his research concludes can be developed vis-à-vis certain contemplative practices and cognitive behavioral techniques; and (3) whether the competency could be isolated to what we each have the ability to influence within ourselves. In other words, its development and enactment aren't dependent on others' actions or behaviors. It is from that orientation our coaching and training programs were born.

I took the liberty of adding "focus" as a meta-skill to the mix of existing competencies—self-awareness, emotional balance, empathy, positive outlook, and adaptability—for two reasons: (1) It wasn't included in the current EI framework, or perhaps its presence was simply implied. (2) It is one of the six emotional styles that Richie Davidson refers to as "attention." I actually prefer the term "attention"; it's a nimbler concept that accommodates our ability to selectively direct our attention irrespective of whether we narrow our focus or expand it or place it anywhere in between, whereas "focus" implies narrowed attention on a specific object. However, since Daniel Goleman had also written on the topic of focus, and we were, after all, using his model of EI as our guide and inspiration, it seemed to make sense to add it—not to mention the fact our ability to maneuver this aspect of our own awareness is critical.

Additionally, I preferred the term "emotional balance" over "self-management" or "self-regulation" because it allows us to speak to and train in the nuances of what it means to be resilient, which is one of the six emotional styles Richie Davidson writes about in his book. A person who demonstrates a high degree of emotional balance is both adaptable, able to pivot, and resilient, which means they can recover more quickly. Moreover, they are also not as likely to get upset as easily or, when they do, not as dramatically. In other words, they experience their emotions more like a blip on their emotional radar screen but are less likely to go full tilt—off their emotional rocker, so to say—when they've gone off course. Like a mattress that doesn't leave a lingering impression of the body lying on it long after the person has gotten out of bed, someone who is able to bounce back mentally from whatever life has in store for them can be said to be resilient. Though we didn't end up with an exact one-to-one match between the two models, it was my best attempt at a crosswalk between our program's model of EI and one that directly tied to a model emerging from relevant insights from neuroscience.

Emotional Intelligence Is Here to Stay

When we look at the heart of what is both meaningful and enduring about emotional intelligence, I am admittedly biased. Within the context of this rendering of EI, the foundational skills hold the greatest potential not only for developing each of the remaining EI competencies but for developing skillfulness in anything we do. We termed the remaining EI competencies that did not meet these parameters "the relationship skills of emotional intelligence": influence, inspirational leadership, teamwork, conflict management, achievement orientation, coaching and mentoring, and organizational awareness.

While arguably important skills to have—though I've worked with plenty of leaders who don't exhibit them who were catapulted to the top of their organizations—they are resultant, or outcome-based in nature. In other words, they are the potential outcomes of having done a lot of things well, many of which hinge on the foundational skills of EI. Whereas others are a function of specific skill-based training and frequency and variance of their use. They could just as easily be updated or swapped out with other competencies or terms to mean basically the same thing or to include skill sets deemed valuable based on the context. But either way, irrespective of the words we give them, we would still be dependent upon one or more of the foundational skills of EI in order to do them well, or at all. My view is if you train the dog, he'll be more likely to behave wherever you take him. An entertaining correlate to that, which I didn't make up, is, "If you like the dog, you must accept the fleas." In my estimation, it's a lot like learning a new language. If you have the basic structure and grammar down, you can go to that country and quickly pick up more vocabulary and soon you'll be improvising, whereas if you go knowing nothing about the basics and try to engage in discussions right off the bat, good luck with that. That may work if you're 10 years old, but probably not if your age is a multiple of 10.

The reason I've taken the time to mention where I am coming from relative to the topic of emotional intelligence is because this book represents an evolution in my own thinking, not only about EI but of my understanding of the neuroscience of emotions and their profound role within perception itself. My own training on the topic of EI stems not only from my graduate studies but from having worked for 25 years in companies like the ones whose competency models helped define this particular articulation of EI. I was responsible for implementing leadership competency models and making sure people's performance reflected them. When I saw this wasn't happening nearly as much as one might think, I realized defining what makes a good leader is a different value proposition than what it takes to become one.

I also observed that one of the most common reasons leaders fail to take on board what they've conceptually learned is due to a lack of specificity and practical application of what they are being trained on and the runway and needed forums to practice these new skills. The way we tend to teach doesn't adequately account for learners' need to practice new habits and skills while they are learning about them. Rather our approach typically emphasizes declarative or intellectual knowledge over and above procedural knowledge or the knowledge about how to do or apply something. We tend to overlook the supporting mechanisms needed to create both the conditions within ourselves and our immediate environment as we apply and learn new ways of being. Like IQ, while helpful to have, just because you have a competency structure that supports an individual development plan or an organizational strategic plan with key performance indicators (KPIs) to chart the path ahead, doesn't guarantee you'll arrive at the desired destination or have a successful journey along the way. Far from it. It takes much more than simply documenting or articulating your goals, although I'm not suggesting it isn't a good place to start. Mapping out a plan is a great first step, so long as you don't confuse map making with the emergent and ongoing nature of change itself.

The key is whichever model of EI we ascribe to, it shouldn't just point the way; it needs to give us specific practices and methods for working with our own minds. Moreover, our emotions are but one factor—albeit a critical one—in the constellation of what determines how we behave. It turns out, our capacity to reframe and shift both our perceptual stance and our interpretation of what we perceive are vital to the conversation. That's the part of the discussion we're delving into now in this book. Whatever we do, let's not leave the EI competencies at the level of mere words or concepts trapped within the confines of a framework or their colorful bubble graphics. Let's also strive to live and embody them!

The Neuroscience of Emotion

While there are many neuroscientists engaged in researching how our emotions intersect with what we understand about the brain, I am most familiar with and take my lead from Richie Davidson's work. And though I've only recently become acquainted with Lisa Feldman Barrett's research, she makes an extremely compelling case in her book *How Emotions Are Made* for the constructed basis of emotions in which she covers vast territory between the historical and current understanding of the human brain, emotion, and perception itself (Barrett, 2017). Her departure from classical notions of emotion processed by a triune model of the brain in favor of a whole brain, constructed view of emotions, resonates with my own assessment of where we have wherewithal and say in the rather complex process of perception and interpretation.[4] She offers readers both a novel and sophisticated articulation of a topic we've had the collective tendency to misunderstand—despite the feeling I had at times like I was wearing an itchy, wool sweater as I had to inch my way out of positions no longer tenable. Meanwhile, my head has been left delightfully spinning as I continue to contemplate and puzzle the practical implications of her brilliant work. Had it not been for me rescuing her book from the bookshelf where it had been peering out at me for well over a year, whispering "read me," the one you're reading now would likely not have had the richness nor depth of scientific understanding to lend to the practical insights and observations underlying the methods I've spent the past six years developing to train our coaches and clients to operationalize EI within their own lives.

And though I'm not a neuroscientist nor have I been able to visit with her yet about her work—though I'd very much like to—I'm admittedly flying a bit by the seat of my pants. I've done my best to synthesize and integrate key insights from her research into how I'm thinking about my own work and theories as they continue to evolve and mature, not to mention how I'm parsing the science with my own understanding of the nature of reality relative to my Buddhist practice. It has been both remarkable and entertaining for me to see the notable parallels between the latest neuroscientific findings on perception and emotion and the insights I've gleaned from having studied and practiced Tibetan Buddhism for more than half of my life—that and the uncanny overlap with certain themes from the remake of *Battlestar Galactica*, a television series my boyfriend coerced me into watching at the outset of the pandemic, which I'm now completely hooked on. All this is to say, let this serve as my apology in advance if I've missed the mark in any way in my attempts to explore the practical implications of any of the scientific insights I've tried to incorporate along with her absolutely remarkable contribution to how we conceive of our own emotions. Now, let's look at both schools of thought on emotion, the classical and constructed views, summarized by me in my own words as she portrays each in her book.

The Tale of Two Emotions: Classical and Constructed

Emotions play a variety of notable functions in our lives, including elevating and drawing our attention to their signals. Like a carrier pigeon, our emotions transport salient messages between the brain and the body, forming a powerful feedback loop. The way the scent of a skunk dutifully follows its owner, our emotions forewarn of their approach in the form of bodily signals and affect as if to let us know they're on the premises. And like a skunk's musky trace, they leave a lingering impression you can almost taste. Emotions set a definitive tone, a palpable atmosphere to whatever is already present. As our emotions make themselves known, their valence and salience flood our bodies like the vibrant colors of a sunset we behold but briefly before its glistening rays of light suddenly fade to an icy blue gray.

Even though we've been trained to use single words to describe how we feel, words like happy, sad, mad, or glad, when pressed, we each define these words, as well as our experience of them, quite differently. The moment we look at emotions from the individual perspective of how we experience them, the way we describe them necessarily shifts away from single-word or one-dimensional descriptions. "Sad" is just a word we assign to an entire complex of sensory signals interspersed with mental impressions evoked in the process.

According to the constructed theory of emotions, in contrast to the classical view of emotions, emotions are created, not triggered. Moreover, they do not have unique fingerprints, footprints, or any kind of print for that matter, other than perhaps the subtle or not so subtle mental imprint they make on us as we experience them. Rather, there is wide variation in emotional expression from one person to the next and even between two instances of any given emotion, such as sadness, happiness, or fear. In this paradigm, the meaning our brain assigns our emotions ties predominantly to our learned behavior about them in various situations and contexts versus any kind of universal or primal existence in which we only need recognize them. In the constructed interpretation of emotions, they are conventions, reflections of the contexts we are a product of. The brain doesn't have an emotion manufacturing plant where emotions with identifiable characteristics are produced exactly the same each time in response to certain stimuli. Rather, when we experience emotion, it's more like your brain has called ahead, having already set into motion what it anticipates you'll need as you're about to tell your boss you're going to quit and go work for a competitor: "I'll take a venti, two-pump adrenaline, no foam courage." But then when your boss unexpectedly breaks down crying and tells you the business can't possibly survive without you, your brain has already adjusted for your boss's cues, dialing in a more context-appropriate response: "Hold up! If it's not too late, I'd like to amend my order. I'll take a tall, two-shot pity, half-pump empathy, slightly forced smile, please." Okay, so maybe an instance of emotion isn't quite like ordering your beverage of choice, but hopefully you get the idea. The brain isn't purely reacting to its external environment; it's predicting and adjusting, calibrating its perceptions as it goes, based on its prior experiences and what it perceives by way of sensory inputs in the moment.

Within the classical view, emotions have been carefully classified and categorized much like a dried-flower or bug collection. Each person—irrespective of culture, geography, upbringing, language, or context—comes prepackaged with a repertoire, an arsenal as it were, of emotions that are consistently experienced and unilaterally identifiable, bearing telltale physiological markers and facial expressions. In the classical understanding, emotions are triggered by external events, and we respond reactively based on a model of the brain as having specific regions that separately oversee our emotions, our higher-level executive center governing rational thought, and our fight-or-flight response mechanism, a throwback to our reptilian predecessors—each distinct area of the brain forever locked in a head-over-heart, stimulus-response tug-of-war. There is also the belief that through cognitive control alone we can bring our emotions under our obeisance, like spirits we summon at a séance, if we just try hard enough.

In contrast, in the constructed view of emotion, the brain constructs instances of emotion, drawing from prior experiences in similar contexts. Our brain casts its bets on what will happen next, setting into motion a response sequence before actually knowing what will happen next. As the brain calibrates its predictions with input from our interoceptive sensations and senses, it fine-tunes its perceptions and corrects for prediction error. In this view of emotions, they do not have an identifiable essence, nor are they universally distinguishable by certain facial expressions or biological markers. Instead, the interoceptive networks of the brain produce our perceptions and emotions through a process of degeneracy in which the brain relies upon different and varied core systems in the brain to produce instances of emotion. Words and concepts not only play a critical role in helping us contextualize and make sense of our perceptions and emotions, but they help us sync up with the experiences of those around us. In this manner, we arrive at a shared picture of reality in which we can effectively communicate with one another about what we perceive and how we feel. Through our brain's capacity for statistical learning and simulation, it dutifully constructs an emergent reality, including our perception of a self.

If indeed the meaning we assign our emotions take their lead from our prior experiences and expectations, shaped and reinforced by concepts that have been modeled for us time and again, then in my estimation we can become cognizant of the mental models influencing how we perpetually and habitually make sense of them. We can decide whether the initial meaning our brain has assigned is the interpretation we'll stick with as well as how we will choose to relate to our real-time sensory experience of our emotions. This prospect is both encouraging and daunting. Encouraging because it means we can unlearn what we were taught we should feel relative to what may be culturally or contextually appropriate in any given situation, and daunting because that's potentially a lot of unlearning we may need to undertake to retrofit and cultivate the kinds of experiences that are more conducive for our aims. Regardless of whether we ascribe to the classical or constructed view of emotions, the end result is mostly the same from a practical standpoint. We still have to deal with how our emotions make us feel and be strategic about the sense we subsequently make of them. That said, the two theories do have varied implications for how we might go about working with our emotions and thus yield different strategies we might use to do so. If we think emotions are fixed, we have far less wiggle room when it comes to how we handle them. But if we know our emotions are constructed and more fluid, then we can assign them whatever meaning we like—that is, if we create the habit of doing so.

Where Does That Leave Us? On an Emotional Cliffhanger

Our emotions are more elaborate than they are simple. Irrespective of the mechanisms by which they arrive or what names we give them when they do, the bottom line is, emotions are a pervasive hallmark of our experience. Their presence acts as a kind of invisible yet palpable navigation system guiding our response. But because we can't see them nor are we fully versed in their detection or intervention, they often elude our conscious awareness and therefore our inclination to recategorize or reframe them. That is where the 12 Self-Discoveries come into play. They provide us with quick methods to spot when our interpretation of them is or isn't helpful, pointing out common mental pitfalls we may be succumbing to and remedies for when we do. Our mental outlook and what unfolds within our mind's ecosystem have a profound impact on us, not just physically but psychologically. What's more, our emotions impact how we make decisions and predispose the course of action we're likely to take as a result of how we interpret them. Thus, our real-time investigation of our emotions and ability to reinterpret or change our perceptual stance relative to them matters as much as our conceptual and scientific understanding of them. How we experience our emotions, the ways in which they color our outlook, shape our outcomes, and impact our relationships for better or worse mirror back to us the working state of our own emotional intelligence.

2

An Introduction to the 12 Self-Discoveries

The inspiration behind the 12 Self-Discoveries comes from many sources, consisting of insights derived from my background in Buddhist thought and meditation and, as an executive, coaching and training people and by noticing the common ways in which we inadvertently create obstacles to our personal growth and happiness. The 12 Self-Discoveries emerged from the observation and recognition of mental patterns at the heart of what causes us to not be able to see what should be obvious to us but isn't unless we learn to observe and pay attention with a different perspective or lens. A few of the 12 Self-Discoveries, though not articulated or formulated exactly as such, were inspired by my training as a Frame of Mind coach, the genius behind whose methods and approach come from its founder and my much-admired friend Kim Ades. The insights I gained being trained in this methodology were further brought to life by my coach Carla Reeves, without whose brilliance I would have unlikely escaped the bowels of corporate America, which is often where companies conveniently headquarter Human Resources—the constipating memories of which I will not soon forget.

Instead of languishing in what had become a rather cramped and increasingly uncomfortable holding pattern, I decided it would be important to jump off every cliff that was standing between me and my fear, which is the path I'm still on today, nearly a decade later. "Leap and the net will appear," is the mantra I relied upon then as I do now to remind myself not to make decisions or take action from a place of fear. What I set into motion then has led me to where I am now, helping people on their own journeys to transform themselves from the inside out, to have a meaningful impact on their own lives, the lives of others, and on this planet.

When we began our efforts to democratize and train people in emotional intelligence, we felt coaching was one of the most powerful and expedient ways to jump-start someone's potential to embody EI. It was in the process of designing and developing the underlying framework and approach of the program that I decided to articulate these insights into what have come to be known as the 12 Self-Discoveries. I had largely already articulated the essence of each in the form of journal prompts and a coaching model I had been using for several years with my coaching clients, synthesizing my training as a Frame of Mind coach, my practice and study of Buddhism, and my insights and experience as an HR executive. I gave them titles I jotted down on scraps of paper, and I drew colorful maps depicting the continuums and scales of each of the motivational drivers and behavioral preferences comprising each sphere of influence of the Motivational Drivers Behavioral Preferences Assessment, which has subsequently evolved and is included in what I now call the MindBody Map.

They not only provide coaches and clients a mechanism to discover what's operative by way of mental models and beliefs beneath the surface of the results they're getting in their lives, they are a vehicle to apply EI—though not actually created for that purpose. When I first shared the 12 Self-Discoveries with the team, what stood out was their common link back to developing one's self-awareness. Yet, from another angle, we could say the 12 Self-Discoveries are the method and result of having developed the full breadth of one's capacity for awareness—not only an awareness of oneself and the context, but, just as importantly, the process by which we make sense of and act on our perceptions. Today, they are an integral part of one of the most rigorous, applied EI coaching and training models in the world, the Emotional Intelligence Coaching Certification (EICC) program. Since their debut, they've taken on a life of their own. I think that's because they resonate with people's experience and lend themselves well toward many applications I hadn't initially imagined or thought of at the time.

The Science of the 12 Self-Discoveries

Over the years, I've had a number of students and graduates of our coaching program ask me whether the 12 Self-Discoveries have a basis in science. Since they weren't formulated with that intent in mind, nor were they derived from anything other than observations of habits of mind that can either keep us stuck or give us the key to what we have influence to change in ourselves, I hadn't yet investigated them from that lens. They were initially conceived of and articulated for coaches and their clients to spur a process of introspection and self-discovery, a methodology for looking at how we habitually organize our interpretation of reality and the extent to which our mental models and beliefs may be standing between us and the internal conditions that make it possible for us to function at our best.

As I share the 12 Self-Discoveries with you in the context I am now, please know I've taken great measures well beyond the original scope of my aims to attempt to examine and situate each relative to what gives them their efficacy from a science-based lens. What I quickly discovered is that it would take me years to fully unpack their subtlety and nuance from a scientific standpoint—and therefore more time than my publisher can reasonably be expected to wait. However, I felt it was an important step to initiate because of the value I place on the intersection of science, philosophy of the mind, and contemplative practice, and most importantly their integrated application. Moreover, my own curiosity to know where the 12 Self-Discoveries sit relative to their overlap with the various disciplines of science impelled my added efforts. I can say that my thought process and understanding of how science may shed light on the 12 Self-Discoveries are more refined for having done it, as time-consuming and at times over-whelming as it has been to wade through the voluminous scientific research that overlaps with one or more elements of each.

In the process of sifting through the relevant scientific publications, I've made a few observations about the discipline of science itself. Where we could collectively do a better job is to connect the insights of current scientific research with its practical value and use in our lives—which is presumably the reason we study anything at all: (1) scientists often leave themselves out of the topics they attempt to study. (2) The conclusions that can be "safely" or conclusively drawn from science are not many, and are, therefore, exceedingly disproportionate to the efforts undertaken to obtain the insights that can be gleaned. (3) Because of the scant output that could be considered ready for prime time, it is difficult to extrapolate much of science's findings into something practicable or actionable, which is a shame because like a fine wine that has been left in the cellar, by the time it's ready to drink, it's either too late to enjoy it or it is quickly replaced by something newer. Synthesizing scientific insights requires a practical lens to distill what can be extracted by someone who isn't motivated by their reputation or standing in the scientific community yet is daring enough to do so anyway given the fact the gaps often far exceed what is known. (4) Finally, science doesn't seem nearly as concerned with the subjective experiences of those studying the various scientific topics, as it is with reaching objective results and conclusions, which is ironic given that the former is what we each have the most direct access to. Therefore, it can feel as though the human experience is being forgotten somehow in the process or sublimated to the priorities and rigors of the experiments themselves. That said, were it not for the discoveries of modern science and the brilliant minds of those who work in its various fields, I wouldn't be alive today to try my hand at translating their insights into practical nuggets for us to use within this context. My aim in taking on this work is to provide a dinghy that connects us from the shore of our experience to the inner frontier of our own minds and like a lighthouse, guides our passage and points us toward what gives us each the capacity to transform our unconscious actions into more intentional ones.

Self-Discovery 1: We Are the Common Denominator

Sometimes we need to look at everything going wrong in our lives and admit to ourselves, I am the only common denominator here.

—Dan Pearce

The essence of the first self-discovery is that we are the source of all we perceive, everything we think, say, and do. There is no aspect of our experience that is not mediated by our own minds. We experience everything through that lens. Imagine for a moment that we're the subjects of a really convoluted experiment—the working title of which is called "Life"—led behind the scenes by a team of comics, scientists, computer programmers, and Ewoks. Too many cooks in the kitchen? Take your pick or fill in the blank with whomever or whatever you suspect may be pulling the strings. Irrespective of source, we've each been given a set of parameters, the outer conditions we each have to navigate. We also have an inherent set of qualities, capacities, and potentialities to work with relative to our respective circumstances. For all we know, we're part of a civilian force of agents who receive a new mission every 75 years or so—sometimes less, depending on the parameters we're given and how we navigate them. If you're reading this now, then you're already in your current assignment—one of perhaps countless—whose duration is unknown. Sadly, we're designed to forget absolutely everything about our previous missions. There have been many service requests to fix that, but headquarters is at an impasse as to whether that's a good idea or not. All we take with us from one mission to the next are our habitual tendencies from our previous mission, the accumulated potentiality—cause and effect—of our former actions, and our capacity to be cognizant and aware—that is, our ability to perceive.

Despite the really screwy setup we're dealing with, we had no other choice than to press play when we received the following prerecorded message just prior to being deployed on our current mission: "Your mission, irrespective of whether you decide to accept it, is to figure out the variables you can influence within yourself to navigate the parameters you've been given. Your challenge will be to discover where you can and cannot exert influence as skillfully and gracefully as you can while minimizing pain and maximizing benefit to yourself and others. Oh, yeah, and you'll need to figure out how to stay alive, of course. That is the heart of your mission. You can try to alter or manipulate the parameters, but your temptation to do so may prevent you from fully exploring the variables of what you have at your intrinsic disposal, within yourself. If that were to happen, you risk getting stuck in various kinds of loops—some more self-referential and repetitive than others; while others, like the endless loop, are infinitely more difficult to emerge from. Your goal is to find your own base case, bringing what's known as the recursive loop to an end, unless you decide to keep getting deployed for the purpose of benefitting beings and helping them find their base case. Until then, you just keep receiving assignments. You'll receive some clues along the way, but don't confuse them with ruses, of which there will be many. As is the case with every new mission, you will have forgotten the essence of your assignment by the time you arrive. It will be up to you to remember and find your way back to the objective. This recording will self-destruct in 10 seconds. Good luck! And don't get stuck!"

One of Many Possible Missions

We start our lives well before we can remember or are cognizant of being alive and having a body. We have to eat, sleep, and go to the bathroom with clockwork regularity. Eventually, others around us will protest if we don't wear clothes, wash our bodies, or brush our hair and teeth—to the extent we still have them. Having a roof over our head, a warm and safe place to stay, and enough food to eat makes doing all of these things more tenable. At some point, we'll need to go to school, to the extent formal education is an option, although we don't fully understand why studying is important until it's too late and eventually comprehend that we have to get and keep a job to pay for our daily upkeep along with anyone who ends up being in our immediate care, like our pets, spouses, children, siblings, or parents, to name a few of the more likely suspects. Either way, finding reliable work becomes necessary when whomever it is who has been providing these things for us suddenly announces, "The free ride is over." For some of us, that comes sooner rather than later and for others money and the items needed to live just appear and keep appearing by virtue of some unknown set of causes distinguishing their parameters from those who have no other choice than to get a job—or suffer the consequences of not having adequate means. This may have something to do with the storehouse of potentialities we come with, but nobody can really be sure because we forgot everything, and we only seem to be capable of seeing a few moves out. We haven't yet evolved to be able to see the infinite number of potentialities we set into motion each time we think, say, or do something that causes a movement in the nonmaterial fabric of consciousness itself, nor the combined magnitude of what happens when our own potentialities meet other beings' potentiality, as well as the outer and inner conditions that have the ability to cause the most unbelievable things to happen all the time. Who knows? How it works is all just speculation, but that it functions, it does.

While we each have been issued a basic set of variables and parameters, we quickly find out that while the variables can and do vary, it's predominantly the parameters that can be meaningfully different, giving some a clear advantage or disadvantage over our fellow civilian agents. Because we arrive without a memory of our mission, we may grapple with the feeling we've arrived in a strange land and are being held against our will or consent for some indeterminate period of time. And while all of this may indeed seem strange—and I can assure you it is—it's not even half of the story. These are just the chapter headings, my friend.

Moment after moment, day after day, month after month, and year after year unexplainable events, harrowing adventures, tales of near misses, and undue hardship punctuated by moments of victory, joy, and happiness form the plotline of our lives and the cast of characters at our side. Pleasant and unpleasant circumstances come and go, relationships we enjoyed yesterday are different from the ones we enjoy today, and even the people we love the most appear and disappear from our lives as if in a dream. Things occur that we have no apparent control over or say in. While there is a mix of things that happen to us each day that are mostly predictable and/or preventable, like being woken up by our alarm clocks, showing up late to class or a meeting, or being reprimanded for taking one too many helpings of mashed potatoes, there is an entire class of occurrences that crop up that aren't within our control. Often, we have a hard time distinguishing between them, let alone gaining proficiency in the ones we do have the wherewithal to influence in our own lives. Even the things in our direct control often still feel out of our immediate control or just beyond the reach of what is detectable and therefore doable.

Sense-Making Machines

Similarly, and in some ways even more befuddling than the parameters we have to work with, are the "random" things generated from and within us. Yet how we interpret and assign meaning to what transpires makes all the difference—particularly in the folds of gray matter encased in a hard bony structure between two fleshy protuberances. The question is, what's going on in the space between your ears? For most of us, we experience a continuous unfolding of pleasant and unpleasant mental impressions, thoughts, sensations, and feelings that run the gamut of temporary experiences, not to mention amok. It's as though our thoughts, feelings, and emotions emerge from some undisclosed location within us and return to some equally inaccessible place. They surface in our mindstream in muddled, disjointed, unseemly, uncharitable, and untimely ways, and with plutonium-like volatility and unpredictability. Our mental activity unfolds in abundance and with such regularity that much of its movement goes undetected by us for long stretches of time. Yet there are other times the mental impressions that unfold within our mindstream and the sensations in our bodies rise to a level at which we can no longer ignore their presence—the more extreme and vocal, the harder they become for us to ignore. And when they teleport their way into our lives, they have a knack for showing up at inopportune moments, like a child's unfailing and uncanny ability to say or do the thing that is most embarrassing to their parents, like trying out new vocabulary words at the dinner table in front of Grandma or at the grocery store at the top of their lungs.

When our mental impressions and sensations register on one or more of the following continuums, valence (positive or negative), salience (intensity), and rapidity (how quickly each of the former appears and disappears), that's usually when we find out about them too.[1] At that point everything they touch quickly becomes contaminated with the residue of their temporary yet potent stain. If what I am describing to you was a riddle and you were to take a stab at solving the riddle, what would you guess I'm talking about? Bingo! You are absolutely correct; I am talking about our emotions.

What I've just described are a number of the ingredients thought to give rise to our emotions. What neuroscientists and cognitive psychologists refer to as affect acts as a kind of petri dish for our interoceptive sensations and mental impressions, thought to be a precursor of emotion. Depending on what our brain prioritizes as important for us to pay attention to, much like paying a visit to the corner psychic who relies on their trusty deck of tarot cards or the lines of our hands to foretell our fate, our brain draws from its concepts, mental models, and prior experiences to decipher and render meaning from the body's sensations and affect.

Many of these processes belong to an entire class of involuntary functions we don't have much if any conscious sway over—at least not relative to the first instance of meaning our brain makes—which makes it a lot like other autonomic functions in our bodies. I don't know about you, but I'm extremely thankful for the many body-regulating, "lights on" tasks that have been taken out of our hands to oversee—although I'm not sure how I feel about this being one of them. But I am glad we can scratch the "blink your eyes" and "don't forget to circulate your blood" off our mental to-do list, among a host of other extremely important functions under the care of our autonomic functions. Plus, there is the fact that a number of these to-do items would make for funny cookie fortunes: "I see catabolism in your near future." Phew, got that one covered.

Even though we have learned to communicate our emotions using single words, and sometimes single, middle-finger digits, how we experience our emotions can be quite nuanced and therefore impossible to capture by a single word or concept. As you know, our emotions can exit as suddenly and quickly as they arrived or as unceremoniously and slowly as though they had never visited. Depending on how quickly they arrive and then depart, a reflection of our resilience or lack thereof, it could either feel like they waved as they drove by or like your adult children who are still living with you. Like a Mardi Gras parade, they pass through with their audacious get-ups and pageantry, guaranteeing a spectacle for all to remember.

We feel their valence and salience physically, as bodily sensations; psychologically, as affect; and mentally, as a procession of free associations, memories, ideas, visualizations, sensations, and impressions, otherwise known as our thoughts, feelings, and emotions. This dynamic triad is like the Three Stooges. Where one goes, so go the other two. They often appear by virtue of a confluence of events that can start with absolutely anything or nothing whatsoever—at least that we are consciously aware of. Sometimes they pay us a visit when something happens to us, like we miss our bus or someone vomits on us. They can come calling when something happens to us physically, like our appendix decides today is the day it's going to burst. A chain reaction of mental activity can be set into motion with the flicker of a thought, a memory, a sensation, or a feeling. In turn, our mental movement can be stirred by what we see, smell, taste, touch, or hear. Any one or more of these external or internal signals can serve as the cue for one or more of the three amigos to emerge like genies from their lamp. Now, if it were a matter of them making periodic or infrequent visits, then no big deal. But things happen all the blessed time, resulting in a flurry of thoughts, feelings, and emotions taking flight within us like a murmuration of starlings.

Where we have our work cut out for us is in figuring out what we have say over. And if we ever hope to have any influence relative to what takes place inside us and how this is connected to the results they produce, we need to figure out by what function and means we have the wherewithal to influence them to begin with. That's a basic recap of our predicament. That's the skinny on where things stand. Now that we have a lay of the land, we can see how, even in scientific terms, we are each the common denominators of our own experience.

When Hindering: We Are the Common Denominator

As you can see, we have our work cut out for us, and it isn't particularly obvious that we are the source from which our experience emerges. When you either don't yet realize this or are unable to act with this in mind, you may experience one or more of the following cues, signals, or patterns in your life:

- You consistently look to blame others or outside circumstances for your hardship or misery.

- The finger is mostly pointed outward in a blaming fashion instead of back at oneself.
- You repeatedly find yourself in situations or relationships resembling ones from the past without recognizing the role you play in the process or in recreating them.
- Certain themes keep repeating themselves and playing out in your life despite your best efforts to avoid them.
- Whether you realize you are the common denominator and source of these experiences or not, you continue to experience them as external to yourself, forgetting that the people and world around you are your mirror.

If you find yourself wanting to argue with any of these points, you may want to take a look at that too. This can serve as good information for you to explore why you feel this way, or what exactly about these notions tweak you. On their own, these statements are quite general, so if you're not sure whether they apply to you, feel free to reflect on them and test them out, observing for yourself whether any of them ring true. If none of these indicators resonates, or you're somehow not yet ready to deal with the ways in which this self-discovery may be playing out in your life professionally, personally, or both, it could be you need more time to observe what's at stake and how it's manifesting in your life again and again.

Self-Discovery 2: Igniting Your Inner Coach

We seek outside the wonders we carry inside us.

—Rumi

We come fully equipped. We have the wherewithal, the capability, and the wisdom within us to move our lives in the direction of what's important to us (see Figure 2.1). It is often the case, however, that we don't see ourselves as the source of our own wise decisions. We haven't necessarily developed the perspective to see how and where we are getting in our own way or the mental dexterity to navigate what we have control over within

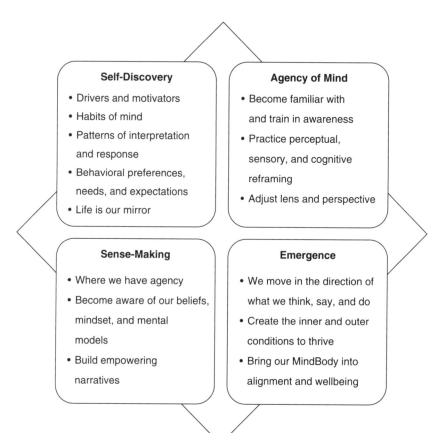

Figure 2.1   Igniting Your Inner Coach

ourselves. When we bring our attention to our habits of mind, our thought patterns, mindset, biases, and beliefs, we can start to connect the dots on how we may be holding ourselves hostage to tendencies that undermine us. We can then begin to work with our habitual ways of perceiving, relating to, and reacting to our moment-to-moment experience. Like a parachute packed and ready to be deployed with a pull of the pin and a tug of a ripcord, we have our own answers bundled inside of us. But we don't know what we don't know, which is why many opt to work with a coach, someone who has been trained to help us see what we cannot yet see about ourselves, someone who can point us in the direction of ourselves. At least until we start to get the hang of looking and seeing clearly what we need to see about ourselves. Until you're able to see yourself as the mastermind behind your own experience, you risk falling into one or more of the following pitfalls:

- You don't necessarily see yourself as a source of knowledge, wisdom, or compassion.
- You may not trust the guidance of your own wise counsel or know how to access that wisdom and agency of mind within yourself.
- You consistently look outside of yourself for the answers, handing over the most important decisions of your life to others, or worse yet may be oblivious to the entire facade and still rely on a blame model.
- You externalize your experiences along the way as opposed to looking inwardly as the source that holds your own answers and highest truths.

The last symptom or indicator can manifest in a variety of ways that despite appearing to be somebody else's fault or doing is itself a root cause of delusion. To whatever extent we rely on others for our happiness, our safekeeping, our wellbeing, or fill in the blank, we stand to be let down. This isn't because people are inherently disappointing or intentionally trying to fail us, but because they too only have direct influence over certain aspects of themselves and their own lives the same as we do. This isn't to say it isn't helpful, essential even, to have a solid support system. While it certainly does help, whenever you've placed yourself in a position in which you are critically dependent on others and their expectations or opinions of you, it places you at the whim of others whom you can't control or entirely rely on. When the things that motivate us come from within us and are intrinsic to how we derive our meaning, they are more reliable, not to mention infinitely renewable. When our motivators are based purely on extrinsic factors, we are handing the reins over to outer circumstances, which often don't conspire in our direction and are outside of our control. Even when we choose to remove ourselves from a situation, doing so can be quite complicated and still we have to make our way in the new context, carrying the same head on our shoulders with all its same tendencies and proclivities.

Often, we can be overheard talking about accountability as if our only access to it must come from someone outside of ourselves. That kind of accountability is limited, uncertain, and unreliable in the end. *The only kind of accountability we can be certain of is that which comes from within us.* This is the advantage of developing our inner coach. We need to learn to trust and seek our own wise counsel. So, where does that kind of conviction come from? What conditions do we need to create for ourselves internally such that self-accountability becomes a habit? What might it look like to show up for yourself? These are the kinds of questions you'll have the opportunity to explore the answers to as you begin to connect with and develop your inner coach. This particular self-discovery also serves as a map for our journey, as depicted in our earlier illustration, shining a light on the steppingstones we'll encounter and traverse along the path, a journey that is by no means a linear one, but one filled with fits and starts in which we end up having to double back—sometimes on a daily basis—to reflect upon and absorb the dynamic lessons life has to offer us. By the time our time together is up, you'll have touched upon each of the following insights relative to your own life and can be sure you got the main points of the lessons "Igniting Your Inner Coach" has to teach you when:

- You trust you have the answers within yourself and believe you have the power to bring about meaningful changes and shifts in your own life.
- You are inclined to look within yourself for the clues, the answers, and the solutions instead of looking exclusively outside of yourself.
- You learn to trust your own wise counsel and to listen to the questions that want to be asked and the answers that want to be found.
- You begin to see the dynamic nature of your own inherent qualities and expressions.

Self-Discovery 3: Perception + Interpretation = Your Reality

There is not truth, only perception.

—Flaubert

Entire disciplines of research and study have as their aim to "crack the nut" on the nature of consciousness, the relationship between the brain, the body, and the mind, and how we make some semblance of sense and order of these gargantuan topics. Our aim is to get close enough to each of these vast topics to understand them in practical terms and see how they impact our lives. If we comprehend how we perceive and make sense of our experience, we can start to see where we have the wherewithal and capacity to navigate all that having a consciousness, brain, and body have to offer. This particular self-discovery is meant to help us parse the main components involved in how we perceive and interpret our experience. It's shorthand for what the value stream map (VSM) of perception attempts to go into greater detail to explain. It is meant to serve as a quick reminder of how the brain arrives at its perceptions, how we subsequently derive meaning based on those perceptions, and where we have influence in the process. Since we'll be delving into the topic in greater detail relative to the VSM shortly, there's no need to say more on the topic here.

In the same way we typically aren't consciously aware of the processes associated with perceiving, we are often equally tuned out to what is happening with us on an internal level. We can go entire days, months even, without having paid much if any attention to what's happening inside of us on a psychophysical level. The fact that we have an entire inner world we don't know much about nor operating guide to help us navigate its mysteries and complexities is peculiar, considering all we've managed to explain, prove, and deduce about so many other subjects over the course of history. We've managed to figure out that the earth isn't flat, that it revolves around the sun (and not the other way around), and to navigate our way through outer space to the moon and back, yet we struggle to understand the inner frontier of our own mind.

As for the topic of the mind, we'll leave the heavy lifting to the scientists and scholars to define consciousness and whether it is the same as the mind and/or the brain, and if one causes, is dependent on, gives rise to, or derives from the other. The aim of our work is to take what we each have direct access to know and observe and fashion it into something approachable, useful, and, most importantly, doable. As one Tibetan master, Khen Rinpoche, puts it, "We must do the doable things."

Even though the Western discipline of psychology is defined as the study of the mind, in practice the mind and brain are often lumped together and even referred to interchangeably. I am not aware of any scientific study that empirically proves the mind and brain are one, the same, or different—though plenty of research studies start from an assumption that a connection between them exists. There certainly appears to be some kind of meaningful relationship between the brain and the mind; however, the depths and details of this are up in the air, figuratively speaking.

For our purposes, I am defining "mind" as the capacity to be aware of our immediate experience, both internal and external phenomena. It's by virtue of the mind's capacity to be cognizant and aware that we perceive, both consciously and even unconsciously, and experience our lives from one moment to the next as a seamless continuity—at least as long as we have the basis to experience reality in this manner. In this context, the terms "mind," "awareness," and "consciousness" are used interchangeably. It is presumably our capacity to be aware that distinguishes us from inanimate objects, which, as far as we can tell, do not have the capacity to perceive or to be aware. As we will explore throughout the book, our minds have many notable qualities and expressions that extend beyond the capacity of being aware. Our aim is to become accustomed to utilizing the observational capacity of our own minds along with its many other qualities as our primary means of connecting with what we have direct and indirect influence over in ourselves. In the event that we are someday able to locate the mind or consciousness in a physical sort of way—though I very much doubt that—it still wouldn't change the fact that we still have to deal with the ramifications of having a mind. The interesting thing about the awareness of our own mind is that we have access to it the moment we remember we do. Even when we forget about our awareness and it switches to more of a passive or functional mode, we are not separate from it. Just by recalling it, we are immediately reunited with our own awareness, one of our more remarkable design features.

Until you learn to recognize and activate what you have influence on relative to the perceptual and interpretative processes by which you create our own reality, you may find yourself getting hung up on one or more of the following obstacles:

- You haven't experienced or recognized the agency of your mind, what you have direct influence over. Not knowing from where it originates, you don't realize it can be operated from the seat of your own awareness by shifting your perceptual stance, nor how to cultivate the capacities you already have.

- You are unaware of the biases and habitual tendencies informing your perceptions and subsequent interpretations.
- You don't question your senses, your perceptions, or your interpretation of what you perceive. Instead of seeing your own perceptions as being highly subjective, your own habitual rendering of reality, you'll instead see them as objectively true and real.[2]
- As a result, you also automatically believe your own stories, that is, the sense you make of your moment-to-moment experience without questioning any of it.

All we each have to rely on is our own perceptions, however subjective. That said, once we realize our perceptions lack objectivity and are our brain's best attempt at navigating its own surroundings and internal conditions, we learn our interpretation of reality is just that and isn't as solid or real as we've come to believe—and neither is anyone else's.

Self-Discovery 4: What Do We Have Influence Over?

In yourself right now is all the place you've got.

—Flannery O'Connor

What we have influence over is the logical starting place for anything we do. Knowing what we do and do not have direct control or influence over is critically important in any situation. It also invites you to think about how you're investing your time and energy and whether those are even things you can control. The only choices we have at our disposal to make are in the present moment. This present, fresh, fleeting moment is the only increment of time we have the possibility to influence. How we perceive what's unfolding in the present moment, and the meaning we make of it, has tremendous influence on the choices we make and, therefore, our outcomes. We are at both the helm and precipice of our perceptions, our interpretations, and our reactions. We never really know how things will unfold. When is the last time you were caught off-guard or taken by surprise with what the present moment brought with it? Try to think of an example now.

Then reflect, "What did I believe I had control over in that moment versus what I actually had control over in that moment?"

The question is not only one of agency, or perception of having volition, which we explore from a scientific vantage point in the next chapter. It's also a matter of discovering what we have at our intrinsic disposal, which is largely what this book is aimed at helping you discover and learn to manuever. But until you recognize and gain familiarity with what you have direct influence over within yourself, what you can rely upon and put to use, you may find that:

- You try to control people, situations, and circumstances over which you have absolutely no control.
- You expend time and energy worrying or perseverating on things you can't control.
- You fail to recognize and consistently act upon what you do have influence over.
- You don't know how to access your own awareness or personal agency.
- You may intellectually know you have the possibility to influence various aspects of your life but do not have the practice, stability, or consistency to do so reliably.

Self-Discovery 5: You Don't Have to Believe Everything You Think

---

Nothing is good or bad, but thinking makes it so.

—William Shakespeare

This self-discovery reminds us to question the veracity of what we think. It can help counteract the intensity of what we may be feeling or thinking, serving as a gentle reminder that just because we think something doesn't make it true nor does it require we give it our continued focus or attention when it may be acting as a hindrance or saboteur.

Before I learned how to meditate, I had no experience observing my own mind. Of course, I was aware to varying degrees of my thoughts and feelings, but I hadn't spent enough time observing my own mind to see first-hand how my thoughts and feelings—any kind of mental movement whatsoever—behave. Only once I received formal meditation training and developed my own concerted meditation practice while living at the Burmese Vihar in Bodh Gaya, India, when I was 20 years old did I come to realize our thoughts come and go, as do our feelings, our emotions, our memories, and so on. The direct observation of my own mind while sitting on the meditation cushion led me to the direct insight that just because your mind thinks something does not mean it's true.

When we spend time observing what unfolds in our own mental stream, how it unfolds, how it comes and goes, we give ourselves the possibility to relate to our own thoughts and feelings differently. The objective of this self-discovery is that we learn to take back the proverbial reins of our own mind. Over the course of the remaining pages, we'll explore how you have the capacity to be at the helm of your own awareness where you can direct and redirect your attention accordingly.

While it may seem obvious or straightforward enough, until you gain experiential insight into how your mind generates its own mental phenomena, you may find yourself falling into one or more of the following pitfalls:

- Until you realize it's your natural tendency to believe your thoughts, it may not even occur to you not to believe everything you think.
- When you are operating from the assumption that your thoughts are true, you're more inclined to give your thoughts and emotions a level of veracity, emphasis, and importance they don't inherently have.
- Because of not being familiar with your own mind, you're likely not aware of the difference between your mind in movement and your mind at rest. Therefore, you don't see the windows in which you can have mental freedom from discursive thought.
- As a result, you may miss key inflection or choice points of when to question your own thoughts or perspective, or when to realize that yours is not the only point of view.
- Finally, to whatever degree you aren't acquainted with the patterns of your mind's own awareness, you may miss the window or opportunity to ignite our own agency.

Until we gain some direct experience of our own mind and how it behaves, it makes sense that we wouldn't see the many underlying mechanisms at play. Absent the ability to maneuver our own perspective, we risk remaining stuck in one view—whichever one our habits select for us—unable to see that more vantage points are available.

Self-Discovery 6: For Better or Worse, Your Focus Becomes Your Reality

---

What you focus on grows.

—Kim Ades, Frame of Mind Coaching

This self-discovery also happens to be quite similar to a quote by George Lucas: "Always remember, your focus determines your reality." Our immediate experience is determined by whatever we focus on. Wherever we place and hold our attention colors our outlook and our reality in that moment. Our mental outlook is a direct reflection of what we pay attention to, how we pay attention, and how we react. I drew inspiration for this self-discovery not from George Lucas—although, during the pandemic, I watched the Star Wars movies for the first time—but from Kim Ades and my grounding in Buddhist practice. Kim is the founder of Frame of Mind Coaching and the genius behind the coaching methodology I was formally trained in. Kim wrote a book on this topic, *What You Focus on Grows,* which in a single phrase sums up this self-discovery beautifully. Focus also happens to be at the core of what various meditation practices aim to cultivate and is one of those key features we each have intrinsic to our own minds which can either bite us in the rear or work on our behalf. Finally, two of my key influences, Daniel Goleman and Richie Davidson, have written extensively on the topic of focus and attention, respectively. In this context, attention is a synonym for our awareness. As implied by Richie Davidson's definition of the word, the ability to selectively direct one's attention, we each have the capacity to direct, place, hold, and redirect our awareness in any number of ways, which we'll explore further when we talk about the qualities and expressions of our own awareness in subsequent chapters.

We each have the propensity at times to perseverate or ruminate on people, situations, and events. When we find ourselves caught, unable to take our minds or attention off of something, it can be worse than having to listen someone talk about something we find terribly boring, or the equivalent of having our brain stuck in a Chinese finger trap. In Tibetan, the word used to describe this kind of grasping or clinging is *shenpa*. When this happens, our minds become like fly paper, attracting whatever may be salient for us, refusing to release its catch from its sticky grip. This self-discovery points to what happens when our awareness becomes so absorbed or fixated on the object of its attention that it becomes the only thing that is visible to us. It's as if our awareness fully inhabits or becomes subsumed and indistinguishable from the object of its focus; perhaps in the same way it might feel to be possessed—plus or minus the physical contortions. Focusing to the point of absorption can be helpful if what you're focusing on is what you want to be focusing on, or it can be really troublesome if whatever you're fixated on isn't particularly conducive or is actively unpleasant. It's like stepping in poop; you'll continue to smell it for some time afterwards. We can say, its smell becomes your reality. Everything else available to you in that moment becomes irrelevant and nonexistent as far as you are concerned. When in that state:

- You find yourself preoccupied by some aspect of your experience, and the more you focus on it, like quicksand, the deeper you go and the more it engulfs you.
- Whatever you may find yourself getting stuck or hung up on holds your attention hostage. You can become fixated on a tangible or intangible object, a thing, a thought, a belief, anything, or nothing at all. The more you cling, the less freedom of movement your awareness has to direct itself toward or focus on other things.
- The object of your focus, be it a person, place, thing, thought, emotion, feeling, or story, pulls you into its grip, creating an emotional suction cup with a valence—be it positive or negative—along with salience, governing its strength or sway over your attention.

- When this happens, you may be unable to find the release valve to loosen your awareness or the power of its grip upon whatever it may be holding onto for dear life. As a result, you not only risk losing perspective of everything else in that moment, but whatever it is you are focusing on can take on an exaggerated and larger-than-life quality.
- When the object of your attention so thoroughly captures your attention, you may give it more credence or power than it deserves or the situation warrants.

To get ourselves unstuck in these moments requires that we cultivate the internal condition of awareness and the habit of either letting go or the facility of other ways in which we can shift our attention. That is exactly what you'll learn you have the capacity to do relative to our own mind and the reframing techniques you have available to enact in the moment.

Self-Discovery 7: What Are You Building Evidence For?

No man who thinks ill, will hear the truth despite a hundred signs . . .

—Rumi

This self-discovery captures what happens when we fall prey to confirmation bias, the Pygmalion effect, or any other multitude of biases we regularly yet often unknowingly give rise to in the process of perception and sense-making. The former is the phenomenon of looking for evidence to support our existing beliefs, often causing us to become blind to all data except the data we expect to see, and the latter, a studied phenomenon by which others perform according to our preconceived notions and expectations of them. Ironically, both kinds of bias mirror how perception is thought to work in the brain. The brain makes its predictions based on what it expects to see drawing from its previous experiences. The brain then calibrates its predictions by consulting with our interoceptive sensations and sensory input, correcting for prediction error. Finally, the brain once again draws on itself to make meaning of this data using the mental models—which are laced with prior data points—to make sense of its own perceptions. Who said it would be easy to come up with a design that lets consciousness move around and experience itself and its surroundings?

The resulting impact is that we tend to look for evidence that confirms what we already believe. Plain and simple. This unfortunately provides the conditions for whatever biases we may be inclined toward to seep into our perception of reality without our detection. These are biases from our prior experiences and what we've come to believe by virtue of our self and social identities. In other words, we naturally pull from what has been modeled to us as well as what we have been taught. While this situation is unavoidable, given how perception itself works, once we are aware this is what's happening and that we do have some say insomuch as we don't have to take the bait of our habitual patterns of sense-making, then we can learn to spot the various clues and train our awareness to notice when it's time to reframe our perspective and/or our meaning. But until you've refined your ability to see the subjectivity of all of your perceptions—all except the unfettered perception of awareness relaxing into itself, the remedy of all remedies—you may notice yourself falling into one or more of these mental kaleidoscopes:

- You tend to put yourself or others in boxes from which it becomes next to impossible to remove yourself or them.
- Your stories and beliefs keep you stuck and have the effect of self-fulfilling prophesies actively working to sabotage yourself, others, and your outcomes.
- When things don't go well or don't live up to your expectations, you may unconsciously add that to the list of damning evidence reinforcing existing negative beliefs or stories you have about yourself or others.
- You may judge others based on very little information and then come to believe whatever it is you may consciously or unconsciously hold to be true about them. This can quickly lead to looking for evidence to support your existing beliefs about them now and in the future.

Our ability to see we've fallen prey to any bias we may have arises out of self-reflection and in asking ourselves on a frequent and concerted basis, "What am I building evidence for?" The stories and meaning we construct from our experience can either create obstacles, or they can free us from confines of our own making. Since no one else is going to sort out the situation for us, we'll need to rely upon both our perceptual and cognitive capacity for reappraisal of what we perceive. In the wisdom of Byron Katie, ask yourself, "Is it true? Is it really true?" and "Who would I be without that thought?"

Self-Discovery 8: Deficit-Based Bias

A pessimist sees the difficulty in every opportunity; an optimist sees the opportunity in every difficulty.

—Winston Churchill

Because our brain displays greater sensitivity toward unpleasant news, our outlook is unduly influenced by negative rather than positive data. And lest we forget, our focus becomes our reality. There are many situations in which we have to work to see the good and the positive in people, including ourselves and situations—unless it's more important in the moment to see and acknowledge some other quality or aspect of your experience which we'd rather focus on. For example, there is a brilliant podcast in which Brené Brown and Susan David discuss the dangers of toxic positivity (Brown, 2021). They offer both caution and insight about the notion that positivity is the sole antidote to all situations or mental impasses we find ourselves in. When the mindset of "everything is okay" even if it's not operates in the subtext of how we process and respond to our emotions, how we may actually be feeling—though temporary—is what's at stake in the matter. I want to be clear this is not what this self-discovery or its correlate, "Seeing the Best in Self and Others," is advocating. Rather, they both have to do with the ability to see and express yourself clearly and to know the lens and frame of mind from which you're operating along with its impact. When you can intentionally discern yourself, others, and situations through various perspectives, you're in a much better position to determine how best to proceed.

The 12 Self-Discoveries are interconnected, each serving in some cases as an amplifier or remedy of the others, with this self-discovery being one of them. As we learned from the previous self-discovery, when our brains become fixated on something or even predisposed to a particular lens again and again, we reinforce these ways of seeing and interpreting without necessarily conceptualizing the potential impacts of doing so. What happens if we only focus on what's not working, the gap, the problem, or what's wrong? We may forget to notice what is working, what's right or life-giving about a person or situation. That can become rough for the people we spend time with, not to mention a source of internal malaise.

When I was getting coached by my coach Carla, she asked me a question that was a game-changer for me at the time: "What's it like to be around you?" She posed the question in the context of how my kids experienced me during a time when I was regularly getting frustrated with my daughter for her propensity to run late for everything. After a while, it became predominantly what I focused on about her, which was a major sore point and source of conflict between us. It ended up negatively impacting our relationship and creating tension within our family dynamic, the outcome of which I'll share in the pages that follow.

Our educational system and certainly our business paradigms reinforce a model of deficit-based thinking in which we are always trying to identify and solve problems. What if there isn't a problem to be solved? Then what? What else becomes possible when not everything is seen as deficient or less than or in need of our brilliant services to fix? These are questions you're being invited to explore the answers to relative to your own experience. Of the following examples in which there is an overreliance upon negativity bias, which ones do you find yourself gravitating toward most often?

- You tend to look for and/or focus on the negative.
- You may adopt a "grass-is-greener" outlook in which you're unable to see or be grateful for what you do have going for you.
- Instead of an inclination to see and ask, "What's right?" you see and ask, "What's wrong or missing?" You may view or talk about everything as a problem to be fixed or solved.
- You may be inclined to fill in information gaps with negative interpretations about the situation or person involved versus remaining neutral or giving the benefit of doubt.

- You tend to focus on the negative aspects to the exclusion of all other perspectives. Because your focus is on the negative, it becomes your dominant lens.

You'll have ample opportunity to work on adding new perspectives to your repertoire of perceptual habits, not just the extremes of having a glass half empty or half full, as you embark on your own journey inward throughout the book.

Self-Discovery 9: Seeing the Best in Self and Others

People deal too much with the negative, with what is wrong. Why not try and see positive things, to just touch those things and make them bloom?

—Thich Nhat Hanh

As I mentioned, "Seeing the Best in Self and Others" represents the flip side of the coin to our tendency toward negativity bias. Being able to spot the life-affirming elements, the unique strengths, talents, and qualities of a person or a situation gives our attention something generative to anchor to. We create the internal conditions needed to feel conducive mental states, such as appreciation, compassion, generosity, gratitude, and so forth. Again, this isn't a suggestion that you make things up or pretend there is nothing wrong when there is, which may be a concern for anyone who may misinterpret this as a call to be fake or inauthentically positive. Instead, it's an invitation to simply notice and pay attention to what is generative and conducive. We cultivate the conditions for civility, openness, and dialogue as a means of better seeing and negotiating our differences. Given our tendency toward negativity and confirmation bias, if we want to be the beneficiaries of all that comes with a generative mindset, we need to practice seeing through that lens. Since we can't control other people or circumstances—only our responses to them—we have the option to look for and appreciate "what's right" versus our natural talent to spot "what's wrong." Because it is easy for us to lose sight of what is positive and beneficial about ourselves and others, until we develop a habit of seeing the best in ourselves, others, and situations, we may develop one or more of the following habits of mind:

- A tendency to forget or deemphasize the positive qualities or what you like about someone, which in more extreme cases can lead to dehumanizing or marginalizing others.
- Your expectations of yourself or others tend to overshadow your ability to see their positive qualities. Instead, you may quickly become disenchanted or irritated with people when they don't meet your expectations.
- You may lack compassion and loving kindness toward yourself or others.
- There is a block to your ability to see what is good, positive, and right about yourself, other people, or circumstances.

Like the other practices you'll be trying out for a spin, I encourage you to give this one a shot as well. Start by noticing where your present perspective may be clouded or negatively biased relative to your key relationships, with regard to your self-perception, and finally to those with whom you actively struggle.

Self-Discovery 10: Emptying Your Headtrash

It isn't what happens to us that causes us to suffer; it's what we say to ourselves about what happens.

—Pema Chodron

I first learned the term "headtrash"—yes, one word—while working for a manufacturing company and hanging out with sales directors. It's a great word that has a very powerful message at its core. It can serve as both a remedy and reminder to let go of the self-limiting beliefs, narratives, and stories we have about ourselves—and others—that aren't serving us or anyone else well. When something important to us backfires or doesn't go as we'd hoped, we have this peculiar tendency to unleash a floodgate of critique upon ourselves. In those moments, we rationalize why this or that thing didn't work out in which we are inevitably the villain in a predetermined ending to a repeating story about why we aren't good enough, why we aren't lovable, why we are all alone in this world, or you name it (insert your poison or your lifelong hang-up). Irrespective of whether this tendency comes from a place of self-loathing or despair, we each seem to have one or two recurring themes in our life that represent the cross(es) we each have to bear.

When you get into this kind of downward-spiral mindset, gently remind yourself, "Be kind to (your name goes here)." Be mindful of what you say to yourself when no one else is listening. Words are powerful. It turns out, what we say to ourselves matters. As we already know, whatever we repetitively think, say, and do becomes habitual. They become our go-to behaviors we fall back on. Our job is to discern the headtrash circulating in our psyche and rid ourselves of the unhelpful beliefs we have about ourselves, even though your specific brand of headtrash may reassert itself, like a paper folded the same way a million times and therefore knows no other way to fold. When headtrash resurfaces, you'll have the sense to know better and the practices available to dispense with whatever is not conducive. Until you make a concerted effort to sort and empty your headtrash, you may find one or more of the following clues you're carrying a load of rubbish around in your head—in much the same way whatever gets digested in your stomach eventually must go the way of all good things:

- You habitually return to old stories about yourself and others, revisiting narratives you've been carrying around and unconsciously adding to over time. These stories are generally not the happy kind—rather they tend to be more of the ilk of Grimm's fairy tales. These can be self-limiting beliefs or full-blown novellas about how you aren't lovable, are an imposter, aren't capable, can never do anything right, and so on and so forth.
- Like a lint roller whose nature is to catch the straggly bits, when left to its own devices your mind can become a magnet for beliefs and stories about yourself and others that, like lint, just need to be discarded. In fact, they may even be actively harming and undermining your sense of purpose, agency of mind, or perception of your own efficacy.

- In the same way you empty the trash wherever you live, you can be aware of the negative thoughts and beliefs you're carrying around about yourself and others. Like anything toxic, these sentiments can build up and begin making even the good stuff around it super smelly—like the pair of Converses you've owned since you were 12.
- Our headtrash can manifest as negative self-talk, self-deprecating comments, or uncharitable statements we say under our breath or out loud. In these moments, we are literally "trash talking" ourselves. Be careful what you think about yourself and what you say to yourself when no one else is listening—*you're* listening. Words, thoughts, and beliefs have power. They have a momentum of their own.

Among the many practices you'll learn to help dispense with unhelpful narratives or beliefs you may be hoarding, learning to see the patterns of what is said and how it's said is a superpower that will allow you to listen in a radically different way—to yourself and those you interact with. You can start now by paying attention to the specific words and language you and those around you use. The interesting thing is people are always telling you what they believe and/or want you to know. Some are more overt and intentional in what and how they say it than others. But if you really pay attention to what is and isn't said, you'll acquire a new way of listening; namely, for the mental models, underlying assumptions, and language that gives meaning to our own and others' perceptions.

Self-Discovery 11: Mantras, Metaphors, and Maps

An idea is a feat of association, and the height of it is a good metaphor.

—Robert Frost

This self-discovery is a little different than the others insomuch as its intent is to provide you with reminders to counteract mindlessness or the habit of setting cruise control from the driver's seat of your own mind. Each offers practical tools and strategies we can use in a pinch when we find ourselves about to get swept up and carried away by whatever confluence of conditions is moving through us. Mantras are sacred utterances integral to the practices of many religious traditions. But in the context that we'll be using the term, a mantra captures the essence of an insight or personal truth. Mantras or sayings can serve as reminders for us in the moment of how we want to show up or respond in specific situations. If someone has a tendency to shut down or wall themselves off in certain circumstances, they might come up with a short phrase they can use the next time this happens, like "Stay open. Be curious." Mantras can be used in moments our habitual response is to do or say one thing when we'd rather practice or respond in another way.

Metaphors communicate complex ideas with depth, clarity, and brevity in a way a single word or description may not. Metaphors have the ability to convey the moral of a story, the wisdom of an insight, or a new way of making sense of not-so-new variables. They provide a richness of language and symbolism that bring the lens of our creativity and imagination alive, affording us a new vantage point we might not be as inclined to access otherwise.

"Maps" is shorthand for the importance of developing an awareness of our body and bodily sensations, as in our MindBody Map. Our sensations are often our first clue that something is stirring within us at an interoceptive or affective level. When we increase our awareness of our bodily sensations and signals, we increase our potential for interpreting and responding to what we feel with greater curiosity and accuracy. For example, if you notice your face becoming flushed, your throat tightening up, and a constriction in your heart center leading to panic attacks each time you're in the presence of your business partner, it could mean that it's time to get a new business partner, or it may point to something else altogether. Either way, it's an opportunity to get curious and ask, "What's happening with me?" Only we get to decide whether the meaning we're initially inclined to make is the interpretation we want to keep. Moreover, when we turn our focus on what we are experiencing interoceptively—meaning having to do with our bodily sensations—like morphine to a herniated disc, it can serve to take the edge off of whatever we are feeling. Why? You guessed it—because our focus becomes our immediate reality. When we change our lens, we are quite literally changing our affective niche—which speaks to what our brain turns its attention toward in the moment.[3] While I wasn't aware this phenomenon had its own scientific definition until I began researching this particular self-discovery, it is what happens when we consciously shift our attention or our physical position relative to our immediate context. Within the context of the 12 Self-Discoveries and the awareness familiarization practices you'll be introduced to that allow you to shift your perspective, having the capacity to shift your affective niche is something you do have the capacity to influence—if not your actual physical environment or circumstances, then your mental and perceptual ones.

Mantras, metaphors, and maps serve as reminders, cues to jog your capacity to recall or remember how you intend to proceed, prompting you in many cases to reframe the meaning you're making in the moment and hence your response. Not realizing you have internal resources available to you can manifest in one or more of the following ways:

- Negative self-talk or self-deprecating comments you say to yourself when things go wrong.
- An inability to tap into your interoceptive or physical sensations that otherwise act as important clues.
- You may struggle to identify or name how you are feeling.
- A tendency to miss the inflection points you have to reframe your meaning.
- The habit of neglecting one or more aspects of your MindBody wellbeing, which is the vessel and vehicle for your perception and everything you do.

We will look at specific ways we can use mantras, metaphors, and maps in our daily lives to remind us that we can reframe and reappraise how we are responding to our own perceptions.

Self-Discovery 12: Happiness Is a State of Mind

The final self-discovery is best summed up by a quote by one of my teachers, Yongey Mingyur Rinpoche: "Happiness comes down to choosing between the discomfort of becoming aware of your mental afflictions and the discomfort of being ruled by them." Happiness, like other emotion words or categories of concepts, describes a temporary mental state—or instance of emotion—consisting of a unique constellation of sensory and mental impressions our brain has anticipated on our behalf relative to our context. Like all mental states, happiness isn't an object we can acquire and keep safely in a box for ourselves. Rather, our mental state becomes a choice in the moment of how we choose to appraise and assign meaning to the signals our bodies and brains curate for us. The initial meaning we assign to what we're experiencing on a sensory basis may or may not be in alignment with the meaning we ultimately decide to stick with. The matter rests with you. The wisdom at the heart of this self-discovery is that you have the ability to respond to what you feel in any number of ways, assigning it the meaning your brain and body give to you or one that may suit you or the situation better. When we don't realize this, we are at the mercy of the mental states our bodies and brains gift to us. Once you realize you have the wherewithal to decide when an emotion, a mood, or mental state has either outlived its expression and intended purpose or is simply off the mark, then you have actualized what you have the ability to influence. We get to make the choice of how long we will indulge and feed our mental states. We can feel whatever is arising for us. We can simply observe and let it pass, we can become entangled with it letting it color our outlook, or we can initiate a shift either in mood or our perceptual stance itself—one that doesn't keep us pinned in a psychological chokehold. However, until we get better at remembering what we have available to us in the moment to shift our perceptual frame, our affective niche, or meaning we assign, we may experience one of more of the following:

- We don't see ourselves as the source of our own state of mind.
- We see our emotions and mental state:
  - As more static and permanent than they actually are
  - As things that happen to us as opposed to something we have influence over and can cultivate, dissipate, or sever at the root
- We don't see the causal relationship between our thinking, our mindset, our beliefs, and our outcomes.

Whatever we may be feeling, whatever our mood or state of mind, it is both temporary as well as a choice as to how we will relate to what's happening within us. While this may not be immediately intuitive or obvious, it is possible to train our mind, our awareness, to ride the invisible waves of our mental elaborations while not getting swept away by its undertow.

The Outcomes of Self-Discovery

Each of the 12 Self-Discoveries provides methods we can use to reframe our perspective and habits of interpretation. They point to specific ways we can activate our intrinsic capacity to be aware, each providing unique gateways to cultivate conducive and beneficial states of mind. If you were to pause to reflect and take inventory of how the following aspects of your life are going, to what degree would you say you could benefit from and are ready to work with your habits of mind?

- Are you making the best possible use of your own life and the unique gifts and talents you have to share? Are you having any fun in the process?
- Are your outcomes and results reflective of what's meaningful and valuable to you, and if not explicitly beneficial to yourself and others, at least not to the detriment or harm of either?
- How would you assess the overall quality of your relationships, not only with those who are near and dear to you but with those you may not be close to or even struggle with?
- To what degree do your own habits of perception, interpretation, and response get the better of you?

If you can answer these questions honestly for yourself, you'll know straightaway where you sit relative to your own mental habits and motivation for working with them.

3

What We Have
Influence Over

We have more possibilities available in each moment than we realize.
　　　　　　　　　　　　　　　　　　　　—Thich Nhat Hanh

Because I've opted to approach the not-so-new topic of habit and behavior change from the angle of what we have influence over among a sea of things we don't, I've needed to make what, at times, is an uncomfortable leap between the realm of how things appear and how we experience them and what, if anything, is understood philosophically or scientifically about the same topics. Unlike the approach I'm taking, scientists tend to steer clear of making leaps deemed unjumpable or highly unlikely to land. Like consciousness, or mind, agency represents one of those chasms. Yet, if we take what we experience at face value, without fully vetting it alongside what we've gleaned from an evidence-based standpoint, we can quickly find ourselves trying to maintain untenable or holey positions or thinking we have agency over things we don't. While I'm not a scientist, I respect science, despite the tremendous gap that often exists between scientific research and the translation of those ideas into practical insights we can apply to our lives.

It's never my first choice to be at odds with scientific evidence or prevailing scientific thought. Thus, I've made a concerted effort to try to understand and incorporate the latest scientific perspectives on the topics that overlap with the ones I've chosen to write about, but from the perspective of what we can extract from these emerging theories to apply to our own lives.

Perception of Agency

One of these topics is the study of agency, referred to in neurocognitive research as "sense of agency," which I recently learned a bit about from reading an article written by James W. Moore entitled "What Is the Sense of Agency and Why Does it Matter?" (Moore, 2016). The upshot of what I learned from reading his synthesis of the latest research in this area of science is that a distinction can be made between our feeling of having agency and how we attribute the causation or outcomes of our own or others' actions. The former is referred to as the *feeling* of agency (FOA), which the author explains is defined as "a lower-level non-conceptual feeling of being an agent" or the sense of agency we attribute to our actions when we are not explicitly thinking about them, whereas *judgment* of agency (JOA) is defined as "a higher-level conceptual judgment of agency" arising when we explicitly attribute actions to ourselves or others. The FOA is thought to be linked to sensorimotor processes, while the JOA, or attribution of causation, is thought to come about by virtue of cognitive processes, such as our beliefs or contextual knowledge related to our actions. An example of how each plays out relative to our day-to-day experience is when something happens we weren't expecting or consciously intending to have happen, it may, or may not, register our FOA, whereas our attribution of causation depends on our cognitive assessment of our own agency (JOA), that is, our beliefs about the situation and whether the specific circumstances seem to suggest we were responsible for causing whatever happened to happen.

In short, we have the sense that we are doing the acting, even though research has shown that our brain registers intent to act, that is, signs of movement, before we actually move. What's more, we aren't consciously aware of having moved until a second or a second and a half after our brain shows its first inklings to move. Basically, our brain prepares to act before we are consciously aware this is the case. Freaky, isn't it? However, according to research in this area, it is our belief and cognitive assessment that determine whether we see ourselves as being responsible for, or the cause of various actions and outcomes. As we will see when it comes to applying the 12 Self-Discoveries, our *judgment* of agency, if not our actual agency, is a critical component.

As you may have noted, neither parameter of agency, FOA or JOA, speaks to whether we *actually* have agency, and if we do, in what ways. Scientists in this field only go so far as to study the neurocognitive basis of agency, that is, our perception of having agency and/or causation. Mainly, this is because it's really difficult to set up experiments that measure overt behaviors, let alone ones that have mental states as their focus. It's probably good I'm not a scientist because I'd be inclined to chalk off the slight delay between our intent to act and our conscious awareness of acting to a design feature that accommodates "just in time" perceptual management. Maybe the motor cortex doesn't require the oversight at a level of conscious awareness that would cause us to need to be aware of what's happening until our conscious involvement becomes necessary. I'm probably wrong to think this design ensures both an effective and efficient use of our neural networks and our body's metabolic resources, while not compromising on quality or losing anything in the process.

Within the parameters of what we presently understand about the research, I'd argue that both types of agency, FOA and JOA, are necessary ingredients—cognitive constructs or not—for anything we consciously undertake as a means to improve ourselves *and* feel good about it at the same time. Whether or not we actually have agency is, well, a mystery for another day, if not the basis for an entirely different book I won't be writing. The final observation Moore draws our attention to in the research on sense of agency is the confusion between free will, also referred to as mental causation, and the issue of motor control, which is one of the primary vantage points from which research experiments try to measure our sense of agency—but not our actual agency. Thus, it's fair to say, we've learned more about motor control than we have about free will itself. However, as the author aptly points out, "understanding the neurocognitive origins of free will beliefs will not tell us if they are true or not, but will help us evaluate whether or not those beliefs are justified" (Moore, 2016).

If Not Free Will, Then Why Not Free Won't?

Of course, I'd like to know, along with the rest of humanity, whether free will is or isn't a thing, which may or may not have played a role in why I majored in religion as an undergrad; though, clearly, the answer I emerged with isn't serving me in this context. I did, however, learn from later speaking with James Moore, the author of the article I read to educate myself on the topic, that while we can't say anything definitive about the role consciousness plays in behavior, there is of course the possibility it may serve the function of helping to explain and provide us with a narrative of our own behavior, one of the side effects of which may be the impression we have free will. He also mentioned research on the phenomenon of "free won't," a theory first put forward by Benjamin Libet whose validity has been debated ever since. Given my training and background, I knew none of this and was so tickled with the idea that I laughed out loud. The theory of free won't is that while we may not have volition beyond the perception we do, we can put the proverbial brakes on whatever it is that may already be in motion. In other words, we can choose to stop an action sequence after it has already begun. I was pretty sold on the idea and, if true, is something that has worked reasonably well for me up to this point, minus those instances in which my self-regulation was a no-show. However, in reading up on the topic further, I discovered a study whose research is summarized in the article "There Is No Free Won't: Antecedent Brain Activity Predicts Decisions to Inhibit" (Filevich, Kühn, & Haggard, 2013). I'm afraid the title sort of gives away what their research yielded when they corrected for what they determined to be errors in Libet's research parameters, but in case it bears repeating, the study found we don't even have free won't to pin our hopes and dreams on.

Even though I just learned about the concept of free won't, I'm already attached to it, like the ginger ice cream I had a bowl of last night and wanted more of for breakfast. I don't know about you, but I'm not quite ready to throw our free won't out the window with our free will. I think it's reasonable to say we don't understand how consciousness is or isn't involved relative to what we can control in our environment, let alone our own agency; although, I read an article in *The Atlantic* that offers some interesting perspectives on what happens when people are primed to believe they don't have free will versus how they behave when we tell it to them straight. Suffice it to say, their reactions range from alarming to more alarming. But we don't want to get too far ahead of ourselves lest it send everyone into existential crisis should they believe the title of Stephen Cave's article, "There's No Such Thing as Free Will," which aptly and elegantly captures various stances and voices on the topic of free will and determinism. One of the voices he highlights is that of Bruce Waller, a philosophy professor at Youngstown State University who wrote *Restorative Free Will*. According to Cave, Waller reconciles both views of reality by pointing out that we have the ability to generate a wide range of options for ourselves that we can pick from without external constraint. Therefore, the fact our biology is constrained to "the causal chain of firing neurons" shouldn't matter. Cave then summarizes Waller's position: "The two views are not in opposition, they simply describe our behavior at different levels" (Cave, 2016). If that isn't the best attempt you've ever heard to make the best out of a bad situation, I don't know what is. It turns out, Waller's position isn't so different than my own, or at least the portion that pertains to how I plan to approach the question of agency relative to what we have agency over.

My view on the topic can be summed up as follows: Whether free will or free won't exists or not, our *judgment* of free will informs our beliefs about it. Our understanding of anything, not just this topic, is only as accurate as our mental models, knowledge structures, and subjective understanding of each will allow for. Our preconscious perceptions don't require our beliefs to be accurate in order to operate. The brain's ability to simulate a picture of reality doesn't appear to be impeded by whether we do or don't have self-agency, or whether we are up to date on the news or the latest research in science; rather, the perceptions our brain generates rely on our cognitive appraisal and interoceptive inputs for context. As highlighted by the most unforgettable four years in American history—I'll let you decide which four-year period—we can hold a whole host of beliefs and ideas, along with their rationalizations, about what is or isn't factually true. It doesn't stop our brain from doing its job. Though there isn't an automatic shutdown feature or beeping noise our brain makes, like a utility vehicle backing up to notify us our beliefs are out of sync with truth, the narratives we generate in the process of either further rationalizing or explaining our beliefs and actions speak for themselves—sometimes quite loudly. Yet, our perceptions are not hampered by whether our expectations, prior experiences, or beliefs reflect an "accurate" picture of reality. Instead, our brain draws from what it has available in curating our perceptions for us.

What we arguably need to be more concerned about is what we each have to draw from relative to our knowledge and experience base. What I have been terming our mental Kanban, which is simply meant to be a metaphor for the just-in-time information our brain has at its disposal to work with. Since there doesn't appear to be the equivalent of an interlibrary loan system or phone-a-friend brain feature available to us yet, when it comes to what our brain has to work with, with respect to our perceptual processes, very much depends on us. While we may be constrained by outer parameters not within our immediate control, our mind is the apparatus from which the elaborate production of our lives is projected. Since we can only draw from the brain we have, we must work within its constraints. Therefore, we should front load it with the knowledge and experiences we not only derive joy and meaning from but that will in all likelihood reflect our choices back to us. As the adage goes, garbage in, garbage out. So, with our habits of mind in mind, we would also do well to discern our own mental models and belief structures, both the ones we are actively aware of and the ones we aren't. The more we pay attention to the subtext and narratives we weave from our experiences, the more we may have line of sight to what may be contributing to their unconscious and habitually generated counterparts. That's precisely what you'll learn how to do using the MindBody Map in later chapters. You'll begin to discern what it is you believe and the mental models you're both consciously and unconsciously aware of.

To the extent you may not feel entirely satisfied with the picture science has painted for us, know you aren't alone; I'm not sure it would be my first choice either. But think back for a moment on the most important decisions you've ever made and the many meaningful shifts and significant transformations you've undergone in your lifetime. I know I've changed over the course of my life, and I'm guessing you have too. I'm also guessing you've accomplished things you're proud of and witnessed loved ones in your life do the same. Even if all of these milestones came about as a result of our responding intelligently and adapting to what we can control within our environment instead of by virtue of having agency, then, as Wallace points out, doesn't this still leave us enough room to work with?

Agency of Mind

As for how I will approach the topic of agency relative to the book, I won't be referring to agency again in the same breath as free will, as I believe it unleashes a hotbed of philosophical, scientific, and religious debate, which, as much as I find it entertaining, is beside the point. Instead, I propose we approach this hairy topic through a different lens and give that which we do have influence over a makeover and a new name. What I like about the term "agency" is that it carries with it the idea of both conscious and intentional choice as well as the ability to act with volition. If we look at what we have within us that gives us that capacity, it's the combination of our conscious awareness, intent to act, and ability to carry out an action without having to rely upon some external source. So, from now on, we'll refer to that capacity we each have as our "agency of mind" and use it to describe the gamut of potential actions we can consciously and intentionally take under the auspices of our own awareness. As we will see in the Awareness Matrix, a framework I've whipped up to illustrate the varying levels of conscious awareness we have to work with, the more autonomic, reaction-based responses or actions we take that we aren't particularly aware of can fall anywhere along a continuum of what we are consciously but passively aware of, to actions we take that we are completely unconscious of. With regard to our perception of agency and causation, I'll look forward to hearing more from science in the years to come as to whether we actually have agency or just think we do.

In the meantime, I'm focused on what we do with the agency we either have or just think we have. But for the sake of simplicity, I'll write about it under two working assumptions: (1) our *judgment* of agency, the cognitive appraisal that we are an agentic self, is incredibly important and core to our motivation, our sense of wellbeing and purpose; and (2) we do have the possibility of agency relative to our conscious awareness—though our ability to enact that agency comes down to gaining dexterity in our capacity to do so. Nonetheless, it is from that basis we can have mindful agency, what I refer to as our agency of mind. I'll of course leave it up to you, the reader, to decide your own position on the matter of free will; but my position and operating thesis, based on my own experience and what I've observed in those I've coached and trained, is our awareness and agency of mind, together, make all conscious action possible.

What's Influence Got to Do with It?

Each of the 12 Self-Discoveries speaks to what we have the capacity to have direct as well as indirect influence over within ourselves and our immediate environment. In this chapter we will focus on this self-discovery through the lens of the value stream map of perception (VSM) as well as the self-discovery that captures the same as is represented in the VSM but in an abbreviated manner: Perception + Interpretation = Your Reality.

If we consider the title alone, "value stream map of perception," we can glean some important points about the purpose and goal of this exercise right out of the gate. To begin with, there is the implication there is something of value to be derived from mapping out the individual segments of whatever process we're attempting to learn about, which in this case is perception itself. That means we need to come out the other side of the effort either having created value or identified value we didn't see before that's already present in the process or system. *Stream* implies there is an ongoing flow of whatever process it is we are mapping. In this case, since we are attempting to map perception, it can be said we're also mapping our own stream of consciousness—or at least our perception as such. Despite the fact our awareness is both intangible and invisible, our capacity to perceive arguably goes hand in hand with our ability to be aware of anything in the value stream of perception. In fact, one meaning of the word "perception" is to be conscious of or to perceive. As to who is doing the perceiving and at what level of conscious awareness are questions we will delve into further when we explore our sense of self.

Self-Discovery: Perception + Interpretation = Your Reality

If we examine what happens relative to sensory input, it may seem that our brain simply reacts to external phenomena or events triggering our emotions and our responses. We already know from a sensorimotor standpoint this doesn't appear to be the case. First let's consider the nature and role of sensory input, which can take the form of incoming stimuli, internal sensations, and mental movement. Our senses take in staggering volumes of data—these days perhaps more than any other time in history—ranging from what our senses perceive relative to our immediate context as well as by our own volition. This latter type of input is characterized not only by what we intentionally choose to focus upon but also by what our zombie-like attention voraciously and mindlessly consumes. Most of the time, we are only selectively and intermittently aware of what our senses perceive, as the brain draws upon this input to validate and calibrate its predictions. If we came with a disclaimer like the ones we see on pharmaceutical commercials, ours might read, "Is prone to delusional perceptions and is on autopilot more often than not."

We are mostly unconsciously aware, or unaware, of what our senses are processing. And it is even more rare for us to be cognizant of our sense faculties as they are doing their jobs of perceiving. For example, we generally don't notice our eyes while they process visual forms, unless there is an obstacle like an eyelash obstructing our view or if our eyeball happens to collide with a bug. Similarly, we tend not to notice the body's internal and autonomic functions that remain mostly hidden to us, like digestion; until, that is, something goes awry, at which point we become hypercognizant about a situation we are otherwise cavalier about. Lucky for us, the brain in tandem with our body keeps its own ecosystem running 24/7, 365 days out of the year without us being consciously aware of its intricate and sophisticated goings-on. I liken it to what a parent does for their child throughout the course of their child's life and how very little goes detected by that child of the parent's herculean effort on their behalf. When it comes to how seamlessly our bodies are equipped to take care of themselves—often despite the monkey wrenches we throw into the mix—it's truly magnificent.

Perceptions Aren't Quite What We Imagined, or Are They?

There is a bidirectional interplay between our brain and our body and the mechanisms the brain employs to read and interpret the body's signals and incoming sensory data. The brain readies itself not only to respond in a context-appropriate way but does so with judiciousness as it takes into account our metabolic resources available to us in the process. Relative to sensory perception and the brain's process of rendering meaning from incoming data, Lisa Feldman Barrett explains how our brain relies upon its own statistical learning and its capacity for predictive analytics to simulate and calibrate our perceptual realities for us (Barrett, 2017). She describes a continuous process whereby the brain anticipates what is going to happen, and then does its best to verify the accuracy of its predictions, drawing upon what it has at its disposal to correct for prediction error. As the brain casts these simultaneous bets, it runs real-time simulations comparing what it anticipates experiencing with our prior experiences, our interoceptive sensations, and our sensory input. The brain must further translate these inputs in order to give them a specific and actionable meaning using concepts, words, and objectives specific to each context we find ourselves in. Understandably, our perceptions are unduly influenced by our prior experiences, as this comprises the data our brain has to work with in the moment. Our brain then selects for an instance of meaning that most closely fits what it estimates is accurate, using input from our senses and our interoceptive sensations as key data points that factor in when it comes to things like our affect and emotions.

Take as an example what happened this morning. As I was making a single cup of coffee using my AeroPress contraption, I followed a sequence of actions I always take. First, I boil the water. Then, I grind the coffee. Next, I place a dollop of coffee grounds inside the bottom of the AeroPress, which is gridded at the bottom where the coffee gets filtered from the AeroPress into my favorite, teal blue ceramic cup. But if I overlook placing a filter in the bottom, like I did this morning, then all coffee breaks loose when I pour the boiling hot water into the press. What these seemingly simple actions and steps to prepare my morning coffee require from the brain's standpoint is, well, nothing short of a miracle—mistakes and all. My brain needed to anticipate and predict based on its prior experiences of making coffee—not with the drip coffee machine, the cafetiere, the percolator, or the French press, but the AeroPress. It had to anticipate each and every step it has learned is part of this process. The fact I sometimes forget to include the filter is both embarrassing and a testament to how tired I am in the moment, not to mention how much I really do benefit from drinking coffee. Errors also serve a valuable function. It means that tomorrow I'll pay greater attention if I remember what a pain in the ass it was to clean up coffee grounds and piping hot brown liquid splattered all over my counter and kitchen floor after forgetting the filter. That's just one task. When you factor in the upkeep and running of our metabolic and autonomic processes needed to keep us alive, our brain is responsible for orchestrating an ongoing menagerie of complex processes and tasks at a magnitude that is hard to fathom let alone comprehend.

Staying Alive—It's a Tough Job, But Somebody Has to Do It

What our brain performs each moment of every day to keep the lights on is no small task. It's not a job most would proactively sign up for, I'm guessing. Our brain has to know where to be, when to be there, and how long it has to do the various tasks it's faced with doing. At the same time, the brain is responsible for overseeing our body's energy sources and reserves in the process. It is through a continuous process of prediction and correction of its estimations that our brain is constantly generating, recalibrating, and refining the mental models and concepts we use to make meaning of our finest creation—our own reality.

If the brain processed information solely on a reactive basis, it wouldn't have the wherewithal to do so efficiently or effectively. It would simply take up too much metabolic real estate for which our bodies aren't designed or equipped to handle. Therefore, the brain has no other choice than to operate as it does, predicting and simulating our perception of reality vis-à-vis a series of critical feedback loops (Barrett, 2017). The upshot of what this means for us is basically a lot has already happened before we become consciously aware of the perceptions we have to work with. We are in many respects both the beneficiaries and recipients of our perceptions as well as our emotions. Because these are preconscious transactions, we don't have much if any direct say when it comes to that end of things. Our conscious awareness is something we show up to the after-party with and it is at that point we have the possibility to influence how we further translate what's available to us by way of our sensory input, sensations, and conceptualizations into our perceptions. Only then does it have a chance to mingle with and shift its stance and meaning relative to its predominantly preconscious perceptions.

In short, most of what we have the possibility of controlling relative to our perception happens at the stage of intentional interpretation and responses to our initial perceptions and interpretations of them. In other words, we can consciously intervene after our brain predicts, simulates, and

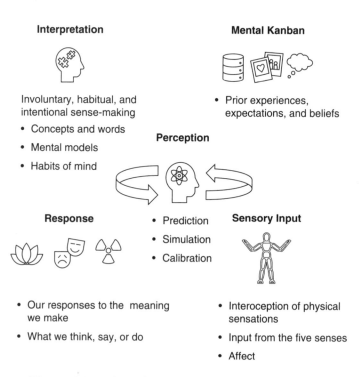

Interpretation

Involuntary, habitual, and intentional sense-making
- Concepts and words
- Mental models
- Habits of mind

Mental Kanban

- Prior experiences, expectations, and beliefs

Perception

- Prediction
- Simulation
- Calibration

Response

- Our responses to the meaning we make
- What we think, say, or do

Sensory Input

- Interoception of physical sensations
- Input from the five senses
- Affect

Figure 3.1 The Value Stream Map of Perception
Source: © Brain Capital LLC.

calibrates the building blocks of perception (see Figure 3.1). The first gate of our influence happens when we become consciously aware of our perceptions rather than passively perceptive. This opens the second gate of possibility, our subsequent narrative overlay. After our brain's initial preconscious rendering of our immediate context, when we endeavor to make further sense of what our brain has whipped up for us, is when our own awareness and dexterity of mind make the difference between us acting on a habitual sequence of sense-making and response or a conscious and intentional one. Since perception is not a linear process but an ongoing and emergent one, the VSM attempts to portray as much with the arrows indicating these constant feedback loops and calibration.

What Exactly Do We Have Influence Over?

Our mental Kanban, or just-in-time inventory, is a metaphor for all of our prior experiences, expectations, and beliefs our brain uses to categorize and formulate its predictions of what will happen next and how that will impact our body budget. To be clear, there isn't an actual repository or singular location from which the brain pulls these prior experiences. The brain employs its interoceptive and control networks and through statistical learning and predictive analytics works with what information it has at its disposal to simulate our perceptions (Barrett, 2017). Irrespective of where this information is stored in the brain or how it is retrieved, we have say in what we decide to add to our mental inventory, the emphasis we place upon it when we do, and how frequently we put it to use. Additionally, we decide what we will consciously pay attention to and for how long.[1]

Remember how I mentioned earlier that our chispa does the picking for us? If your chispa keeps reaching for a beer and chicharrones, know the result will likely be a big belly unless you offset this habit with daily living-room salsa—and not the kind you eat with chips. If you're a World War II buff like my 15-year-old son, chances are you're very knowledgeable about every aspect of what happened in each battle and turning point of the war. In this way our interests seem to pick us, yet we still have say in the matter. I don't know about you, but as a teenager I didn't ever think I'd like sex, for example, until I learned there was an entire discipline called metasex and quantum sex—I mean physics—replete with topics I am interested in, like where we came from and the nature of the universe and so on and so forth.

With each new experience, we are adding to our inventory of knowledge, application, and understanding, which, in turn, makes up what our brain has to draw from. Slow going perhaps, but nonetheless something we still have influence over. If we take the approach that things can be learned simply by studying or reading about them, like sex or physics, then we're leaving out an entire branch of learning, which is referred to as procedural knowledge. This is the kind of application-based learning that comes about through doing or applying something repetitively. When we only seek to know something with our intellect alone, we remain like a rock at the bottom of a river, which despite being immersed with water continuously moving over it, inside it always remains dry.[2]

We Can Change Our View

One of the mind's unique capacities is to be able to take different perceptual stances relative to what we are aware of. We can place our attention on tangible or intangible objects. We can narrow or widen our focus or rest our attention anywhere in between. You have at your disposal many perceptual perspectives or stances you can take. Much of the time we are focused on external, tangible phenomena more than we are on what's happening on an internal basis. Gaining dexterity in the many stances our awareness can take requires practice. We generally have to train to direct our attention inwardly in order to get acquainted with and grow accustomed to our own minds, which is the meaning of the Tibetan word for meditation, "gom." In other words, we're getting used to our own minds.

Our capacity to act from a place of conscious awareness and to have the wherewithal to take different perceptual stances is critical to doing anything well, let alone anything intentionally. I've italicized the above sentence because I'd like to ask you to re-read it and as you do, really take in its meaning. If someone were to tell you doing anything well in life requires you to be able to exercise the dexterity or agency of your own mind, and you were to believe it, then wouldn't you make it a priority to train in your capacity to do so?

One of the challenges we all experience is that we aren't built to focus all of the time. One, it's metabolically expensive and two, at some point, it can become a proposition of diminishing returns. There's a reason we have the capacity to do things while in a state of being passively perceptive to inadvertently aware. But what if there were a stance our awareness could learn to take that is both open and aware, at ease yet awake? In Tibetan Buddhism, there is a natural awareness we can learn to rest or abide in that has those and many other qualities. While this particular way of being aware has many names in Tibetan, depending on the context in which it's being used, the term "open awareness" sums it up quite nicely. It's not the kind of awareness that's uptight, restricted, narrow, taxing, or exhausting. It's the opposite of those habitual perspectives. While it's one among many views we can learn to take, it is one that allows for conscious awareness in a manner that isn't conceptual or taxing for the brain the way focusing can be if we're made to focus for long periods of time without having another mental stance to call upon.

Our minds have a wandering nature and go on frequent walkabouts. In fact, it may very well be that they're out and about more than they stay in or remain put. Between this and the tendency for our awareness to recede beneath the threshold of what we are consciously aware of, we spend a predominance of our time on this earth with our minds wandering in the direction of its distractions, becoming fixated at times and opaque and absent at others. The funny thing is until we grow accustomed to observing our mental phenomena as they appear and disappear against the backdrop of our own awareness, we tend not to notice how much our minds spend in motion, nor how much mental activity they actually generate. While some claim to be able to control the thoughts or feelings that bob to the surface of what they become aware of, it just takes meditating a few times before it becomes clear we don't actually have control over what pops up. Only once you've spent enough time paying attention to what's unfolding within your own mindstream do you come to realize you don't have control over what comes up by way of mental movement, such as thoughts, feelings, emotions, memories, ideas, and so forth. That said, you can train in noticing and observing what comes up. You can come to know the mind's movement. In fact, you can employ any number of methods, such as dropping a thought when you become aware of it. You can also try to notice where the thought comes from and where it goes. You can count breaths until you become distracted and then start again. I've always thought it might make more sense to count thoughts since we have so many of them, and they're what tend to distract us anyway—but I'm guessing even then we'd quickly lose track. Meanwhile, your mind's movement and activity doesn't ever really stop. It's just a matter of how far its activities recede into the background of what you are consciously aware of.

Even though we don't really have control over what comes up by way of our thoughts or mental movement, we have the capacity to learn different strategies for relating to whatever comes up. We can learn to relate to our thoughts in a manner in which our awareness of them creates space in which we get to decide how we will relate to their impact on us. Just by becoming aware of the thoughts or feelings in our field of reference and having at our disposal new ways of relating to any mental commentary and interpretative overlays they may inspire, we can play a more conscious role in what is otherwise an illusory dance unfolding in our own mind.

The Rudder of Our Own Mind

Going back to the origins of the word "mindfulness," in Sanskrit *smṛti*, in Pali *sati*, and in Tibetan *dran pa*, each carries the meaning of recalling or remembering, among a number of other meanings for the same word. My favorite among them, however, are "non-slipping of mind," "remembering to recall consciousness," and "remembering with longing" (Rangjung Yeshe Wiki – Dharma Dictionary, 2003). What gives us this ability? The mind has the capacity to act as its own rudder, steering itself toward whatever it remembers or directs itself toward. When we are in a state of being passively perceptive or barely aware, the rudder of our attention is directed for us by our immediate internal and external cues and our habitual responses to each. However, when our minds are conscious and present and we have presence of mind, we can direct the rudder of our awareness in any number of perceptual stances of our choosing. We will get into greater detail on these stances when we discuss the natural qualities and expressions of our own awareness.

When we are in the mode of being passively perceptive, we default to whatever has become habitual or routine for us, including the cognitive patterns or mental models we use to make meaning of our direct experience. Where do those patterns come from? For one, our upbringing, the immediate and surrounding contexts in which we were, as we say, reared. Funny term, isn't it? Come to think about it, I definitely feel "reared" by my upbringing and various experiences throughout my life. We learn from seeing, doing, and repeating. Everything we've been taught and experienced, advertently or inadvertently, sits in our mental Kanban (not literally but figuratively), making itself accessible to our brain in a just-in-time manner to make sense of its own rendering of reality. So, in those moments in which we handle something skillfully or well but aren't necessarily conscious of our intent to be skillful, it happens by function of what we've learned and enacted repetitively until it becomes a thought-action sequence we can handle in passive perceptive mode. Our minds and our bodies just kick in and say and do the right and appropriate things. This isn't the same thing as doing something with mindfulness, or presence of mind. Similar to other habits, until we've established being mindful as a go-to way of being consciously aware, we must rely upon the rudder of our attention. In other words, it requires we orient from a place of conscious and intentional awareness.

Thus, while we have the capacity to have direct influence over our own presence of mind, like anything it takes practice to be able to do so in the moments we need to most. The mind often behaves like a naughty or unruly child. I should know: I was one and have four of them—not minds but children. When we issue our mind, or one of our children, the command to be still, it gets even more restless, jumpy, and antsy. When we say don't think, the mind goes into overdrive, producing more mental movement than we ever thought possible. When we say be nice, it sticks its tongue out at us and at others. Unless we become accustomed to our own mind, its ways and habits, we risk it becoming rudderless. When we aren't able to pilot our own mind, it drifts, its destination uncertain. With a rudder, our mind can take us where we want to go, or at least it can keep redirecting us until we eventually get there.

I don't know about you, but my mind manages to wreak havoc on itself pretty regularly and more often than I'd like on those I care about. Even though we may regularly make a mess of things by some unskillful combination of how we express ourselves or by our actions, the reins sit squarely in our hands at some series of points prior to doing or saying the thing that gets us in trouble. The only times we don't have direct control is when our response is one of an involuntary nature or our reaction is so swift it might as well have been. When we introduce awareness and our conscious attention into the equation, it increases the possibility for us to intervene on our own behalf. If we're not able to avoid the impending misstep, then perhaps we can create enough distance between our assessment and our reaction to allow for the kind of response we can be prouder of. In other words, we figure out how and when to put the brakes on. To be clear, this isn't to suggest we deny how we feel, it's that we use our awareness itself to relate to our initial perceptions in a manner that allows for a different interpretation and therefore a more conscientious response. We are quite literally using the rudder of our own awareness to steer our perspective in the moment, which by default sets us on a different course of response and action. It's the mental equivalent of physically adjusting your body to be able to see a different perspective, but without having to physically move. In Buddhism, remembering we have our awareness at our disposal to shift our view is called mindfulness. Our awareness has a rudder built into it. As we'll see when we look at the qualities and expressions of awareness, there are many options available to us with respect to how we can adjust our view from the seat of our own awareness.

Stimulus and Response: A New Paradigm

Up until very recently, I would talk about how between stimulus and response we can exercise our agency. You may be familiar with the famous Victor Frankl quote, "Between stimulus and response there is a space. In that space is our power to choose our response. In our response lies our growth and our freedom." I used to explain that it is in these spaces, these inflection points, if we manage to seize them, where we have the possibility for direct influence. However, based on the constructed view of emotion, the brain doesn't react strictly on a stimulus-response basis. Rather, our brain simulates its best guess of what's going to happen in an anticipatory fashion.

Instead of simply reacting to incoming input, it is through prediction and correction of prediction error our brain conceptualizes and sets into motion its interpretation and response. In other words, we may not be responding directly to the stimulus itself, but to our anticipation of events and our best guess of how we will need to respond. Once our brain has simulated what it believes will happen, using the data it has at its disposal to do so, namely our past experiences, it factors in input from our senses and interoceptive sensations to account and correct for prediction error. Since this is presumably a never-ending cycle of prediction, calibration, and correcting for prediction error, it's hard to say exactly where the inflection points are in which our conscious awareness has the capacity to intervene. Irrespective of how we talk about perception, neither model precludes us from introducing awareness into the mix as a means of preempting or mitigating for an unskillful response and opting for a better one.

For instance, when you say or do something you know isn't going to be received well but you do it anyway, that's when the ability to act upon any glimmer of awareness you have in the moment would be the most helpful. But that's also when it's usually the hardest to do. Unless we train in our own awareness, our capacity to reposition our awareness when these moments come up, which they do many times within a single day, it simply won't happen, not even by accident. For many, the prospect of taking this level of personal accountability for their actions can be overwhelming. However, it represents the difference between giving up what we have influence over, defaulting to our habits of minding and behaving, or exercising our own agency of mind to select for a more conscious and well-considered response. Which will you choose, the "red pill" or the "blue pill"?[3]

Our Means

There is a single gateway to what we have the possibility of influencing within ourselves, and that is our conscious awareness (see Figure 3.2). Here, you'll see the various perceptual processes and functions we have the possibility to influence along with their unconscious counterparts that preside over our lives when we don't enact our conscious awareness, ranging from what we are passively perceptive of to processes considered preconscious to

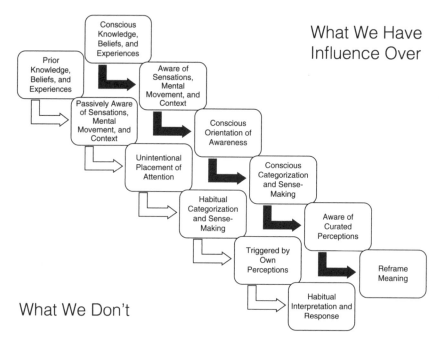

Figure 3.2   What We Have Influence Over and What We Don't
Source: © Brain Capital LLC.

unconscious. As you can see, there is quite a lot that we do have both direct and indirect influence over, two broad categories of which we can employ in the moment to exercise our agency of mind. The first is shifting our "view" or perceptual stance, which we spoke about earlier in this chapter and will address in greater detail in later chapters. The second involves us reframing our meaning using one of two broad methods: (1) using our awareness of our bodily sensations and signals and recategorizing their meaning to arrive at greater emotional granularity; and (2) using our awareness of our mental models, beliefs, and attitudes to interpret our perceptions in a conscious and intentional way that hopefully serves us and those around us better.

However, each of these techniques first requires us to have the presence of mind in the moment to remember to enact it. To the extent we've developed maneuverability within our own awareness, we can use its inherent qualities as methods for working with our various habits of mind. Our own awareness is the gateway to all other contemplative and cognitive techniques, tools, and strategies we have at our disposal to work with our perceptions. Anything we wish to do intentionally requires our awareness and conscious involvement. We either need to employ our awareness in the moment or already have a habit of skillfully responding to that particular set of variables—which certainly isn't a given.

Our ability to spot what we do and do not have direct control over is vital. Each of the 12 Self-Discoveries provide methods we can use to reframe our meaning in the moment and reminders of how we can enact our inherent wisdom. Only when we start to notice and work with how we are constructing our own reality do we start to regain our footing in a process that otherwise can feel mostly out of our hands. Our ability to recategorize the meaning of the physical sensations associated with our emotional valence and salience and to reframe our interpretation of what's happening is an opportunity to infuse our actions and words with judiciousness, empathy, and compassion, among many other equally beneficial ingredients. Short of our ability to do this, humanity has virtually no chance of preempting or mitigating the deleterious effects of jealousy, hate, divisiveness, and us-versus-them thinking. Without adequate training in awareness, how we treat each other, our basic human kindness and dignity, will remain unsteady. *Changes in behavior require changes to how we see and how we relate to what we see.*

What We Can't Control

What in your life are you expending energy trying to control but is not actually within your control? Do you find yourself trying to control other people, their emotions, or the outcomes to a variety of situations you don't actually have control of? If so, what are these things? There is a parable often shared in the context of learning about meditation and one's own mind within the Tibetan Buddhist tradition. In rural areas of Asia, water buffalo and cattle are often led by a nose rope. The rope is attached to a ring between the nostrils, which is a very tender area. If the ring is pulled or tugged even slightly, it's excruciatingly painful. The lesson at the heart of the metaphor is that we don't want to hand over our own nose rope. Metaphorically speaking, the rope represents those things—people, circumstances, even our own thoughts, emotions, and mental states—we allow to drag us around by our proverbial nose rope. The moral is, we need to learn how to take back our own nose rope when we notice we've handed it over. As you reflect on your own life, where in your life do you need to take back your own nose rope? In other words, are there areas in which you are not taking accountability for or leveraging the things you can control, like the sense you habitually make of your perceptions, your reactions, your words, your actions, or your attitude? Unless we take every naturally existing opportunity to develop our awareness, we won't be in the position to exercise what we do have direct influence over. We won't be able to keep a hold of our own nose rope.

While it may be obvious to you what you do and do not have control of, it has been my experience that we inadvertently try to exert control where we don't have any or miss the mark when we do. While my aim isn't to produce an exhaustive or all-inclusive list of what we can't control— despite its sobering potential—I think it's worth taking a moment to note areas in which I've observed myself and other people hit a brick wall. For starters, let's discuss the expectations we each claim to be free of. In the same way SPANX promises a trademarked *flat gut, great butt*™, our expectations offer us the illusion of being invisible while remaining abundantly present, neatly folded and tucked away behind the veneer of ego's seamlessness. Of course, we can learn to notice, dial back, or reconfigure our expectations—or simply decide we care more about what's at stake than our own agenda. But each of these scenarios requires us to be conscious of what our expectations are to begin with. Even when we say we don't have expectations, in fact, we do, although they remain mostly silent until they're not met and don't become personal until they do. If our brain could speak to us unmediated by our mouth—what we generally refer to as thoughts and feelings—our expectations would be our brain's, and perhaps our ego's, way of articulating what it thinks should happen, based on what has happened before in similar situations. From our brain's point of view, when our expectations aren't met, it's simply the brain's incredulousness that what it expected to happen didn't. *If our expectations are the output of our brain's predictive capacity, bias is the by-product of the assumptions and influences it's operating under relative to its sense-making capacity.*

Our expectations stem from what we've observed or have been formally taught and are basically the headlines of our prior experiences.

Whether based on our moral, religious, or philosophical views, or our upbringing, socioeconomic status, or education, the threads of meaning our brain predictively assembles from a lifetime of input is, well, mind-boggling to say the least. The brain naturally does what computer scientists have attempted to achieve with artificial neural networks built to mirror the capacity of the human brain to process hundreds of billions of interconnected inputs at the same time (Frankenfiel, 2020).

When our expectations aren't met, one of two things typically happens. We either come to realize what our expectations were to begin with, even though we could have sworn we didn't have any, or we get cranky and lose our patience. What's more, we often read into other people's intentions as to why they haven't met our expectations, forgetting they probably aren't aware of our expectations—after all, how could they be when we weren't even aware of them ourselves? If they've purposely or inadvertently violated what we care about, it's most likely in service of getting their own needs met. Typically, it has very little to do with us—unless the person is motivated like my 15-year-old son is, which is to get my goat—to see how his mom, spokesperson for emotional intelligence, will react. Alas, when the reality sets in that our expectations have failed to be met, we may then try to exert control or power over the person who has failed to predict our needs in the process of predicting their own. This can end poorly for both parties. Take the following anecdote from my own habits of mind, part B to the story I mentioned in the introduction to the Self-Discoveries.

All Good Things Come to Those Who Wait[4]

My daughter was born a day early but has run about 10 minutes late ever since. Who knew that would be the price we would all pay to have her arrive a day in advance? Her propensity for lateness began impacting me and her brother when she was in middle school. I used to have to drive her and her brother to their school, which was across town. My daughter's habitual lateness was met with strict measures by her school if she wasn't in her classroom, butt in chair, by the first and only bell. I guess people didn't nickname it "Rigidview" for nothing. Kids who didn't arrive on time sat in the front entrance on a bench for the entire first period. While I could have learned to live with that as a natural consequence for my daughter, when it started impacting my son and me—when I still had a job I had to be on time for—it was less and less workable. We tried everything: setting alarms earlier; taking showers at night instead of the morning; setting out clothes the night before—even though it was a uniform and therefore didn't yield much choice or variation to begin with. We tried having my daughter go to bed earlier. But nothing helped. It turned out neither did getting upset, yelling, or losing my cool. My son, who was just six at the time, would calmly set his backpack down, cross his arms as he leaned against the doorway to the garage, and just shake his head as he watched me blow a gasket while my daughter raced around the house as though she had become a contestant on *Wipe-Out* as she completed what felt like round seven of an invisible, yet seemingly real, gauntlet of her own making each morning before we were allowed to leave the house.

Around that time, I started working with a coach for the first time—I was accustomed to being the one in the coach's seat but never the other way around. After my coach listened to me talk about this situation a number of times in our coaching sessions, she had me do two things. First, she had me get out a piece of paper and draw a dot on it. She then had me draw a circle around the dot and a second circle completely around the first circle, until I was left staring at what looked like a bull's eye—no doubt a foreshadowing of either the insight or impending doom to come. She asked me to write everything I had direct control over in the inner circle with the dot in it. I assumed the dot was me, though I never asked. Then she had me note all the things I could think of that I did not have direct control over and write them in the space between the two circles. When I ran out of ideas, she asked, "How about your daughter's perpetual lateness? Which circle does that go in? How about the kids' school living up to their reputation?" And so on. Once we'd established that I didn't have control over my daughter, her tendency toward lateness, or what at times felt like the school's cold-hearted but consistent response to her lateness, my coach asked me the following perspective-altering questions: "What if you didn't try to protect your daughter from the natural consequences of being late? What if you left her at home while taking your son to school on time if she's not ready to go?" I thought to myself, "Great idea! Where the hell have I been? How did I get four kids without having a lick of sense in my brain?" Oh, yeah, that's how I got four kids. While quite painful, the next question she asked me has proven to be an eye opener to this day and a bone-shaking question for me at the time. She asked, "Michele, what's it like for your kids to be around you, do you think?" My heart sank to my belly button—though the two are admittedly much closer now—and my eyes welled up with tears, as they do every time I recall these words.

The gift my coach gave me by asking me those few seemingly simple questions was the shift in perspective I needed to be able to see where my expectations had been getting in the way of my relationships with those I cared about most; namely, my kids. Trying to change my daughter's relationship to time along with my own failed attempts to alter the time-space continuum each morning by yelling was, in the end, a futile manner to go about things. Once is all it took, by the way, after leaving my daughter at home the next time she wasn't ready to go to school on time. I didn't yell or become irate. My heart felt tight leaving her at home, but I decided in this instance that letting the natural consequences play out was the right thing to do. Next thing I knew, my hand just waved goodbye, as did my son's— though his far more enthusiastically. While it didn't solve her proclivity to be late, it did elicit a new behavioral response. The incompatibility between her desire to do well in school and risk being stranded at home facilitated her initiating a temporary truce with time. Whenever I find myself getting worked up or carried away, I still make a point of asking myself, "What's it like to be around you?" This has become one of many personal mantras I use to remind myself to shift my view and see what new things can be seen when I do. How might you answer this same question for yourself?

While everyone could certainly benefit from having a coach like Carla, eventually shifting your view comes down to establishing yourself on a first-name basis with your inner coach. Your own awareness is your inner coach you can always turn toward. In the lineage of Tibetan Buddhism I practice, as part of a practice called "Calling the Guru from Afar" we make the heartfelt aspiration and plea to our Guru, "Quick, look upon me with compassion." It's an extremely profound practice with many layers of meaning, the innermost of which reminds us we are never without the Guru when we are resting in the natural face of our own mind (Thaye, 1998). From there, all of our best qualities unfold. By establishing practices that allow you to familiarize yourself with your own awareness, you'll eventually start to notice your own habits of mind and be able to catch yourself when you're up to your old shenanigans. Little by little, you'll learn to recognize the many disguises of your habits of mind and how best to greet each and every one of them, invite them for a cup of tea, and then guide them on from the console of your own conscious awareness.

While there is plenty that isn't in our direct control to influence, as you can see there is plenty that is. Since we can't do anything about the things we can't control, we would do well to focus on what is within our direct capacity to do something about, which almost always originates in and from ourselves and comes down to our ability to make different choices on a conscious basis. When it's possible to exert indirect influence, as in the example of what we feed and reinforce by way of our mental Kanban, we can and should be selective and intentional with whatever we add to the mix. When you find yourself in a difficult moment or a frustrating or complicated situation, it may be helpful to start by asking yourself, "What, in myself, in this present moment, do I have influence over?"

4

You Are the Common Denominator

The closer you come to knowing that you alone create the world of your experience, the more vital it becomes for you to discover just who is doing the creating.

—Eric Michael Leventhal

Where is the one place from which we cannot escape? Where do we spend the entirety of our lives? In this body and in this mind. Many of us go through our entire lives trapped in the confines of our own habitual ways of processing and making sense of what we perceive, not even realizing the role our interpretation of reality plays. *Once we realize our own awareness is the exit strategy from an escape room of our own making, we start to catch glimpses of the invisible mental attitudes and constructs holding us hostage to those aspects of ourselves we're not yet consciously aware of.* Within any given moment of our lives, we experience a nearly constant stream of perceptions, thoughts,

87

feelings, and emotions, for which we have our brain, our social condition-
ing, and our prior experiences to thank.

If each day of your life were captured by an episode of your favorite
Netflix series, what would the day you're having today be entitled? What
would you name the series? What would you witness as you observe your
own life from the vantage point of someone looking in from the outside?
If there were headlines of this series, what might they be? How might you
describe to others what takes place in the series of episodes that when
viewed together comprise your life? What notable qualities and hangups
do you as the main character have? What as the main character do you not
see that is obvious to everyone else? If you could give the main character—
presumably some aspect of yourself—a piece of advice, what would it be?

Like a movie set, we arrive on the scene of our lives again and again
either fully present or only partially present, like a stunt double who just
shows up to perform the dangerous or controversial scenes. All the while
we alternate in and out of conscious awareness, not knowing where we've
arrived from, how we got there, or where to depart for next. That is the
life we lead each day. We wake up again and again, until of course one
day we don't. No matter how varied the sets we find ourselves arriving
on the scene of or the fellow actors with whom we end up performing
our roles, we have roughly the same repertoire of habitual responses we
employ. Within each new context we find ourselves, we do our best to
adapt to the parameters we are given, be they predictable or unpredictable,
straightforward or formidable. Yet, the mental habits we employ to make
sense of these ever-evolving parameters aren't nearly as visible to us as the
outer circumstances we're navigating. If we want to know that part of who
we are better than we do now, we must unpack some of that mystery for
ourselves and become aware of our typical arsenal of moves. It's incumbent
upon us each to investigate and discern the option sets and mental models
we habitually default to and employ as we move through our lives, blink-
ing in and out of awareness. If we don't do this for ourselves, I promise you
nobody else will. The question I leave you with is this: If we are the stunt
double, arriving only when the stakes are high, who is in charge the rest of
the time? Who are we the stunt double of? Who is the leading actor? Is that
person competent, effective, and reliable?

Imagine that for an hour or two you go about living your life completely unfiltered—like brewing a pot of coffee without a filter. You ignore the social norms and niceties, which basically serve the same function as a coffee filter, which have been impressed upon you from as early as you can remember. The filters we've been taught, of course, serve many functions, one of which is to prevent us and others from having to choke on clumps of gritty coffee grounds—metaphorically speaking. While perhaps an overly simplistic analogy, you get the idea. But when it comes to our habits of mind, it is the more subtle and nuanced filters we are focused on. Going back to the coffee filter metaphor, what kind of water did you use to brew the coffee? What mechanism did you use to brew the coffee? What type of coffee did you select? How finely or coarsely did you grind the coffee; did you drown it with some sort of creamer, sweetener, or both? All of these things ultimately impact what type and flavor of coffee you end up with, right? We need to reach this level of certainty and precision with regard to our own minds, our awareness, how we perceive reality, how we make sense of what we perceive, and, in turn, how we use and act upon that information.

Perception Is the Axis Mundi

In the same way our wherewithal and wisdom exist as possibilities within us, so too are we each the common denominator of our own experience. Our perception is the axis mundi, or reference point, from which everything unfurls. Our intrinsic capacity to be cognizant and aware gives us the possibility of being able to perceive and observe the ever-unfolding display of our own mind and its interpretation of reality. You are the magician that gives rise to the "magic show" you call your life. This is none other than you. The finger of our results, our outcomes, the quality of our relationships, and our overall wellbeing (or lack thereof) always points back at (insert your name and likeness here)! When we look more closely, our experience in each moment is a reflection and outcome of:

- How we experience and react to ourselves—our perceptions and interpretation of our internal and external landscape: our thoughts, feelings, emotions, and inner dialogue; what we say, and what we do.

- How we experience and react to others—their perceptions and interpretation of their internal and external landscape: their thoughts, feelings, emotions, and inner dialogue; what they say, and what they do.
- How we experience and react to the cues in and around us.
- How others experience and react to us.

Our task is to start observing the direct link between the results we're getting in the various areas of our lives and how we perceive and react to the world and people around us. Take a moment now and reflect on what it is you believe determines the outcomes you're getting in your own life as well as the quality of your relationships. Identify and describe whatever you believe is responsible for the results you are getting or have gotten in your life up to this point. Then, reflect upon how your habits of mind impact your relationships and how others experience you.

Perhaps you know someone who believes they have no control in response to their own emotions or what happens to them in life, someone who sees themselves completely at the mercy of their present circumstances; someone who somewhere along the way has unwittingly adopted a victim mentality. How might this perception shape their experience? Now, think of someone who goes through life trying to control the moods or actions of others to fit their expectations of how things should be. How do others experience them? Visualize what they might say or do and how they make the people around them feel. Now, apply the same thought process to your own beliefs—naming what is operative in your core belief system, whether by default or consciously chosen. What do you believe about yourself? Do you see yourself as someone with volition and agency? Take a few moments to reflect upon what you believe about yourself and how this impacts you, your relationships, and your results.

Observe how those around you react to your presence and to what you say and do. Are you able to discern any immediate feedback the world and others provide you with? Do you see any common patterns or themes? To what extent might this be a function of how you perceive yourself versus how others may experience you? As you take the time to observe and listen to the feedback your life and those around you are giving you, notice your urge to fill in the gaps with explanations or narratives.

We Are Our Own Frame of Reference

Scientific methodology has historically relied upon a picture of reality that can be objectively known and studied uninfluenced by the subjective perceptions and methods of those attempting to study it. In other words, science is predicated upon there being an object that can be objectively studied, observed, and measured. However, despite the priority science places on understanding the phenomenal world from an empirical standpoint, how can we know phenomena objectively when everything we perceive is mediated by our subjective perception and interpretation of them? I certainly wouldn't be the first nor likely the last to point out the problematic and to a large extent unavoidable predicament of the scientific process itself. My point in highlighting this conundrum is that it's precisely the same dilemma we find ourselves in as we search for meaning about ourselves and within ourselves.

Within Buddhist thought the term "relative or conventional truth" is used to describe what lies at the heart of our mistaken belief in an objective, permanent self and our habitual tendency to perceive reality through a subject-object lens. In other words, we are deeply conditioned to perceive our experience through this mode of subject-observer and object-observed. This is mirrored in how we experience reality as a sentient, conscious being navigating our immediate context using our connections to the outside world via the five senses and to other sentient beings, who provide us with the concepts, language, and mental models we use to create meaning to interpret our ever-changing context. Buddhists would assert that there are actually six sensory inputs—but who's counting?—the same five we acknowledge plus consciousness. In any event, we experience ourselves as the owner of this mind and this body. Thus, it's not surprising we fall back on this construct, the same dualistic approach, when it comes to everything we do, including the scientific process itself. Both stances capture how most of us go through life unaware of or not wanting to acknowledge the subject-object frame through which we perceive reality in which we are the observer and everything we observe, the objects, are separate and distinct from ourselves.

Because we don't give this way of being or perceiving much if any conscious thought, we not only lose track of ourselves as the actor who is doing the acting, we aren't inclined to see ourselves in the capacity of an observer much of the time either. Instead, we spend most of our lives passively perceiving and reacting to our environment. We are the magician who misses our own tricks. We also do not tend to see our outcomes as direct or indirect consequences of what we habitually think, say, and do. Rather, we have a tendency to disconnect our actions from the results they produce both by way of consequences and the habitual tendencies from which they emerge.

According to Everett's relative-state formulation of quantum mechanics, what we see is the world relative to our own state. In short, he describes a universe of possibilities in which each perception is subjective to the observer.[1] Buddhism agrees what we each perceive is our own subjective experience of reality, while we mistakenly believe what we see to be empirically or objectively true. From the Buddhist perspective, the phenomenal world can also be experienced from a nondual perspective in which there is no observer and no object to be observed, only awareness unmediated by a perceiver. Buddhist philosophy refers to this way of perceiving reality as "ultimate truth," whereby subject and object collapse into awareness itself, free from an observer. For that instance, our awareness and capacity to perceive isn't trapped within the constraints of a subject-object view of the world. For that moment, we are neither focused outwardly nor are we focused on what's happening inside our mindstream or our body. It's the mental equivalent of what would happen if we removed our exterior context and our interior context at the same time yet kept our capacity for awareness. Even with training, this perceptual stance doesn't tend to last long due to our habitual tendency to perceive reality according to the way our design naturally lends itself to, but let's just say, hypothetically, this way of perceiving did persist. What if our own awareness, free from subject-object focus, free from observer and observed, was our default? What would happen? Our awareness wouldn't have any context, or affective niche, other than itself to perceive and be aware of. Presumably, we might then experience and embody the qualities of our own mind, our awareness, of consciousness itself—whichever name you prefer to assign our capacity to be aware, to know, and to perceive. Life as we are used to experiencing it would change, wouldn't it?

Awareness unmediated by an observer causes the foundation of what we normally hold as objectively real and true to fall apart. In that instant, our perception of being an observer with something to observe simply collapses. The observer and observed become jobless, and for that instant, there is no one doing the seeing and nothing that is seen, apart from awareness itself—which isn't something we can pinpoint or find. It isn't an object. Yet it is the basis of our capacity to experience and can be experienced in its own right. Quantum theory, at least in Everett's interpretation, supports the notion that what we see and experience can only be said to be a reflection of our own state. Moreover, according to Lisa Feldman Barrett's constructed theory of emotion and how the brain predicts and simulates its own version of reality versus solely reacting to stimuli in its environment puts forth a similar view in which she says, ". . . we are the architects of our own reality" (Barrett, 2017, p. 40).

What we can take from all of this is that our frame of reference, and what we conclude about it, holds profound implications for how we make sense of what we perceive and the actions we are inclined to take because of those views. We each have beliefs about the nature of reality and our position relative to it. Whether we are aware of what those beliefs are depends on whether we've made a point to explore and articulate what we believe or whether we've made a habit of behaving according to our unconscious beliefs about our perception of reality. It turns out this matters greatly and is one of the many clues we need to gather and piece together about ourselves, for ourselves, in order to gain a full picture of what's operative with respect to our own mental constructs we use to make sense of our moment-to-moment experience.

At a minimum, these various ways of understanding reality and our position relative to those perspectives should inspire us to ask questions we haven't yet thought to ask ourselves and a willingness to explore the implications of what our insights might yield by way of practical and actionable wisdom. Each of us only has direct line of sight and access to our own highly subjective perspectives, which is why it is good to go into anything we do resisting the urge to cling too tightly to our own views as being the only ones that are correct or deserving of merit. Since our only option to study our own experience is from the standpoint of what we can directly observe about it using our own awareness, the cognizance aspect of our mind, we should expect it to yield both unique and valuable insights. We all share patterns by virtue of having roughly the same hardware and parameters to work with, including shared frameworks of meaning, such as culture, concepts, words, and language—all of which allow us to approximate a shared experience of reality, even though our perceptions and beliefs about that reality vary greatly enough that our response to those differences in belief cause us to harm and kill each other, oppress and subjugate one another. Unless we're given the idea or impetus to, most of us aren't naturally inclined to make the mental leap; our beliefs are largely a function of our social influences and contexts as well as our repeated use of those concepts and mental models each time our brain simulates its own reality.

In order to learn about the invisible forces that shape, define, and give rise to our habits of mind—our thoughts, emotions, beliefs, biases, mindset, and habitual ways of making sense of each—we need to employ the same precision of observation used in the scientific process to observe our own experience—subjective as it is—of absolutely everything we have the capacity to be aware of and perceive. The invitation you're being presented with is to investigate your own internal landscape using the various views you have intrinsically available to you. By engaging the practical methods, frameworks, and practices discussed in this book, there isn't any reason you can't practice discerning, making sense of, and transforming your own habits of mind.

L'Ego My Ego

It would seem not everything we do in our lives is exclusively in service of our body budget—unless our psychological needs also fall under its auspices. That may just be my ego talking; though, I can understand how one might arrive at this conclusion, particularly if they were to believe consciousness is predicated upon having a brain and a body. However, even with this understanding of reality comes the need to account for our sense of self, our perception that we have agency, and our belief in the concept of "I"—what I am referring to in this context as our ego. This isn't Freud or Jung's definition of ego, but rather a belief in an objective self, an "I" in contrast to other people's selves and I's. What purpose does our belief in a self serve? Does our perception of being a self in body serve a purpose, or is it simply an unexpected yet pervasive side effect of our practical design? I'm pretty sure we're not going to work out a complete or even partial answer to these rather riddlesome questions in a chapter whose subheading is a play on words borrowed from a seventies commercial in which two teenagers are fighting over an Eggo waffle—bantering back and forth, "L'eggo my Eggo."

Nonetheless, here is the upshot of what I've gleaned from living on this planet for nearly half a century: People will push themselves well beyond what is humanly or physically possible for a cause, for a purpose, for something they believe in, or for someone they love. While science hasn't yet successfully managed to put its finger on ego's origins, its purpose, or function, Buddhist philosophy certainly has taken a compelling stab at it—the complete study of which would entitle you to at least one PhD. Irrespective of whether ego is under the direction and command of our body budget or whether ego is holding our body's budget hostage to its aims, we'll not likely read about it anytime soon in scientific journals. One of the psychological purposes I suspect it plays is in rationalizing our own point of view, the decisions we make, and even our own existence. Ego receives ongoing existential validation primarily owing to its subject-object frame of reference through which it is perpetually reinforced as we carry out all aspects of our lives.

Our Sense of Purpose and Being, Nature's Insurance Policy

Not dissimilar to earlier discussion on our sense of agency lending itself toward us feeling as though we indeed have a purpose, it follows that one of ego's roles is to shore up the continuity of our physical and psychological experience, giving us each the distinct impression—whether true or not—of being a discrete self that exists. When we believe we are a self with an identity, that belief serves as the impetus and basis upon which we seek purpose—outside of our immediate concern of remaining alive. Our belief that we are a self, placed on this earth to fulfill a purpose, acts as a kind of psychological, if not biological, insurance plan, one that despite whatever hardships we may face are by design built to provide us with compelling enough reasons to keep choosing life over its alternatives. The correlate to that is that to be human also means there are times we don't want to stick around anymore. I don't know a person on this earth who hasn't at some point in time thought they would be better off dead than alive. If we struggle to find even just one "why" as to why we want to be here, just one tiny reason, like that cup of Earl Grey tea with honey we enjoy each morning or our cat who falls asleep in a purring turban on our head each night, some small gesture of our existence that allows us to access life's magic, then at that point, we're at the mercy of our own beliefs.

In the tradition of Buddhism I practice, we believe taking life is one of the worst things a person can do, let alone taking one's own life. There is the belief that doing so creates such a negative and powerful imprint in one's own mindstream that a person may be inclined to take his or her life again and again for many lifetimes to come. If having to live again and again isn't enough of a deterrent, try that on top of being inclined to do yourself in each time. That's a fate worse than having to watch *Groundhog Day*, the movie, over and over. But if you believe you're just going to be reborn again and are uncertain of the circumstances of your rebirth, recognizing future circumstances may be even worse, it makes taking one's own life a much less compelling option knowing you'll have all the same habitual tendencies as you did in the past, plus this additional one. Someone who holds this particular worldview is more likely to slog on through, learning to work with the factors that may, at times, make them not want to be here anymore.

Bottom line, had I not believed what I believed when I believed it, I might have become another casualty of suicide at least a few different times in my life. It turns out our beliefs matter! And our belief in a self absolutely has consequences. In Buddhism it is owing to this mistaken albeit pervasive belief in a discrete self, along with the sum total of cause and effect this perceptual stance accumulates, that is the impetus for us being reborn again and again. Who knew having a reference point could be so impactful? It makes sense on some level, given that nothing produced leaves the system it is a part of; only when we dismantle the system does what it contains and perpetually produces also collapse.

I think it is important to add, since I brought up the topic to begin with, that suicidal thoughts and tendencies that spring from any number of serious mental or physical conditions, such as anxiety, depression, or chronic pain, to name a few, have as much of a basis in the mind as they do the body. Therefore, working with each in modalities of care that match the severity of the need is imperative. When someone is suffering from one or more serious conditions that may cause them not to want to remain alive, that's probably not the time to improvise. It's important to seek the care of those who can offer expert support to fit the situation accordingly. However, knowing what is at the heart of your own beliefs, your self-identity, is a good indicator for how you may behave when such thoughts surface—as I believe they do for everyone at some point over the course of their lives.

As abruptly as I began this section, I will conclude it. As a Buddhist, while I believe ego is the root of our confusion, I also believe ego has a very effective continuity plan in place for itself. Irrespective of whether each of us has a desire to undermine ego or is perfectly happy to believe we exist, we're all in various states of the same predicament. While we are here on this planet, we might as well have a purpose, particularly one that isn't deluded by beliefs that cause us to want to harm one another, in effect edging each other out. Instead, we can use our belief in a self to construct a purpose that benefits self and others. As long as we have the perception of ego, me, and my, what other choice do we have but to embrace its use on the path, even if that path for some of us is to dismantle it? Even if our sense of self replete with a purpose serves roughly the equivalent of having a security blanket and an existential binky, neither of which we're quite ready to part with, so be it. Our belief we have a purpose does in fact serve a purpose, though perhaps not the one we might have hoped or expected. However, since most of us still believe in a self and experience our life from that vantage point, we might as well put our perception of being a self to good use.

It's up to you, to me, and to everyone else to decide what footprint they will leave on this earth. The fact we can each question the nature of our own existence speaks to a level of awareness and agency that feels as empowering as it does exasperating at times. Even though purpose and aimlessness are opposite sides of the same conceptual coin, we can work with what we feel, knowing each concept or emotion we experience is temporary. If we can shift our perspective just a smidge to be able to see ourselves as agentic selves in our lives in which we can employ our own intrinsic capacity to be awake and aware, ready to observe whatever unfolds within our own mindstream, that's what puts us each at the helm of our own habits of mind and in charge of the perspective and lens through which we experience our lives.

5

You Don't Have to Believe Everything You Think

You are the sky. Everything else—it's just the weather.

—Pema Chodron

We have the capacity to notice our thoughts and whatever passes through our field of awareness. Our attention can follow our thoughts, or we can abandon and let go of them the moment we notice their movement. We can examine them, as we look for their origin or try to follow them to discover where they disappear. We can become lost in our thoughts, swept up in the current of their movement within our own mindstream. We can ruminate or perseverate on our thoughts. We can question or doubt our thoughts, or we can accept them at face value. We can put stock in them, believing them to be true, or we can get curious and test whether they hold merit. And we can look into the natural face of our own awareness that perceives them to begin with. These are just a few possible ways we can position our own awareness to relate to our thoughts and mental movement. But perhaps most importantly, we can invite a new relationship to our own awareness and whatever appears in the field of our perception, such as bodily sensations, thoughts, feelings, emotions, concepts, memories, and ideas.

When someone first learns how to meditate, within a Buddhist context, we don't typically make a point of distinguishing among the various kinds of mental phenomena. We don't necessarily make a point of differentiating between categories or types of mental movement, such as thought, feeling, emotion, memory, or whatever comes up within one's mindstream. When we are getting used to the experience of noticing our own minds, the intent isn't to categorize, classify, dissect, or interpret, which is what our brain is normally accustomed to doing. When our minds are calm, like a lake with no movement, we have an opportunity to experience our awareness and its natural qualities in a way that is different from how we experience our minds when they are busy like Grand Central Station at rush hour.

The objective when we practice calm-abiding, or Shamatha, meditation is to allow our minds to settle, to become still and calm. To create the conditions for this to happen, we remain open and aware, gently placing our attention on the natural cadence of our breath. Our awareness is like our breath. It's very subtle, and there is nothing visible to see. Our breath leaves its trace as we feel the air move through our lungs or experience its movement in us as the rising and falling of our chest, or we may feel the sensation of air passing through our nostrils and mouth, evidence we are in fact breathing. Due to habit, our mind quickly becomes entangled in its own movement, either with the appearance of mental phenomena that unfold within our mindstream or external objects that draw our attention. Just the subtle act of our own awareness noticing its own appearance or movement is enough of an impetus to cause us to notice and to bring our attention back. We don't have to be heavy-handed or yank our minds around as if we were training a dog to heel. For those of you who have ridden a horse before, you may have learned if you forcefully pull the reins or are rough with the horse, your results are mixed at best. It becomes a battle of wills. We simply need to shift, sit forward, sit back, or gently press into the horse with our knees and lean in the direction we want the horse to go. Our minds are no different.

When learning how to meditate, we're often taught to notice and let go of our thoughts while anchoring our attention to our breath or an external object. Training our attention to come back to the breath or an object of focus each time it wanders off or becomes distracted is attentional training. In the same way Kegels strengthen the muscles of the pelvic floor, when we train the aspect of our awareness that can move, direct, and place itself, we are using the dexterity of our own awareness to pay attention in different kinds of ways.

The reason we typically start with calm-abiding meditation is because it makes it easier to experience your own mind when there isn't so much hubbub. While there are other practices we can engage in that allow us to begin noticing other aspects of our own mind, if you were asked to do so in the middle of Grand Central Station at rush hour, it would be more difficult. That said, when you are ready to start familiarizing yourself with the natural qualities of your own awareness, you can start by sitting in a dignified position as a means of welcoming your presence of mind. You're neither slumped over in a heap nor are you strained or stilted. In the same way a parent might summon kids from playing outside home for dinner, let the act of taking a few deep breaths in and out signal your mind to come home as you imagine gathering back any strands of your attention that, like the rowdy children, are now abandoning their activities and making their way toward home. This also allows you to locate your breath in your body. Let your awareness rest gently upon the invisible cadence of your natural breath, like a hummingbird that barely touches the flower from which it's sipping nectar. Meditating in this way allows us to connect with our own capacity to be aware. When our mind settles into itself, we start to notice its various qualities, with no particular object held in mind apart from just becoming aware of our capacity for awareness itself. We sometimes refer to this aspect of mind training as open awareness. Though we can experience the qualities and expressions of our awareness, we generally aren't accustomed to looking or to paying attention to our awareness in this way. Try noticing for yourself what qualities are present within your own awareness using the aspect of your mind that allows you to have the ability to perceive and know whatever arises.

Regardless of which practice you use to try out your awareness wings, eventually you'll start to notice its subtle expressions and qualities. You start to notice even the most minute movement or shifts in its expressions—when it expands its scope and becomes diffuse, or when it becomes fixated and fully absorbed and consumed by the object of its attention. You'll notice when your awareness is bright and awake or has the character of being dull or heavy. The more you become accustomed to your own awareness and capacity for perception, the more you gain access to your agency of mind, your mind's ability to move and adjust itself as well as its own perspective. When we gain familiarity with all the different ways we can be aware, our sensitivity to and awareness of our mind's ability to shift itself and its stance relative to the internal or external context can have the side effect of us noticing minute fluctuations or changes. We may feel a single hair that has fallen on our knee or detect when our attention moves ever so slightly, revealing subtler and subtler substrata of mental commentary and elaboration.

The value of getting used to your own mind is that you begin to experience mental phenomena for what they are, temporary appearances in your mindstream—your mind moving and nothing more. In those moments, our thoughts, feelings, perceptions, and sensations lose their normal air of importance and concreteness. When we practice letting go, we're practicing the mental disposition of nonclinging. Training our mind to release its Vulcan-like grip makes it easier when we're faced with something we're perseverating on in our day-to-day lives. Forming the mental habit of just noticing gives us a taste of what it feels like not to cling so tightly to begin with. We start to see that despite the big to-do and splash our thoughts often make of themselves, they are just as empty and invisible as the air we breathe. They are no more tangible than the clarity of awareness that perceives them. Like writing on the surface of water, they appear and then quickly disappear, if we let them. There's no need to use methods that would have us catch and release them. There is nothing to catch and nothing to release. Even though there's no "thing" to perceive, we can and do perceive whatever unfolds within the field of our perception. Yet, when we try to pinpoint a particular thought, or any kind of mental movement whatsoever, we can't actually locate them. They elude the capacity to be caught. But when we look directly into the source from which our thoughts or mental movement arise, the mind that perceives, the one observing, whatever you may have been perceiving by way of mental movement instantly vanishes like a snowflake hitting the surface of water.

But unless you make the effort to create the conditions to experience this for yourself again and again—namely, by establishing a consistent practice of meditation or mental training—all you've just read will remain at the level of writing on paper, a concept, a mental construct instead of a direct experience of you noticing and getting used to your own awareness. The amazing thing is we can learn how to be much more nuanced and precise in how we work with our own minds and our own awareness. To be clear, meditation isn't about chilling out or inviting the mind to become dull. If it were, we would just call it that, training in ordinary mind, dullness, or sleep itself. The objective isn't to space out; it's the opposite of that. The objective is to wake up and learn to relate to whatever unfolds in the open space of your awareness in a manner in which you aren't handing over your nose rope again and again to your thoughts, emotions, or whatever experiences may surface. Meditation also isn't the time to force anything, like you might a foot in a shoe. It's about allowing the mind's own awareness to relax into itself, to get used to itself. In the same way breathing relaxes the body, let your awareness settle its own activity. If you spend more time in the presence of your own mind, you'll have more options available to you in the moments when the ride gets a little wild and it's more like a rodeo.

The Meaning We Make

While we rarely choose how we will initially perceive a person or situation, we can choose how we relate to what we perceive and steer whatever overlay of meaning we're prepared to assign from there. For instance, if upon seeing someone outside your window, standing on what looks like your property line at 11 o'clock at night, flashlight in hand, your brain might jump to conclusions, just like mine did as I tried to figure out why someone would be standing so unabashedly close to my property line so late at night in close to zero-degree weather. As I peered out the window, I realized it was my new neighbor standing with their dog between our properties.

Initially, I found myself irritated and had the rather instantaneous reaction, "What the hell? Why are they taking their dog—which better not be as barky as the other neighbor's dog—to go to the bathroom on what looks to be the edge of my property?" As you can see, my first thoughts weren't particularly charitable. Instead, my mind quickly filled in the blanks and read ill intent into my neighbor's behavior, which was likely never there to begin with.

But then just as quickly, I found myself remembering what it's like to have a dog. Dogs—I think to myself in my head—they just pee and poop wherever suits them best. It's then up to their owners—or their neighbors—to sort it out. My thoughts moved to how much I love my dog Brownie, and how much I miss him since he went to live with family in Mexico. My next thought was, I bet my neighbor may be slightly irritated at their dog for having to go to the bathroom this late at night, especially given how cold it is, and at the need to get all decked out in winter wear. Then, I felt slightly badly about my initial assessment. That's when I noticed the neighbor could see me watching their every move. I waved and quickly turned out my light. This is an example of how through reframing and a modicum of empathy we can proactively reassess a situation and our initial judgment or narratives about it. Moreover, who knows what was going through my neighbor's mind or their dog's that whole time? We'll never know, but it's probably fair to say neither the neighbor nor their dog's line of thinking even remotely resembled the meaning I was initially inclined to assign their actions or feelings.

In this example, how I perceived what was happening and then chose to make sense of what I was seeing in large part dictated my response. I was able to regain my mental footing relatively quickly. By keying in on common points of shared humanity and with a bit of nudging from my side, I was able to steer my interpretation in a direction that allowed me to relate more charitably to my neighbor and their dog. I was able to get to a mental space of understanding despite my original inclination and perception of the situation. But I could have just as easily allowed my mind to take an entirely different path that would have yielded a very different understanding and outcome. For example, I could have opened my back door and yelled at my neighbor, "Get the hell off my property!" as I continued to mutter things under my breath or speak my mind: "I don't care if you're my new neighbor or not. Go take your dog to poop on your own lawn. What's the matter with you?" And in parting, I might have offered up, "I sure as hell hope this isn't going to be a nightly ritual for the two of you," no doubt closely followed by, "Oh, by the way, I'm Michele, your new neighbor. I just wrote a book about emotional intelligence. Nice to meet you."

Yet these are exactly the kinds of mental predicaments and situations we find ourselves in throughout the day, every day, 365 days a year. As we know from our experience of reframing our interpretation of what's unfolding in the moment, we do have choices in how we choose to make sense of and act on what we initially perceive. The meaning we initially assign to what we perceive doesn't have to have the last laugh—or bark. Our perception is a function of whatever our brains deliver up, and, like take-out, sometimes the order gets screwed up or the soy sauce and chopsticks are missing. It's then up to us to have enough presence of mind to remember not to say or do the thing that is going to create a kerfuffle for us or others. We can get in the habit of reflecting in the moment whether the way we've assessed or interpreted a situation is conducive to our aims and those involved, or whether our interpretation of events is going to put us smack dab in the middle of shitstorm. In practical terms, this is what it means to train the rudder of our own minds, that aspect of our own awareness that reminds and guides us toward how we want to show up.

It Is Written

In the context of the Emotional Intelligence Coaching Certification (EICC) program we've created, journaling plays a central role. There are many reasons for this. For one, journaling gives coach and client an ongoing forum to observe what's percolating by way of patterns of thought and mindset. It allows clients to reflect and integrate how they're making sense of what happens to them, and what's unfolding in their lives. The journals become one of the ways we teach our coaches and clients to unearth their own habits of mind and spot which if any of the 12 Self-Discoveries is operating as a pitfall or ally. We train our coaches, who, in turn, train their clients to learn to see themselves and their lives with new eyes and from different perspectives. Both coach and client practice observing their experience through the lens of each of the 12 Self-Discoveries. As they do this, they practice what it means to activate their inner coach, which is synonymous with what happens when someone develops the capacity to move and direct their own awareness. *In the absence of awareness, we are rudderless. In the absence of a rudder, we are governed by our existing mental models and habits of mind, and, in turn, their corresponding outcomes.*

How we relate to our own thinking, our beliefs, and our emotions sets the tone for how we will show up each new moment, and how we will relate to ourselves and others. Technically, the point is not just that we have thoughts, beliefs, or emotions, but how we relate to them. It's how we act on their meaning that ends up making the difference that counts, setting the trajectory of our outcomes and results. In a very real sense, our psychological and physical wellbeing are deeply interwoven with our habits of mind. They are part of the same ecosystem influenced by and within itself and by the ecosystems of other people and our physical environment. Each has a profound and undeniable ripple effect on the other.

Our awareness is the catalyst for what we have influence over within ourselves. It is through our own awareness we are able to work with our habitual tendencies and ways of perceiving reality. Where the journaling comes into play is not just with regard to what we know about its positive side effects of increased wellbeing and introspection; it becomes the primary tool we use to help our clients learn to spot their underlying assumptions, mental models, biases, and beliefs. We teach them to become aware of the potential pitfalls of how they are presently relating to and making sense of their perceptions and experiences. Through the journals, both coach and client get to see the client's specific choice of words, how they describe themselves, others, and the situations they find themselves in. Once they learn to see these patterns, they can also choose to reframe the meaning they're presently assigning to what's happening in their lives. They start to see themselves at the helm of their own experience versus at the mercy of it. They learn to use the qualities of their own awareness to navigate the open seas of their experience.

Over the course of what is typically a 6- or 12-week coaching engagement, the client journals in response to prompts covering each of the 12 Self-Discoveries. They experiment with applying specific practices to increase the dexterity of their awareness and the various ways they can use their awareness to relate to the variables within themselves and their respective contexts. With practice, clients eventually learn how to spot the underlying mental models upon which their beliefs hinge and, in turn, their results unfold. They learn to work in the currency of the mental paradigms of belief they unconsciously use to categorize and make sense of their perceptions.

Valence, Salience, Rapidity, and Duration

Journaling helps us become aware of our underlying belief structures, valence (positive and negative), and salience (strength and force), and acts as a bellwether to observe the pathway our affect and emotions take and their impact as they move through us. I was surprised to learn in my research for this book that valence is a term used in neuroscience and psychology to describe our positive and negative affect (see Figure 5.1), as is *arousal*, but I thought better to stick with the term I typically use to describe the intensity and strength of emotion, which is *salience*. I've used both terms for years, not knowing there was a scientific correlate and not having fully grasped or understood the role of our affect. You may recall affect is basically the output of our interoceptive sensations and sensory inputs after our brain has put into motion its best guess of how we will feel and before our brain conceptually assigns our affect meaning on its way to becoming an instance

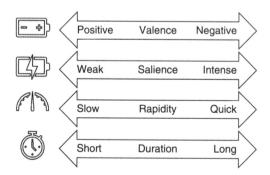

Figure 5.1 Valence, Salience, Rapidity, and Duration
Source: © Brain Capital LLC.

of emotion, although not all sensations or sensory input become affect and not all affect becomes emotion; only that which rises to the level of significance, valence and salience, does our brain determine to act upon and assign meaning. We teach our coaches and clients to pay attention to the valence and salience of what comes up for them in their daily interactions, in their own mindstream and physical sensations, as well as their journal entries. In this way, they start to see patterns in how they experience their emotions and, in turn, the sense they're inclined to make of them.

In Figure 5.1, "rapidity" speaks to how quickly our affect and emotion arrive on scene—like that guy who messages you before you even play your first word on *Words with Friends*, which during the pandemic apparently replaced bars as a means of picking up a prospective mate. In addition to how quickly our affect and emotion make their presence and accompanying thoughts and sensations known, "duration" speaks to how long our emotions and their entourage of sensations and affect take to subside, which is usually tied to their strength to begin with. To whatever extent we keep rehearsing or stirring the pot of how we feel and adding layers of meaning to the mix, it can either increase or decrease the valence, salience, and duration of what we feel. In Richie Davidson's work, he defines resilience as the rapidity with which we recover from a setback. The way I am using the term here is roughly the same idea, which we might refer to as emotional balance in the context of emotional intelligence. In sum, valence and salience describe the speed, energy, and intensity with which we are flooded by interoceptive sensations and affect as well as their duration.

These four components are indicators, evidence of what our brain has set into motion and predisposed us to feel. In this way, our interoceptive sensations and affect are a mechanism for the bidirectional communication between our brain and our body, offering key data points upon which we extrapolate meaning that guides our actions. Since much of what I've just described falls under the threshold of what we are normally consciously aware of, it requires practice on our part to become aware of these variables.

Richie Davidson explains how we can increase our interoceptive self-awareness by tuning into and noticing our bodily sensations. In our work with clients, we teach them how to key into and detect the signals and cues their bodies are giving them, including their valence, salience, rapidity, and duration, not dissimilar from the way canaries were historically used by coal miners to detect when there was the presence of noxious gases in a coal mine. Our bodily sensations are often our first clue that something strange is afoot at Circle K (never mind, an obscure *Bill and Ted's Excellent Adventure* reference that seemed to fit nicely here). They are tools we can use to notice the inner conditions that give rise to and go hand in hand with our sensations, affect, and emotions. They each represent specific ways we can put our awareness to work, giving it a specific job. The practice of identifying words and emotion concepts to describe what we are feeling as we key into our bodily sensations in the moment can counteract the tendency we otherwise have to perseverate, to take things personally, or to ascribe a level of meaning to what we are feeling it may not have or need to have.[1] It can also serve to dampen both the valence and salience of what we are experiencing in the moment, clearing a path for whatever we're feeling to pass. Keying into one or more of these elements also provides us with an opportunity to train and fine-tune our awareness in these moments. If we look at why this method neuroscience terms recategorization is effective, it allows us to assign meaning to what we feel in a conscious and considered way as opposed to whatever our perception and initial interpretation whip up for us. It gives us input and say, where we might not otherwise have any.

As we discussed in the previous chapter, our perception and belief in a self puts us in a dualistic relationship with everything that isn't us. We either like something and feel varying levels of attraction toward it, or we dislike something and feel to varying degrees repulsed by it. If we are neutral toward it, we take a standoffish or indifferent attitude. This is basically a description of how valence and salience play out in our own experience. So, if you notice yourself feeling drawn in and enamored, or repulsed and wanting to reject, or to remain aloof or neutral, that is your clue there is valence present in the mental or affective stance you're taking in that moment. The more extreme you feel in either direction is its salience. Finally, the speed with which your mental impressions arrive, hang around, and then depart, like your grown kids or parents when they come to visit, speaks to their rapidity and duration.

There is no doubt, we are valent, salient beings. We spend nearly all of our waking and sleeping hours engaged in this dance of liking, disliking, and feeling indifferent toward ourselves, others, and our experiences. Not surprising, I suppose, given we are used to relating to everyone and everything that isn't us in a way that predisposes us to perceive and process reality on these terms. So, while it can be a challenge not to take things personally at times, this may just be what inadvertently happens when we have the impression we exist as discrete and separate from everybody and everything else. In those moments when we feel we've been singled out, wronged, or treated unfairly, our valence, salience, and rapidity are more likely to go off the charts and stay off the charts, much like my contractions did with the birth of my daughter.

Off Your Rocker

When we are out of our heads or not in our right minds—whatever saying suits your demeanor when you're not at your best—we do have options available to us, including the decision to do nothing at all. Let's review the following methods relative to what we have influence over (see Figure 5.2).

Since our thoughts and feelings tend to take their lead from each other, we can use cognitive reframing and recategorization of our sensations to shift the meaning we make of what we think and feel. Cognitive reframing is a fancy way of saying we alter our thinking relative to our initial thoughts and perceptions. Similarly, recategorizing our sensations means we alter our interpretation of how we feel, using our capacity for interoception—an awareness of our own bodily signals and affect—to reassign their meaning.

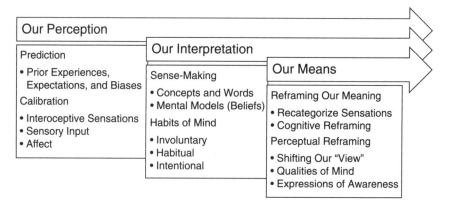

Figure 5.2 What We Have Influence Over
Source: © Brain Capital LLC.

In the first example, we use our cognitive capacity to reason our way out of the conceptual box we've put ourselves in, whereas in the second example, we use our awareness of our bodily signals and emotion concepts to reclassify how we feel. The 12 Self-Discoveries provide us with methods to reframe our meaning. They prompt and remind us to shift our interpretation of events in the moment—not only by shifting what we are thinking or feeling, but how we make sense of the variables to begin with.

If we're not able to use cognitive reframing or recategorization to shift what we think and what we feel relative to whatever has come to pass, we can rely on our awareness for help in reframing our perspective, what I've termed "perceptual reframing" in Figure 5.2. For this, we can employ any number of awareness practices, which we'll try our mind at in the upcoming chapter. Each method we will explore enables us to change our perceptual perspective or vantage point relative to any situation, including the stance we take relative to our own awareness. By shifting how we're seeing and perceiving, we see possibilities we hadn't seen before and therefore hadn't factored into our response.

Finally, we do always have the option simply to disengage, distract ourselves, or physically change our relationship to whatever is happening in the moment, which neuroscience tells us is an immediate remedy to give our brain new parameters to adjust to. So, while it probably won't make the situation disappear altogether, in the most immediate sense that's exactly what it does. However, as anyone who has ever been married, had a job or children, or been a friend, son, or daughter knows, you're still on the hook for resolving whatever situation you stepped away from. Physically removing ourselves from a situation is the alternative when we're not able to shift our awareness to achieve a mental equivalent of the same outcome.

Each of the 12 Self-Discoveries falls into one or more of these three categories of tactics geared toward operationalizing our own emotional intelligence and ultimately increasing our personal effectiveness working with our own habits of mind. At the heart of the self-discovery we are learning about in this chapter, "You Don't Have to Believe Everything You Think," we get to decide the level of attention, power, and energy we give our own thoughts and emotions. Our bodies are constantly providing us with feedback, data that if ignored can have negative consequences on our ability to regulate our physical and psychological wellbeing. Becoming entangled in our thoughts and feelings is optional; experiencing them is not. But learning how not to perseverate and to instead take back our own nose rope takes practice in noticing in new ways. It takes a shift in our awareness and remembering we have the mental wherewithal to work with whatever comes up. We don't have to believe everything we think, nor do we need to get swept away by our emotions or mental commentary in response to either. By learning to relate to emotion as energy moving through us, we can use each opportunity that emotional valence and salience raise within us to train in our awareness of each.

6

Your Focus Becomes Your Reality

Like a mirror, our attention reflects the object of its focus and quality of awareness. Isn't it true our immediate experience is determined by whatever we place and hold our focus on? Like our emotions, whatever our attention becomes fixated on colors our outlook and how we experience our reality in that moment. If you're upset and someone prepares a tasty meal for you, you're unable to enjoy even a single bite. Similarly, if we have a habit of expecting or looking for particular behaviors in people or situations, how can we see anything other than what we are focusing upon or waiting to see? If we place emphasis on being compassionate and kind, even our gaze and expression will soften and our interactions with others become gentler. As the adage goes, "Be careful what you ask for," and the correlate here would be "Be careful what you focus on." The good news is we can take responsibility for what we focus on, but it requires practice.

How do we train our attention? We train our attention by bringing our awareness back again and again to the object of our desired focus, like our breath, the work in front of us, the person we are listening to, the road we are driving on, and so on. This includes being able to redirect our attention when we realize we have become fixated to the detriment of ourselves or others, usually marked by our mental state becoming the loudest voice in our heads, or our emotions seeping out like toxic waste and impacting us and those around us. Like a herder whose flock has wandered off, first we need to notice our presence of mind is no longer present, and then like the herder who gathers the herd back, we call it back.

Our ability to selectively direct our attention is critical for everything we do, whether we are making an important decision, listening to an ebook while driving on the autobahn, chopping broccoli, observing a spider weave its web, learning to speak Latin, or offering words of encouragement to someone when they get fired and their spouse leaves them. The ability to direct and course-correct our attention is akin to the functional relationship between driver, steering wheel, and vehicle. If there is no driver, no one is present to steer the vehicle. Similarly, if there is no steering wheel, then the driver doesn't have anything to steer with, and the direction of the vehicle becomes uncertain, not to mention precarious. Eventually, the vehicle will veer off course, meeting with disaster. Similarly, if we aren't consciously directing the reins of our attention, there isn't anyone else present who will do it for us. This is either when our existing habits come into play or our trusty autonomic nervous system, which is predominantly geared toward directing mission-critical tasks like making sure our heart continues to beat—a prudent design choice, given how reliably our attention gets sidetracked or wanders off—as you can see happened with the construction of this sentence. If we could pay someone to pay attention on our behalf, most of us would get a job so we could afford to have someone else do that for us. Then, we wouldn't have to worry about directing our own attention. But alas, all humans are equally deficient in this area and technology hasn't yet offered entirely viable or reliable alternatives. So, for now, we have to do it the old-fashioned way—all by ourselves.

In moments of perseveration, when your attention becomes fixated or stuck, your perception and experience also become distorted—like the warning message on the side mirror of a vehicle, "Objects are closer than they appear." When you are undone by your perception of something some-one has said or done, you may discover all you're able think about is the story you are telling yourself about it or them. In that moment, you cease to relate to events in a way that is conducive. You quite literally experience a loss of perspective. When we get carried away by the momentum of our own emotion, we can become hyperfocused on the object of perceived threat such that our perception becomes fixated. In such moments, all we can see is what we have come to believe about that person or situation.

Any Reality but This One

The other phenomenon that can occur when we're trying to selectively direct and hold our attention is we can easily become engrossed in realities, virtual or otherwise, different from the one we are physically located in. We are immediately transported to new landscapes, scenes, and experiences as we play a video game, watch a movie or television series, daydream, or even read a book—to the extent we even do that anymore. Despite our seeming inability to focus on the things in need of our attention, we have a tremendous capacity to focus on distractions of our choosing or alternate realties meant to direct our attention away from our present-moment lives. We excel at distraction to the point we don't really know how to be with ourselves or others, and when we are by ourselves, without an immediate source of distraction—our smartphones, computers, tablets, e-readers, or televisions—it's as if we experience a kind of agoraphobia of our own minds.

Even when we attempt to focus our attention in earnest—if, that is, something else doesn't grab it first—our experience of directing and holding our attention often lasts for such brief periods of time that it's easy to lose track and slip back into more passive ways of being aware that are more akin to being on autopilot. We're going to explore each of these habitual ways we have of relating to what we experience in greater detail as we learn how to position our awareness for maximal positive, conscious influence and impact. I've developed something I'm calling the Awareness Matrix, a model that attempts to summarize what we do and do not have conscious awareness of and the mental processes that take place at each level of consciousness—at least what we understand of them. It's my practical attempt to help us discern what we have the capacity to be consciously (intentionally), unconsciously (preconsciously or subconsciously), passively (habitually), and autonomically (involuntarily) aware of.

Awareness Matrix

We have varying levels of conscious awareness we bring to any situation depending on the context, as illustrated in the four quadrants shown in Figure 6.1. Whatever transpires on an unconscious basis can either describe when we are simply unaware of something we have the capacity to be aware of, or it can describe specific cognitive or sensory functions we are unconscious of that even if we wanted to be conscious of fall beneath the threshold of what is accessible to our conscious awareness. The Awareness Matrix attempts to capture both meanings of the word "unconscious." The y-axis depicts what we are minimally to maximally consciously aware of, whereas the two quadrants that fall below the x-axis represent what we generally have nominal to no conscious access to. In other words, each of

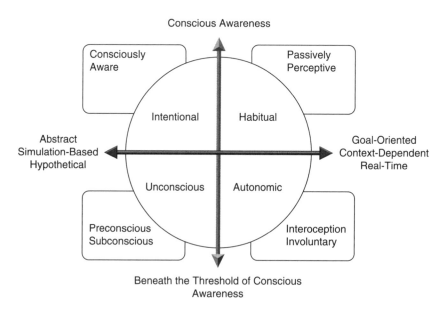

Figure 6.1   Awareness Matrix
Source: © Brain Capital LLC.

these two zones captures cognitive and sensory functions that range from being unconscious yet still accessible to completely inaccessible to our conscious awareness, or detection.

If something is preconscious, for example, it precedes our conscious awareness of it, like a memory before we recall it. Even though we aren't presently conscious of it, it is accessible and to varying degrees within our conscious reach. Unlike the preconscious functions that fall within our conscious reach, our subconscious functions range from being not readily accessible to inaccessible to our conscious recall or awareness. Within most scientific coffee klatsches, the term "unconscious" is still the preferred term to use versus "subconscious." However, I chose to distinguish the terms here to be able to capture functions that range from accessible to inaccessible within the overall category of unconscious processing.

In their research paper "The Unconscious Mind," John A. Bargh and Ezequiel Morsella note the following as organizing elements that guide the processes and actions of our unconscious mind: our motivational drivers, behavioral preferences, societal influences, prior experiences, and others around us whose behavior ends up providing a blueprint for our own unconscious responses, particularly when we are experientially blind—or have no experiential template for what may be situationally appropriate (Bargh & Morsella, 2008). While we don't know what all takes place within the unconscious mind, many posit there are both goal-oriented, context-specific activities as well as ones that are more abstract and simulation-based in nature, such as our brain's capacity for statistical learning. In either case, just because something is inaccessible to our conscious awareness doesn't mean it is any less important, intelligent, or sophisticated than those functions accessible to our conscious awareness. In fact, it may be just the opposite—the functions that occur outside of what is consciously available to us may not only be more sophisticated and complex than the cognitive functions we have the capacity to be aware of, but they may even be the source from which most of our conscious actions are derived.

If I were a neuroscientist, that's where I'd want to spend my time. I'd want to understand the interrelationship between the functions that take place inside and outside of our conscious reach. One of my favorite books, *Subliminal: How Your Unconscious Mind Rules Your Behavior* by Leonard Mlodinow, happens to be about this topic. It was in reading his book that

I became even more curious than I already was about what capability we have to influence our own lives, behavior, and outcomes on a conscious basis, considering all that isn't within conscious reach, let alone our control. The book served to highlight what I care most about and that is what we do have the capacity to influence because it gives us something we can work with. This has in many ways been the underlying question fueling my work for some time now and ultimately the impetus for me in writing this book. As it turns out, I'm not the only one who thinks our influence may kick in at the level of conscious processing and intentional sense-making, after our brain curates our initial perceptions and upon receipt of what our unconscious mind whips up for us. The authors of the article mentioned earlier summarize the position of several other researchers who posit that "the role of the consciousness is as a gatekeeper and sense-maker after the fact" (Bargh & Morsella, 2008). While I wasn't familiar with this research until writing this book, I'm glad to know there are those in the scientific community who may agree we have plenty to work with on a conscious and volitional basis that is of value and consequence.

The Awareness Matrix highlights not only what happens on a pre-conscious, subconscious, and unconscious level, but what takes place on an autonomic and involuntary basis, which to varying degrees also falls below the threshold of what we normally have conscious access to. These consist of functions that are for the most part goal-based and real-time in nature and therefore aligned to and dependent upon context-specific inputs that have our physiological wellbeing as their primary focus. Like other functions that take place on a preconscious level, we can train ourselves to increase our interoceptive awareness of our bodily sensations and other sensory-based functions that might otherwise fall outside of our conscious awareness.

Top of Mind

With respect to the upper quadrants of the Awareness Matrix that fall within range of what we have the capacity to be consciously aware of, the zone that depicts our habitual functions accounts for what we are passively to subliminally aware of, "subliminal" in this context referring to functions that fall beneath the threshold of what we are consciously aware of in the moment but aren't by default inaccessible to our conscious awareness. I've chosen to distinguish subliminal processes, which have simply faded away from our present-moment awareness but are theoretically accessible to our conscious awareness, from our subconscious or unconscious functions, which are largely just inaccessible to our conscious awareness. Another example of when we are passively conscious is when our senses take in information relative to our immediate environment or vis-à-vis our interoceptive sensory input at a level we aren't necessarily consciously aware of or are to varying degrees only passively aware of. Only when their valence or salience rise to a level we actively and consciously perceive them, do we tend to give such input their title, *emotions*.

It is likely owing to the homeostatic advantages and economics of our predicament that we spend significant portions of our waking life in the habitual quadrant. You may have noticed I didn't emphasize in what I noted above the extent to which we have conscious awareness of our habitual functions because, by definition, a habit is something we aren't entirely conscious of while doing it. But as we've been learning about throughout the book and relative to what we do have influence over in the VSM, there are inflection points when we can consciously intervene relative to our own habits, which is largely the focus of this book. The more our awareness slips into the mode of being passively perceptive or unaware, the less opportunity we have to impact our own outcomes. It's precisely in those moments our ability to summon our conscious awareness increases the possibility for greater influence over the variables of perception and sense-making that set our responses on a particular trajectory. However, in order to access the conscious-awareness, on-demand features of our own mind, we need to practice maneuvering using the medium and dexterity of our own mind. In the absence of intentionality, we rely on guiding factors—what we call *habits*—to carry out action sequences we otherwise remain mostly oblivious to. When we are simply unaware of what is taking place above the threshold of what we have the capacity to be consciously aware of, it not only speaks to what we have the possibility of bringing into our conscious awareness, but what we have the opportunity to train ourselves to become aware of, which is the main, if not entire, aim of this book—to be able to discern for yourself and put into play what you have influence on and by what mechanisms and means.

Within the quadrant of what we are intentionally and consciously aware of, we not only have the capacity to be aware, we can also navigate our lives with maximal agency and efficacy by virtue of operating from that space. The more time we spend being aware in a conscious manner, the greater opportunity we have to nudge our habits of mind and work with whatever our conscious awareness comes into contact with in the moment. When we are operating under the guidance of our conscious awareness, we possess the optimal internal conditions to unfold the qualities and expressions of our own awareness as a means to benefit ourselves and others. Ultimately, it is within this quadrant we are able to access our present-moment potential and emergent capacity. As we spend more time training in the variety of ways in which we can exercise our conscious awareness, we can even become cognizant of phenomena and/or functions we would normally have minimal access to, such as various stages of dreaming and light sleep as well as interoceptive sensations and our affect, the valence and salience, that precedes our emotional responses.

X's and Y's

Both the x- and y-axis and what they represent are designed to have multiple functions in the Awareness Matrix. They function as continuums, on the one hand, with the y-axis measuring what we are minimally to maximally consciously aware of, as well as functions we perform that fall along the same scale ranging from involuntary, inadvertent, to voluntary. Similarly, the x-axis depicts functions ranging from goal-oriented, real-time, and context-dependent to those that are abstract, simulation-based, and hypothetical in purpose. I strongly suspect—though it's only my conjecture—that as we move more toward abstraction, we also become less subject-object oriented, meaning we lose the "observer effect," in which there is an observer and something to be observed. At the extreme end of the abstraction spectrum, I also posit we may operate on more of a closed-system basis, as we run simulations based on information that is presumably already in the system, so to say, and aren't necessarily taking in or factoring in real-time inputs that would cause us to have to adapt to a more dynamic context, unlike when we are operating in more of a context-dependent, open-system mode that requires us to be able to adjust and adapt to real-time variables. Similarly, any concept we normally have of being a "self" moving through space and time also falls by the wayside as our awareness and subconscious processing become more abstract and hypothetical, such as when we are dreaming.

Conversely, the further we move to the right of the Awareness Matrix, the more our processes and actions are oriented to time-bound, goal-oriented, context-dependent scenarios, all of which require us to adapt and course-correct on a real-time basis in response to evolving circumstances. Irrespective of which types of functions are governed by which end of the spectrum, both operate to varying degrees simultaneously depending on the context—for example, if we are sleeping or awake, at rest or in motion, and so on. Moreover, each type of function takes place to varying degrees under the auspices of our conscious and intentional awareness or lack thereof and therefore, on a voluntary, inadvertent, or involuntary basis.

The Awareness Matrix is not perfect. I'm positive it has flaws, as it was born out of my attempt to synthesize my own user interface with awareness and the relatively little I've studied about each of these individual topics from a scientific standpoint. Like the value stream map of perception, the Awareness Matrix represents a working model of how these varied functions work relative to each other and relative to what we have the capacity to be consciously aware of, as the title suggests. It's my best effort to understand and piece together the insights from the vast body of scientific research available on each topic of which I've only just begun to touch the surface and conceptualize what it might look like when integrated in both a functional and practical manner. Thus, I don't want to give the impression there are hard and fast lines that can or should be drawn between the many variables I've tried to capture more broadly and generally within the model. Rather, we should keep in mind that it's a working hypothesis of functions and processes that occur to varying degrees simultaneously and interdependently, the complete details and complexity of which remain under the lock and key of our own brain, whose job it is to optimize in whatever manner it sees fit.

Putting the Awareness Matrix into Practice

Part of being able to determine what you have influence over is understanding where training your own awareness can help you navigate your present-moment experience. As you consider where most of your time is spent in the Awareness Matrix, I invite you to reflect upon how familiar you are with the one thing you always have with you—your own awareness. How much have you really investigated and gotten to know your own awareness and all it naturally affords you? When you bring your conscious awareness to various situations in your life, whether they be conversations with loved ones, colleagues at work, peers, friends, acquaintances, or people you've not yet met, what's the result? Do those communications go better? Are they substantively different than when you just show up to conversations on autopilot or lacking intentionality and conscious awareness? Similarly, when you have a task you need to complete or an important project you're responsible for, is there a meaningful difference when you bring an intentional outlook as you complete that task and carry out each of its steps? What happens when you're not coming from a place of awareness? Are you even sure what the difference is like? These are important questions you can use to gauge your relationship and familiarity with your own capacity to be aware and your proficiency in bringing it to bear on different situations in your life. Familiarizing yourself with your own mind, and the capability and capacity of your own awareness, is the topic we'll explore next (see Figure 6.2).

The Qualities and Expressions of Awareness

Unfortunately, we don't have much exposure to the different ways our mind is equipped to position itself relative to its surroundings, its inner landscape, or inherent qualities and expressions—particularly, not in secular or mainstream settings. This isn't a criticism as much as it is an observation, consistent with the relative nascence of mindfulness in the West, where the practices are often introduced and practiced divorced from their philosophical study and meditative contexts, which have had the benefit of

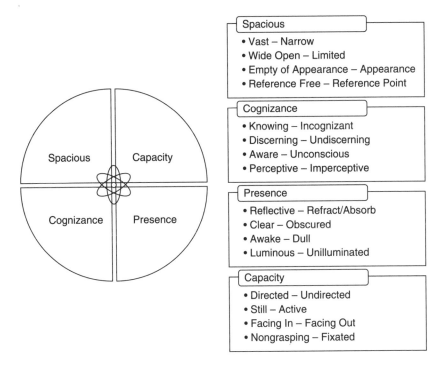

Figure 6.2 The Qualities and Expressions of Awareness
Source: © Brain Capital LLC.

several thousand years of being carefully steeped and passed down through established lineages of practice and structured systems of ethical thought. As I debated whether it would make things better or worse to delve into the topic of awareness absent these important ingredients, I realized the momentum of mindfulness in the West is happening and will continue to, with or without my voice added to the mix. In my estimation, it is important to have secular-based practices whose design and intent is to maximize our capacity to benefit beings by virtue of having more specific and accurate means to achieve that aim. So, it is from that intention and view I am sharing my own understanding and how I've come to think about these topics based on my own rather limited experience of Buddhist thought and practice as I've attempted to practice the instruction I've received from my teachers. Like anything with potential to benefit, there is also the potential for harm, either through misuse or misunderstanding. Absent a solid grounding in ethics, or devoid of the intention to benefit and a commitment not to harm, anything we do can quickly become misguided. Thus, I feel it is important to state my own intent, which is that whatever I share that may be of benefit and creates the causes of happiness is a result of what I have correctly understood and applied from my teachers. By contrast, whatever I may convey that brings about the opposite, though not my intent, is result of my own lack of insight and understanding.

The Zone of Awareness, "Zone A"

What we have access to be aware of on a conscious basis is depicted in the upper left quadrant of the Awareness Matrix, which I will refer to here as "Zone A." Our conscious awareness, a word I'm using synonymously with the word "mind," has unique qualities that embody how we experience its many expressions, which are both descriptive and indicative of its nature and capacity.[1] Whether we've realized it yet or not, we can position our own awareness, and therefore our perspective, on whatever we place and hold our attention or redirect it toward, which allows us to experience its various expressions in the present moment. Even though I'm describing each of its qualities and expressions separately, they are not separate. In the same way a diamond has many facets or sides, they still all belong to the same diamond. Similarly, we can become familiar with the various aspects of our own mind and learn to use our awareness itself as a method, a path, and key to unlock our inherent qualities and capacity, or agency of mind.

Like anything we are hoping to gain proficiency in, let alone stability, we need to be specific about what we are training ourselves in. Many people practice and teach mindfulness in both secular and religious settings. The perspectives, expertise, and training they bring to the work varies as greatly as their backgrounds. My orientation to the topic is twofold. My own meditation practice has been situated within the Tibetan Buddhist tradition for the past 29 years—though I consider myself to be a beginner. While fluent in the concepts, I am not an expert; nor am I qualified to train anyone in formal Buddhist meditation. When it comes to secular-based contemplative practice, what I often refer to as training for the brain, I've relied upon the research of Richie Davidson and his team at the Center for Healthy Minds and Healthy Minds Innovations. My work is necessarily influenced by my own meditation training and study of Tibetan Buddhist philosophy, whose practical application has helped in making sense of the nuanced and contemplative aspects of my work.

When we pursue contemplative meditation absent a spiritual or philosophical grounding in its methods, we should call it what it is: an attempt to familiarize ourselves with our own habits of perception using what we have at our immediate disposal, which is our own awareness and powers of observation. By engaging in exercises that allow us to see what we normally do not pay attention to, we open up the possibility to see in new ways and from new perspectives. Much like the stretches and warm-up exercises you would do before engaging in physical activity, these are practical examples, metaphors, and reflective exercises meant to familiarize you with your own awareness and the varied stances it affords as a means to tune into and work with your own habits of mind and what you have the possibility to influence within yourself. I've taken the liberty of creating a practical framework to provide you with an introductory glimpse of how the interface of your awareness already operates and can, with formal practice and training, be developed according to your preference of what context in which you may wish to seek further instruction.

Should you wish to undertake formal meditation practice and training, you should seek training from a qualified meditation master or instructor, someone who is not only trained to teach others but has their own practice. I don't know about you, but I wouldn't seek instruction on jumping out of a plane from someone who had either never jumped out of a plane or had jumped only a few times. There's a reason why meditation teachers often spend years in solitary retreat and yet even when they do will often not act in the capacity of a spiritual guide offering meditation instruction. In other words, the bar should be quite high. Be wary when the bar is set so low you can trip over it. That said, you are allowed to look at your own mind and to become familiar with your own awareness. Otherwise, what the hell good does it do to have a mind, or the capacity of awareness to observe and come to know it if we don't have enough interest or motivation to get to know its qualities and capabilities?

Our results are meaningfully different when we conduct our lives under the auspices of our conscious awareness. By contrast, when we live our lives absent awareness, it has the effect of us living our lives in a kind of blur—what we refer to as the habitual zone, or "Zone B," of the Awareness Matrix—that is when we employ the minimum threshold of awareness necessary to go through our lives. When you move from a state of being passively perceptive to a state of being consciously and intentionally aware, your relationship to yourself, others, and the outside world shifts. Awareness allows us to shift not only our own perspective in the present moment, but our interpretation of what we perceive. Our perception behaves differently when we have access to views or stances that we don't otherwise exercise. Equally important, gaining a level of agency over our own minds allows us to embrace more conscientiously what it means to be the common denominator of our own experience. So, let's dive in and learn how each of these continuums can increase the dexterity of our own awareness as we become familiar with each.

Mindspace

Our minds have an open and spacious quality to them (see Figure 6.3). Like the sky, we can experience our own awareness as having no boundaries or limits. Our awareness has the view of being vast, wide open without center

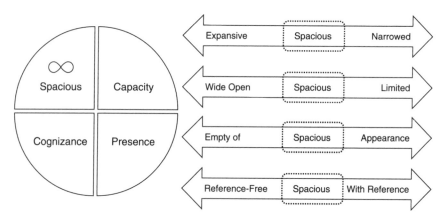

Figure 6.3   Expressions of Spacious Awareness
Source: © Brain Capital LLC.

or edge. Like the space and air that surrounds us, its nature is accommodating. It fits everything. Within it, everything is contained. Anything can appear within the field of awareness, both imagined or thought forms, as we term them in Buddhist philosophy, as well as visible, or physical, forms. The spaciousness of our own awareness can either have an absence of imagined or physical phenomena, or it can contain and include them. Had you ever thought about space in this way before, let alone spaciousness as a quality your own mind possesses?

What happens when we restrict the space we're in? It can become quite cramped. There is less room to accommodate whatever is present. Even our movement within it becomes more restricted. Imagine you move from a big house to a tiny home. Now, you need to get rid of at least half of your things in order to make everything fit, or you can cram them into storage. This is what happens to the spaciousness of our own minds when our attention narrows to an extreme—in other words, when we perseverate, cling to, or focus our attention on the object of its focus to the exclusion of everything else within our field of awareness. This could be an experience, another person, a thought, an emotion, an object—anything whatsoever. The space that was once available to hold and accommodate other things diminishes, not in real terms but in terms of what we experience in that moment. As our awareness becomes hyperfocused on the object of its attention, its spacious quality narrows, moving from roomy to limited.

This can be good or bad, conducive or unconducive to our aims. For example, when we pay attention and really focus on what someone else is saying to us, our frame of reference zeroes in on what this person is telling us, although our attention can also wander off while we are listening to this person. It's as if our awareness recedes without our conscious detection into the background while its illuminating quality allows whatever is arising or that we choose to focus upon takes shape and form within our perception—even if what we are perceiving is illusory and not a physical form. In other words, we lose track of our own awareness, the medium that makes all experiences possible, and for those moments experience whatever unfolds. Our minds move from one distraction (or point of focus) to another continuously to the extent we become blind to our capacity to perceive and to be aware. The fact that we are aware and our awareness makes all experience possible suddenly is like news to us when we discover what should be obvious but simply isn't.

As we've said before, our affect is like a magnet, in this case for our own attention. That's why when our affect reaches a threshold—a level of valence or salience—at which it grabs our attention, it's difficult for us to ignore its call. In classical terms, we might say this or that person or thing triggered us. From a constructed view of emotions, our attention is predisposed by our brain's best guess of what and how we'll need to pay attention next. Bottom line, our awareness in those moments can quickly become engrossed in the experience of its own valence or salience, appearance, and movement. That's what gives emotions the current and momentum they seem to have. It's like a two-year-old or your boss who is screaming for your attention. Let's say you're engaged in conversation with a friend, who is so impassioned—telling you about the incident with their two-year-old or their boss—that spit flies out of their mouth and inadvertently onto you. Most of us would become distracted—even if only for a moment. And if you're a germaphobe, you may stop listening to the person altogether, not because you're not interested in their story—though, that may also be the case—but because your attention has shifted from listening to pondering the consequences of your friend's spittle that just landed on you.

The degree to which we experience something as extremely positive or extremely negative is mirrored back to us by the strength of an instance of emotion and the accompanying sensory experience that goes with it. That emotional event will persist as long as our awareness remains wrapped up in what is essentially the valence and salience of its own perceptions. What's more, depending on the meaning we assign it, our interpretation of events after the fact either continues to feed what we're already feeling or it can diffuse it. It's one thing if your friend accidentally spits on you, but if they spit on you on purpose, that's a game changer relative to how you are likely to respond. The more intense our perception of an experience is, the more we disapprove, dislike, or reject whatever is happening; our mindset takes the shape and character of whatever our perceptions about it are. In those moments, our awareness acts like a mirror for our own salience and valence. The more our awareness narrows in on or becomes completely caught up in the object of its attention—in this case our own instance of emotion—the more we lose the spacious view our awareness normally affords us. But if we position our own awareness such that its object of focus is itself, which by nature has no reference point, whatever we are perceiving in that moment collapses into itself. In that instant, there is no observer and nothing observed. There is just awareness of awareness. That's what is meant by "free of reference point" relative to this particular expression, or view, of awareness. Like an ouroboros swallowing its own tail, this is the momentary equivalent of us finding our own tail. That said, because we have the habit of perceiving in a manner in which there is an observer and something observed, this view or way of seeing quickly reasserts itself.

The various expressions of our awareness are depicted as continuums for clarity's sake; however, its various qualities are happening all at once. While they can't be separated, we can intentionally pay attention to each aspect and notice what our stance may be relative to each in any given moment we look. You can use the following questions to get started as you observe the qualities and expressions of the spaciousness of your own mind across the following continuums of awareness:

Expansive–Narrowed
- Is your outlook one in which you can see all possibilities? Or is your view narrow in scope? Which perspective would be most helpful for you to take in this situation?

Wide Open–Limited
- Does the situation call for expanding your awareness or perspective? Or have you limited what you are aware of?

Empty of Appearance–With Appearance
- Is your attention focused on what is appearing by way of mental activity and/or your surroundings? What would an absence of thought or holding something in mind be like? To what extent could it be helpful to see what's present as one of many perspectives or possibilities?

Free of Reference–Reference Point
- Do you notice when your mind is operating from a self-other perspective, in which there is an observer and observed? What happens when your awareness is free of a reference point, when the observer turns its awareness toward itself?

Mindsight

In the same way our awareness has a spacious and wide-open quality, it has a cognizance quality, giving us the capacity to know and to perceive (see Figure 6.4). Like a spotlight that reveals whatever it comes into contact with, our mind has the capacity to be aware of and cognizant of whatever comes into our field of awareness.

We can be aware of our bodily sensations, affect, and emotion, or incoming data from our senses. We also have the capacity to be aware of internal or imagined phenomena, such as thoughts, dreams, memories, visualizations, or ideas. The cognizance aspect of our awareness allows us to perceive both physical forms and mental appearances or impressions. Let's investigate our mind's capacity to know. What do you notice about your own mind right now? Take a few moments to look. Your job isn't to focus on anything external by way of objects or any kind of thought forms or mental movement. Instead, be like a detective who has been instructed to notice the discerning quality of your own mind. Start by noticing your own awareness. Notice in such a way you're prepared to report back on what you observe. Take a breath in and as you do, notice the aspect of your mind that is aware, just ready to perceive, to know, to apprehend. As you breathe out, let your

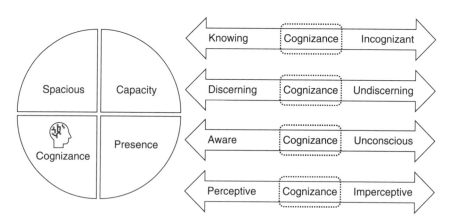

Figure 6.4   Expressions of Cognizant Awareness
Source: © Brain Capital LLC.

awareness expand into its spacious quality. Within that sense of spaciousness, notice its cognizance aspect. Whatever crops up in your mindstream by way of thoughts or mental movement or sensory perceptions, simply notice the ability your mind has to be aware of whatever comes up. Do you notice your mind's readiness to perceive, to become acquainted with absolutely anything that comes into its field of reference? In a moment, I'll ask you to close your eyes, and when you do, notice whether your mind still perceives. Try it now for a minute or two. How does your mind perceive when your eyes are shut? How is this different than when your eyes are open?

How would you describe what you experienced? Did you pick up on anything new about your mind's capacity to know? If you had to describe the quality of this knowing, what words might you use to describe it? The mind's inclination to discern, to investigate, and to know is similar to a cat that can't help chasing after the red dot produced by a laser pointer. Have a cat? Go try it. Don't have a cat? Look it up on YouTube. The moment you move the red dot around, the cat instinctively chases after it, trying to catch it. The cat thinks the red dot emitted from the laser pointer can be caught, and therefore it tries to catch it. We can't say the red dot doesn't exist. Clearly, the cat wouldn't be chasing after it unless the red dot was visible. But we can't say the red dot solidly exists; otherwise, the cat would be able to catch it. What we can say is that the red dot is both visible yet uncatchable. The cat can see it, but it can't capture the red dot in the same way it can catch and play with a toy mouse, for example. That is more or less how our own mind behaves. Like the cat, its inclination is to chase whatever appears, but like the red dot, our awareness can't be caught, although it can be experienced. If the red dot could chase itself, that would be like the awareness of our mind attempting to catch itself. Here are some questions you can ask relative to the cognizance aspect of your mind in day-to-day situations as you practice paying attention to your perceptual stance across the following continuums:

Knowing–Incognizant
- As you're going about your day, are you aware of what you're perceiving? What happens when this knowing quality of mind recedes into the background, and you're no longer actively aware?

Discerning–Undiscerning
- Do you notice when your awareness shifts between discerning its inner and outer context to when what it discerns goes undetected by you?

Aware–Unconscious
- How often throughout the day are you consciously aware of what is happening and what you are doing versus when you default to being passively perceptive or unaware of yourself, others, your surroundings, or some combination thereof?

Perceptive–Imperceptive
- Under what circumstances are you conscious of what you are actively perceiving? When does what you are aware of tend to fade from your direct awareness or view?

Mindlight

The mind's presence is like a torch whose function is to illuminate. When the torch of awareness is lit, it effortlessly reveals whatever is in its presence (see Figure 6.5).

Sometimes what's present is a thought, a feeling, a sound, or an object. When the mind is calm and settled, it has a reflective quality like the surface

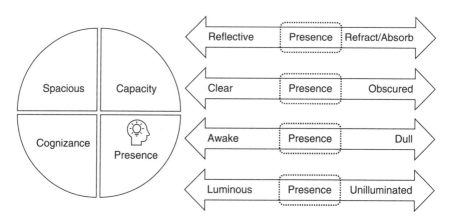

Figure 6.5   Expressions of Presence of Awareness
Source: © Brain Capital LLC.

of a lake in which there is no turbulence whatsoever. The reflective capacity of our own mind is like the water's capacity to act as a mirror. Yet the
moment we throw even a tiny pebble into the lake, stir the sediment beneath
its surface, or introduce a variable that changes its calm surface, the lake's
mirror-like, reflective qualities become distorted and take on an appearance
commensurate with the nature of the disturbance. That is how our mind
behaves when its mirror-like, reflective nature becomes otherwise engaged,
whether by virtue of movement, appearance, distraction, or disturbance.
Like the lake whose motionless surface transforms into ripples or waves
when it has been perturbed, so too does our awareness change from being
reflective when it splinters off from itself, becomes absorbed, or readjusts
its stance as a result of any number of factors. In the same way, the ripples
are still the lake even though they may take on the temporary appearance
of something distinct and different from when they were indistinguishable from the lake's serene and calm surface. Similarly, the mind's reflective
nature can change.

Though our minds may at times become dull, sleepy, or distracted, our
awareness is always available to us as the mechanism by which we are able
to perceive both outer and inner phenomena as well as the only thing that
can perceive itself. Isn't that phenomenal? Unlike so many other things that
come and go, the fact that our awareness is intrinsically available to us is
incredible. It may very well be our saving grace, if we can use it to become
softer, kinder, and more skillful with ourselves and others. Our job is simply
to recall it and learn how to maneuver its stance. When we remember, or
recall our awareness, it is instantaneously present.

But training our awareness is a bit like training a puppy. The puppy may
bite you while attempting to play, not knowing its own strength. It may
run amok in the park or neighborhood when it gets loose, and it may have
many accidents before it learns not to pee on your favorite rug or chew up
your favorite pillow or pair of shoes. The good news is that, like a puppy, our
mind can be trained and like the puppy it is incredibly loyal. If we couldn't
train our own mind or it only showed up some of the time upon being
summoned, it would make for a very short and decidedly different kind
of discussion. Here are some questions for you to reflect on with regard to
your own presence of mind and its attributes:

Reflective–Refract/Absorb

▪ To what degree is your experience a reflection of what you want your life to be about? Do you need to turn your reflective capacity inward and become more introspective? What happens to your mind's reflective capacity when you become distracted? How about when you become absorbed or engrossed?

Clear–Obscured

▪ Where in how you perceive have things become clouded or obscured? What could benefit from being made transparent and clear?

Awake–Dull

▪ Does your mind have the qualities of being awake and present? Or are you dull or sleepy?

Luminous–Unilluminated

▪ What are you not seeing that you would be able to see if your awareness were lighting the cave of what you don't see about your own experience?

Minding

The fourth main quality of our mind is its capacity. It can move and direct itself. If our presence of mind allows us to be awake, the cognizance aspect allows us to be aware. While the spacious quality of our awareness accommodates everything, its capacity is like the conductor that directs its movement or attention (see Figure 6.6).

So, what kinds of things can our awareness do? Our awareness can be directed toward physical objects as well as imagined ones. Moreover, it doesn't have to be directed toward anything at all. It can be still and calm with no movement, or it can race from one distraction or object of attention to another. Our awareness can and does become fixated, sometimes on purpose when we choose to focus on something. There are other times when it becomes fixated on the valence or salience of our sensations, our affect, our emotions, or thoughts. By contrast, there are times when our mind is unfixated, when it isn't preoccupied or grasping after anything in particular. When we let our minds rest as they are, without having to maneuver or navigate or without a job to do, its various qualities become more apparent and visible to us.

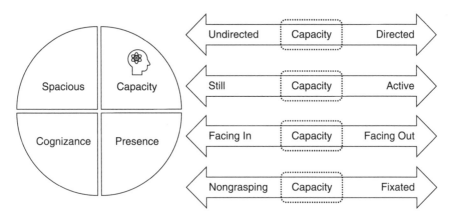

Figure 6.6 Expressions of Capacity of Awareness
Source: © Brain Capital LLC.

As you experiment noticing your own mind, practice noticing how you can adjust your own perceptual stance, your perspective, and your view from within your awareness:

Undirected –Directed
- Is your attention directed and focused? If so, on what? Or is your awareness on a walkabout, roaming free wherever your experience takes you? Is your awareness in sync with your body and what your body is doing, or not?

Still –Active
- Is your awareness calm and still? Or is your awareness active, moving in the direction of whatever appears in your mindstream, sensory experience, or outer environment?

Facing In–Facing Out
- Are you operating from a subject-object, self-other vantage point? Is your attention facing outward, on external objects, or is it facing inward on what's unfolding in your own mindstream? What happens when your awareness faces itself?

Nongrasping–Fixated
- Is your awareness or attention in a state of perseveration or clinging? Or are you moving through your experience unencumbered, free from grasping and fixation?

Now that you've had a quick introduction to each of the main qualities of mind and its capacities, let's review what makes our awareness unique. We said the mind is awake and aware. It reflects and illuminates. It can transform from being reflective to refractive; it can move in the direction of and become absorbed in the object of its focus. It is open and spacious, able to accommodate anything whatsoever. Our awareness performs many functions, even though we can't physically see or grasp onto it like we can a physical object. Despite being intangible, our awareness can become fixated. It can also break itself loose from whatever it is clinging to and redirect itself accordingly, turning its focus outwardly, inwardly, and even back on itself.

Compassion

What's the opposite of relating to ourselves and the world through a subject-object frame of reference? Relating to ourselves and the world free of reference point. When our awareness is free of its regular self-other stance, it creates the conditions for us to perceive and relate to ourselves and others in a radically different way. Right now, most of us have favorites, people we love the most on down to those we don't consider loving at all. The fruition of mind's qualities and expressions are wisdom and compassion. This is not a directed kind of compassion in which we have someone as our focus. Rather it is compassion without reference point, an orientation that by its very nature is all-inclusive. This is the kind of compassion that goes well beyond empathy or the kind of territorial love we normally direct only toward our "tribe"—to be defined as you wish—whether that be our family, loved ones, peeps, amigos, or (fill in the blank). When our awareness is free of reference point, it is the most inclusive stance we could possibly embody. When we're not operating from a subject-object orientation, there is no "me" or anyone doing the acting in relation to or on someone else's behalf. There is only awareness itself with all of its qualities simultaneously manifest. That is the greatest kind of compassion there is. But until we can exercise that kind of compassion, we need to work within our self-other frame, realizing that while it may be a construct, it still allows us to give rise to all manners of good qualities—albeit in a dualistic frame. Start to notice how open you are to the idea that all beings are equal. All beings possess the same natural capacity for awareness, suffering, confusion, and all the rest. See if, little by little, you can start to make room for people whom you don't already love and care about. See what if any new perspectives that affords you.

7

What Are You Building Evidence For?

People put a lot less effort into picking apart evidence that confirms what they already believe.

—Peter Watts

It's our brain's job to make sense of itself as a physical being moving through space and time. It must interface with everything it comes into contact with, both inside and outside of itself. If someone gave us the job of building a human, it would be really tough. Rarely do we stop to ponder how incredible the human body, brain, and mind are. We just inhabit our bodies and go through life as if everything is normal, boring even, a hassle at times, drudgery at others. In order to make this thing we call a body work, the brain has to do some pretty sophisticated maneuvering. It uses what it has at its disposal to navigate what's needed both physically and psychologically, tapping into an elaborate system of feedback loops and signals to process and act upon the internal and external information it needs to navigate the situations it encounters. Imagine being the one left in charge of this ongoing operation and communication that allows our brains and bodies to function 24/7. Wait a minute, you are the one who has been left in charge. Imagine if your brain and body merely reacted. They wouldn't have enough notice to do all they would need to do effectively and efficiently. So instead, your brain anticipates and simulates what it thinks is going to happen next. Upon what does your brain make these conjectures? Its prior experiences. But as we often say, best-laid plans, or no good deed goes unpunished. Sometimes the brain just plain screws up.

Like yesterday morning, for example, when I nearly killed myself tripping over my own scales moving in a half-asleep mode from the toilet to the sink. I think I'm better navigating in the dark than I am when I have to get up for the day. When our brain makes an error or miscalculation with its predictions, it quickly attempts to correct for these errors. To do this it calls upon what it has available to it to do so; namely, incoming data from our sensory input and data from inside our bodies, our interoceptive sensations and affect. But absent translation, these signals are difficult to make heads or tails of. Our brain needs to make sense of and integrate these data points to have something it can act on and know what to do with. Much of this happens automatically without us giving it the slightest bit of conscious thought. But a fair bit of sense-making and interpretation can and does have to happen at a level we become consciously aware of and proactively, or retroactively, involved with, which brings us to the topic of this chapter and self-discovery, "What Are You Building Evidence For?"

As we know from our own experience, as much as our brain gets right—which it does to an astonishingly effective degree—there is a fair bit it gets wrong, especially when it comes to how we interpret our own perceptions. We are often blind to when our snap judgments or biases predispose us to a skewed point of view. While this is to be expected given the predictive leaps our brain must make, the implications of this are that we have to be extra diligent when it comes to teasing out the inaccuracies and fallacies of our interpretations. When left unchecked, we tend to gather evidence to support our assessment of the context and whomever we find ourselves in the company of. Mostly, this happens without us even being consciously aware we are doing it. For instance, let's say we meet someone who doesn't make a great first impression on us, which I'm sure has never happened to you. The next time we see this person our perception is typically influenced by how we experienced them the first time.

Or let's say you've assessed someone you know, maybe a sibling, spouse, or one of your adult children, as having the table manners of an ogre—an actual ogre like Shrek. Whether it's true or not and by what standard or measure you've arrived at that conclusion is hard to say, although it probably included some combination of lumping them in with ogres based on your previous interactions with ogres, your beliefs about them, and your expectations about how they should have behaved at the table but didn't, or at least not up to your standards. Although it's true that in many cultures it's considered rude to slurp and burp and make loud eating noises at the table, in others—ogre culture being one of them—it's expected and can be taken as an insult to the host if you don't. Fast forward to the next time you're sharing a meal with this person; you may inadvertently look for evidence of their ogre-like manners. You may even look to see if the person has other notable flaws, making them eligible for entry into a different mental category you've cordoned off for those whose manners are so bad they make ogres seem polite. In short, we risk becoming blind to all data except the data we expect to see. This phenomenon is referred to as confirmation bias in which we (consciously or unconsciously) look for evidence to support our existing beliefs about ourselves, others, or situations. A close cousin of confirmation bias is the Pygmalion effect, which basically refers to the studied phenomenon in which our expectations shape and influence not only our perception of another person but their actual results relative to our expectations of them. We'll look more closely at the impacts our beliefs can have not just on ourselves but on others when we explore the following self-discoveries later in this chapter: "Deficit-Based Bias," "Seeing the Best in Self and Others," and "Emptying Your Headtrash."

Perception Is in the Eye of the Beholder

Another way in which we tend to see variation in people's perceptions is when it comes to how different people who have witnessed or been privy to the same situation assign meaning to it. If you ask 10 people who witnessed the same event what happened, there are going to be some common themes and observations that get surfaced of course—especially if they've been brought up in or exposed to similar experiences, settings, and influences. However, if you ask them to get more granular about why the situation occurred the way it did or what insights they gleaned, they are likely to give you answers that reflect more about who they are and what they believe than about the situation you've asked them to describe or evaluate. In other words, our interpretations tend to reflect our self-identity and social influences as much if not more than the facts of what transpired.

For the rest of today and tomorrow, see if you can pay attention to the initial impressions you have of others and/or the situations you find yourself in. If you've never met or interacted with a particular person before, what are your initial impressions? With those you know well, a spouse, family member, or co-worker, pay attention to the valence or salience that comes up for you when in their presence and your underlying opinions about them when you're around them. Where does the valence of how you feel when you are around this person register? Do you feel more positive than negative, or more negative than positive? Is being around this person conducive for you and for them, or not so much? Notice whether you've already made up your mind about how they are or aren't. Have you already passed judgment on their character? Have they already passed judgment on yours? Do you afford some people benefit of the doubt while not extending the same leeway or mental space for others? If so, examine why or why not. Also, pay attention to whether your assessment of a person or situation is related to your expectations and the degree to which those expectations are or aren't being met. Then, take a few minutes to journal about what you find yourself paying attention to or keying in on about them, and whether it's a function of your building evidence for what you already believe, or whether you're coming at your perception and assessment with a fresh perspective and new eyes. Ask yourself what the impact is of what you believe. Does it help the relationship or hurt it? Do you see any immediately obvious areas you'd like to work on shifting or hitting the redo button on?

Here is a recap on what this self-discovery can look like when you realize that the evidence you're building and the stories you're telling yourself about the scenario or people involved may be getting in the way:

- You see when you are falling into confirmation bias or the many other types of bias and begin to push back on and challenge our own stories.
- You begin to spot the stories you're telling yourself more quickly before spending days or months going down the rabbit hole.
- Instead, you proactively build evidence in the direction of stories and habits that serve you better or that create positive momentum in the direction of the kinds of relationships you want to have with yourself and other people in your life.
- You begin to see the habitual tendency to make sense of your own experience by rationalizing your perceptions and beliefs. Because you recognize this tendency, you aren't as inclined to take what you believe at face value but rather as a single perspective or interpretation.

Deficit-Based Bias

Never give a negative thought an inch or it will take a mile.

—Matshona Dhliwayo

The brain is built with a greater sensitivity toward unpleasant news. Responding negatively is so automatic it can be detected at the earliest stage of the brain's information processing. Take, for example, the studies done by John Cacioppo. The brain, Cacioppo demonstrated, reacts more strongly to stimuli it deems negative; there is a greater surge in electrical activity. As such, our attitude is more heavily influenced by negative than positive data (Berkovic, 2017). Presumably, our proclivity toward negative input serves the underlying purpose of keeping us out of harm's way. Remember, our brain has the responsibility of moving us through the world and ensuring we not only interpret what's about to happen, but how we will need to respond. Thus, it has developed critical systems that allow it to get a head start and then quickly interpret and respond to situations. The unintended consequences of this phenomenon are that we have a knack for seeing what's not working, the gap, what's wrong, or what's missing. Not only may we have the habit of perceiving people or situations in a light that may be less than charitable, but once we form our initial impressions, they usually don't get any better.

Deficit-based bias is one of the brain's many go-to mechanisms for making sense of its own perceptions and experience. None of us asked for this to be the case, but that it is, it is. We discover we possess many marvelous design features and an equal number that may give rise to a feeling of buyer's remorse. This self-discovery may well be one of those—great when it serves us and a real pain when it doesn't. But since presumably no one is keeping tally, a ticket hasn't yet been submitted to request a review of the unintended negative consequences with the hope of an upgrade. Thus, we each have to be our own monitor as we go about our daily lives. To that end, take notice of where you see your deficit-based bias at play in your own habits of perception and interpretation. Where in your life, in your relationships at work and at home, are you seeing through deficit-based goggles? Journal about what you see relative to your own negativity bias tendencies. Get very curious and reflect about the impact this kind of seeing and interpretation has on your immediate experience, your results, and your relationships.

Deficit-Based Bias in Organizations

Deficit-based bias can often be seen in how organizations and the leaders who lead them are taught to navigate day-to-day business. We have entire disciplines and fields of study designed to solve problems, gaps, inefficiencies, and so on. This isn't to say this is wrong, by the way. We do of course need to be able to discern what's working and what isn't and to take action to address and make improvements or course corrections. That said, seeing everything through the lens of being a problem can itself be limiting—detrimental even. We start to see aspects of ourselves, others, and situations as perennially problematic and in need of timely correction, whereas if we shift our perspective to a mindset of ongoing, continuous improvement, the time horizon we have to make all these incremental improvements lengthens. We can take into account there is no point at which we arrive; rather, we just keep emerging, attempting to make the best of what each new moment has to offer, and what we have to give.

Like anything we are trying to shift or change in ourselves, it takes conscious awareness and intent to recognize we're going down the same rabbit hole and then consistently practice reverse-engineering what got us there in the first place, and then how we might gracefully handle our temporary mental predicament. Here is where shifting our perceptual perspective, or awareness, relative to whatever we're experiencing can be immediately applicable and useful. However, if shifting what we perceive by means of adjusting our own perspective and awareness isn't as accessible, we can look at what's available to us by way of cognitive reframing.

Take, for example, someone you presently have difficulty interacting with or being around. Maybe it's your boss, a colleague, a frenemy, one of your siblings, a parent, your neighbor, or your child. Picture this person in your presence now. Among the many things about them you actively struggle with, imagine them saying or doing the thing that drives you bonkers. As you visualize whatever it is they say or do that causes you to want to push the eject button on them or you, what comes up by way of notable physical sensations? What surfaces by way of thoughts, feelings, or emotions? Try noticing how you feel in terms of valence, the positive-negative continuum. Take mental note of the level of salience this holds for you—the strength or intensity of what you're feeling—along with how quickly what you're feeling comes up and how long these feelings typically loiter on the premises. What perspective could you take when you're interacting with this individual or when something they've said or done sends you into a tailspin? What resources do you have within yourself that you can call upon in moments like these? Let's look at what have you accessible to you by way of *perceptual* and *cognitive reframing* strategies.

Perceptual Reframing

Of the various qualities and expressions of your own awareness, how could a change in your view create the conditions to shift your perspective, giving you a fresh set of mental parameters to work with (see Figure 7.1)? Of the following questions you might ask yourself, what stance would invite a new interpretation and way of relating to this individual?

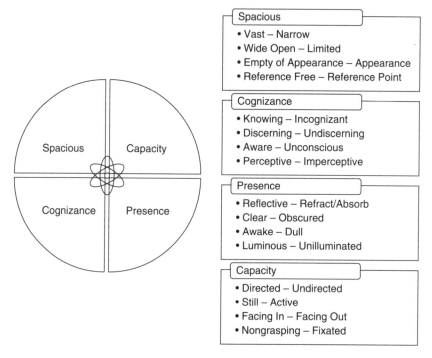

Figure 7.1   The Qualities and Expressions of Awareness
Source: © Brain Capital LLC.

- Could my view benefit from being more spacious? In what ways might my self-other vantage point be skewing my perspective? Am I overly focused on myself and my expectations at the expense of others or vice versa? To the extent my view of the others involved, or the situation, may be limited by my preconceived notions, what might be possible if I could broaden my point of view?

- Where can I implement greater discernment? Is there something about this person, how I'm feeling about them, or our relationship I am either not consciously aware of or am misperceiving? What, if anything, might I not be apprehending or understanding about one or more of the variables involved?

- Am I seeing things clearly, or is my perspective clouded, obscured, or mistaken in some way? If so, in what ways? To what extent, if any, might my reaction be a projection of some aspect of myself I've rejected or a reflection of my own story?

- Can the situation benefit from me looking inward, either toward my own awareness or by reflecting on my role in what's unfolding? Is my mind calm and steady? What might it look like to move in the direction of this person, to say or do the thing that improves our relationship? Is there anything I've become fixated or overly focused on to the detriment of being able to perceive other points of view or the priority I place on the quality of relationship or mutually conducive resolution to the situation?

When it comes to implementing one or more adjustments to our awareness as a means to shift our perspective, we can either literally take space by removing ourselves from the situation, or we can create mental space by allowing our awareness to embody its natural spacious quality. We can invite any of the qualities of mind to be present, such as our ability to discern the situation clearly, which may include seeing where our own point of view or interpretation may be biased or skewed. We can think about what's at stake and our intentions, inviting conscious awareness of each. We can do this by taking several deep breaths, imagining with each breath we are infusing our perspective with whatever form of wisdom is present within our own awareness—our inner coach—whichever expression has the capacity to offer us support and act as a natural remedy to our present mental outlook or predicament.

Cognitive Reframing

In cognitive reframing you're employing mental reasoning to change your own mind. You're using thought to change thought, concept to shift concept. Since there is no limit to the concepts you can employ, only a limit to your creativity or imagination, you may wish to start by experimenting with implementing one or more of the 12 Self-Discoveries. Each invites new ways of seeing and relating to your own habits of mind when you're at an impasse or stuck in an unconducive line of thought, or when the manner in which you're perceiving and making sense of a person or situation isn't helping.

Take negativity bias as an example. We are physiologically predisposed to view our experience through deficit-based bias, which makes it even more challenging as we work against the grain of our tendencies. Nonetheless, if we don't want to give our negativity bias any more latitude or voice than it already has, then it may require a shift in our perspective. Instead, we may want to practice the opposite, seeing the generative elements in people and situations, which is the next self-discovery we'll explore. As a means of quickly and effectively discerning where you may want to dive in and how you can orient yourself when you do, it can help to ask yourself a few simple questions:

- What do I have direct control or influence over?
- What is my intention?
- What objective(s) or outcome(s) am I trying to achieve?
- What's at stake?
- What would it look like to act in alignment with my values, and what is important to me in this situation?
- Is what I'm about to say or do going to bring harm to myself or the other individual(s) involved?

When Helping: Deficit-Based Bias

As we develop greater proficiency in adopting whichever lens may be the best one for the job, we gain the following agency over our own minds:

- We are able to shut down our tendency toward negativity bias when it crops up, and we aren't forced to see and interpret our experience through only that lens.
- We catch ourselves trying to solve "problems." When we catch ourselves using language that presumes something is problematic, we are able to shift our language to include the possibility of other options. When we use language more appreciative by nature, we tend to ask different questions that lead in the direction of positive inquiry. When we shift from asking "What's wrong?" or "What's the problem?" to "What's right?" or "What's working?" and "Where's the opportunity?" and "What's possible?" we alter the nature of the inquiry itself as well as its outcome.

- We are quickly able to look past the "ugly wrapping" of the challenges we're faced with and as a result can unwrap whatever gift is waiting inside, to paraphrase a saying of a friend. Even if the gift has a message that may be less than encouraging, we're able to find meaning in difficult situations and pivot our mindset accordingly.

Emptying Your Headtrash

The curious paradox is that when I accept myself just as I am, then I can change.

—Carl R. Rogers

We each develop coping mechanisms and stories as a way to work with and make sense of rough patches in our lives. Eventually, however, these ways we've developed to deal with the adversity we face no longer serve their original context or intended purpose. While they may have at some point in time, they may not be conducive strategies for you now. But somehow that is lost on us, and we are simply too close to the situation to see it for what it is. The conditions that give rise to our response in one moment often shift and change before we do. Our means of dealing with those circumstances can lag our awareness or acknowledgment that what worked for us then isn't working for us now. What may have been appropriate in one scenario may not be a plug-and-play in another.

We can inadvertently fall into the trap of thinking every bad thing that's ever happened to us ties back to or is a result of this or that character flaw we've either been told by others we have or that we ourselves have come to believe we have. This can surface when we experience disappointment or defeat. We then tell ourselves and others the reason this or that thing happened is because we aren't lovable, we aren't good enough, we can't do anything right, or fill in the blank with your favorite bad thing you often think or say about yourself. Without even being aware of it, we then revisit these stories after something negative occurs, or when we become discouraged. We say things in those moments to ourselves about ourselves that we wouldn't dare say to anyone else. We engage in negative self-talk, uttering things under our breath like, "I told you it wouldn't work out." Or we admonish ourselves in the second person, "You shouldn't have put yourself out there like that or taken a chance on (fill in the blank)."

These become the stories that fuel self-doubt, creating steeper and steeper barriers between our aspirations and our belief in our ability to bring our dreams to fruition. In the same way we learn to brace ourselves for disappointment, we unconsciously sabotage ourselves by looking for evidence to support the self-limiting beliefs we have about ourselves. Our headtrash can take the form of stories and scripts that make their way center stage in our imaginations. They become like well-rehearsed lines that loop in our brains, like the lyrics to a song we can't shake.

Mental Hygiene

We wouldn't purposely not bathe or brush our teeth for extended periods of time, right? So why don't we perceive the need for the same kind of hygiene for our own minds? His Holiness the Dalai Lama speaks of the need for mental hygiene, and he's right. While it's impossible to eradicate all bias, as it's a feature of perception itself, cultivating awareness is the only thing I'm aware of that can help counteract these tendencies and negative consequences that arise from navigating the world with bias. Just like we have a tendency to accumulate belongings and clutter over time, so too do we have a tendency to accumulate mental models that no longer serve our purpose or aims. Therefore, like going through our closet periodically, we have to intentionally revisit our belief systems, dust them off, and determine whether they still fit.

I recently taught a course to a group of coaches and leaders on the the 12 Self-Discoveries. When it came to the concept of headtrash, I was explaining our headtrash often takes the form of self-deprecating comments, but what I inadvertently said instead was, "Headtrash often takes the form of self-defecating comments and beliefs you hold about yourself." While not the words I consciously meant to use, that's exactly what headtrash is! As you practice observing and journaling about the various stories and self-limiting beliefs you may be weaving about yourself or others, try to identify and articulate what is at the heart of the story or belief, along with what evidence you are building wittingly or unwittingly to lend to your own or others' conviction in that narrative. Think about whether this story or belief is serving you well or not. If not, what might serve you better, and what evidence will you need to search for to confirm your new story or belief? Pay attention to where your thought patterns and habits of mind consistently take you. Which ones do you find ensnare you most frequently and in what situations? When you get caught up in headtrash, are you able to spot it? When you engage in negative self-talk, do you recognize it as such? If you weren't getting caught up in these mental traps and pitfalls time and again, what else might be possible? What else might you have room for? You'll know you've moved the needle on this particular self-discovery when:

- You notice when your headtrash is asserting itself and strike back by implementing the strategies you've learned to build and reinforce evidence of your positive qualities.
- You don't engage in negative self-talk, and when you do, you catch yourself and switch up the dialogue to those things that would be helpful to think about and say to yourself instead.
- You know yourself well enough you can spot when you're up to your old tricks of downward spiral thinking, negative self-talk, or engaging in amassing an arsenal of evidence against yourself and instead will do something right then and there to change course.

Seeing the Best in Self and Others

Everything that irritates us about others can lead us to an understanding of ourselves.

—C. G. Jung

Given our tendencies toward headtrash and confirmation and negativity bias, coupled with whatever we obsess over or cling to getting accentuated or magnified, we have to be diligent when it comes to training and focusing on seeing the generative qualities in people and situations; that is, if we acknowledge and believe that *for better or worse, our focus becomes our reality.* When we get stuck in a downward or negative spiral, our aims usually aren't served by exploring whether the staircase reaches the basement. Rather, if we see ourselves going down a one-way street the wrong way, we don't keep driving against traffic. Instead, we can examine whether engaging in the negative momentum of our emotion brings us or anyone around us any benefit whatsoever.

When all we can see is the negative, the downside, the gap, and the missing link, the invitation is to practice seeing the qualities, the upside, and the humanity in people and generative possibilities of situations. This is what we can think of as applied empathy or compassion. What is empathy or compassion if not the ability to exercise our capacity to connect with the best aspects of ourselves and others? This approach of learning to discern and appreciate the life-giving elements of situations and people is particularly helpful given that we can't control other people or outside circumstances—we can only control our response to them. When we are struggling with a person or a situation, there are at least a handful of choices available to us in that moment. We can change nothing about how we perceive the situation or person and continue to let our mental outlook drag us around by our nose rope, or we can shift what we choose to focus upon. For that, you can employ one or more of the practices on reframing your meaning—the sense you're making—or your perceptual stance relative to it.

In coaching clients and leaders over the years, I've seen that they often start the coaching engagement with goals like wanting to become better listeners or developing greater self-awareness or increasing their effectiveness with others. But often clients aren't thinking globally about why they're getting their present results, or why the relationships they have with key people in their lives—both at work and home—may be hitting a wall. In the coaching I've done, there has not been a time when the conversation didn't quickly turn to the client's desire to improve one or more of their key relationships. We often get stuck in the habit of directing our attention toward the elements about that person or our interpersonal dynamic with them we don't like or isn't meeting our expectations. But as we discussed earlier in the book when I shared my story about my daughter's proclivity for running late and the ineffective manner I was handling it, we often don't recognize when it's our expectations that are standing between us and having a good relationship with someone in our lives.

Once we realize it isn't a case of this person actively wanting to disappoint or fail us, as much as our own expectations not being met, we can see the value of making an effort to see the best in another person as well as being clear about our aspirations for the relationship. What inevitably happens when we apply an appreciative inquiry lens in which we proactively connect with our own and others' qualities is we become reacquainted with what we like, love, or admire about that person. When we expend at least as much if not more energy looking for evidence of what is right, good, or life-giving, our locus of attention shifts, and our mental outlook follows.

We humans are funny. All we have to do is give our mind a job and most of the time, it will do it—no questions asked. If you give your mind the job of finding things that aren't working, your mind will hop to it, churning up the data you asked of it. Similarly, if you give your mind the job of searching for what's working or to find a solution that requires a positive, forward-going, and fresh perspective to an old obstacle or growth edge, it is also capable of doing that—even if it's not as accustomed to doing so. When we practice shifting both our perceptual and cognitive orientation to what we are perceiving and gleaning from a situation, we end up increasing our mental agility, that is, our ability to shift our own perspective to be an ally versus an inadvertent foe.

I've witnessed clients saving their marriages, establishing more positive relationships with their children and loved ones, and learning to work effectively with colleagues they once couldn't stand to be around. They're able to do this when they can envision, articulate, and act on their best intentions for the relationship—not to the exclusion of how they feel, but in a way that holds the tension between their own expectations and their aspiration for the relationship. It's not that everything suddenly goes right and nothing ever goes awry again; our lives don't suddenly become a Disney movie, which I'm pretty sure we wouldn't want to have happen regardless. All of our same tendencies crop up to whatever degree they have a foothold in our thinking and our habits of minding. But the difference is when they do, we're ready to apply a perceptual or cognitive shift to our perspective, thereby impacting our interpretation and actions that follow. Our actions and outlook tend to follow our mind whether we're aware of it or not. Our influence in this situation is to get to know our own mind and our own habits of perception and interpretation.

Then when we see ourselves reacting on the basis of someone not meeting our expectations, we get better at spotting it. This is the case even more so if you regularly journal. You're able to go back and read your journal entries relative to one or more of the 12 Self-Discovery journal prompts and home in on where this type of thinking may be cropping up either in your relationships or in how you are making sense of your experience. You can only do something about it if you recognize something needs doing. That's how the 12 Self-Discoveries are designed to work—as reminders that you have a choice. You get to decide on a conscious basis the sense you choose to make, the mental models you rely upon to do so, and where there may be an opportunity to switch things up for yourself a bit—not always being so predictable about how you'll interpret or respond to certain people or situations. Ultimately, we can make choices that move us in the direction of what is conducive to our own and others' wellbeing.

Hit the Road, Jack[1]

You may have a desire to see if staying in your current job or relationship can work. If that's the case, then it may be worth reacquainting yourself with its positive or generative elements. But if wiping the cobwebs out of your eyes doesn't do the trick nor does trying to rekindle la chispa or rediscover the magic, then there is only one person who can decide whether it's time to move on, and that's you. When you've established that staying isn't a matter of not being able to see what's good but is more a function of there just not being enough good, or the right things present, then you may well be due for a change in scenery and/or company. The main point I am trying to make here is if we abandon ship too quickly, particularly without experimenting with trying on a few different lenses, then we will never know if the reason the relationship is failing is a result of any number of reasons that are in fact workable. When we practice seeing with a lens of appreciation and gratitude, allowing ourselves to connect with what is good and right about a person or situation, we invite the conditions for authentic connection and can benefit from the life-giving elements of our new and old relationships alike. However, there are times in our life when, even after swapping out a negative lens for a well-considered one, the relationship or situation we're in turns out to be untenable. Note, this strategy isn't appropriate in all situations, especially where abuse or harm are part of the equation. In those situations, no amount of trying to see what's positive will fix the collateral damage or is worth waiting to see if the situation will improve. Only you know your situation well enough to decide what's best for you or even whether seeking professional help may be an appropriate thing to do.

When We "See" Each Other

What does it mean to see the best in someone else? It means we see people not only for who they are now but for who they have been, and who they are when unencumbered. It means we afford them the same positive regard and grace we do those we love or hold in high esteem. When I work with clients who are having difficulties with other people, which is always—if not in their personal lives, then in their professional lives—I encourage them to practice paying attention to the qualities of the person they're struggling with. For every fault, I ask them to find at least three positive qualities. We don't need to force things or make things up that aren't true. We do, however, ideally need to be able to find some redeeming quality. If you're truly struggling to find something positive in that person, that's when using your awareness to zoom out may be in order. Take stock of the fact that despite this person's unlikability or even despicableness in your eyes, they are still a sentient being who possesses the same capacity for awareness you do. They long for happiness, safety, and security, just like you do. They suffer and have unmet needs and expectations, just like you do. They've endured disappointments, betrayals, and hardship just like you have. They've likely suffered physically and psychologically at some point in life. Like you, they are subject to the same laws of the universe, sickness, old age, and death. They experience impermanence in the form of losing people they cherish or circumstances that once brought them joy. If we can't connect on the level of our basic dignity and humanity, what hope is there for a better world? We have to start somewhere.

If you notice yourself reacting negatively to your perception of something someone else has said or done or by their very presence, ask yourself why. What about this person irritates me? Do I object to something they said or did? Is there anything they could have done differently that might have resulted in me feeling differently? Each time you ask a question, try what's known as the five-why process in Lean. That's where you ask a question then turn your answer into the form of a question and ask it again. Do this five times or until you get to the heart of what you feel may be the reason you don't like this person or why you may be reacting to them as you are. Often this practice will help you to get to the root cause, helping you bypass symptoms or side effects of the core issue. Eventually, you'll often uncover an expectation you didn't realize you had that's not being met, or a value or belief system that is somehow being tweaked.

Moreover, you may find there is something about this person, one or more of their behavioral traits, that may be more like you than not. When this happens, we can feel pinched or impinged upon, particularly if it's a trait that suddenly puts you on the receiving end of what it might feel like to others to be around you. Maybe you have a bossy streak or are a frequent interrupter or both. When faced with someone who gives your bossiness a run for its money or in whose company you can't get a word in edgewise, you may get a taste of what this feels like to be on the receiving end. This doesn't always mean what you observe in someone else is automatically a reflection of your own behavioral tendencies, of course; whatever you've keyed into about the other person is giving you information about the valence or salience of your perception of them. Bear in mind, they likely feel that from you.

The good news is you have more than a few choices available to you in these situations. You can pause and observe; notice your internal thoughts and any bodily sensations you're experiencing. You can invoke one or more of the qualities of your own awareness you have at your disposal to shift your vantage point, or you can see which if any of the 12 Self-Discoveries can be helpful to you in that moment. When you're operating under the auspices of your conscious awareness, you increase the option sets you have available to you in that moment that allow you to respond in a manner that reflects your values and intent.

When Helping: Seeing the Best in Self and Others

Here are some indicators you've gained headway pertaining to this particular self-discovery:

- Instead of noticing what's wrong, missing, or a gap, you start to notice what's right, what's present, and available to you.
- You switch from a scarcity model to an abundance model.
- You are once again able to see your own and others' strengths and choose to focus on the generative aspects life has to offer all around you.
- You tune out the noise or turn down the volume on the stories or beliefs that aren't helpful.

8

Happiness Is
a State of Mind

Happiness comes down to choosing between the discomfort of becoming aware of your mental afflictions and the discomfort of being ruled by them.
—Yongey Mingyur Rinpoche

Do you see yourself as being at the helm of how you respond to your mental states and emotions? Do you feel better equipped with strategies to recognize unconducive states of mind and to work with them using any number of strategies we've explored up to this point? As we shift into learning how to spot and work with our own mental models, let's take a closer look at what's operative at the level of what we believe about our mind, our habits, and our ability to transform each.

Breaking Free from Behavioral Inertia

In the same way awareness is a prerequisite for us to do anything consciously, our ability to take actions that create the optimal conditions for shifting our behavior are critical to our ability to bring about meaningful changes to our habits of mind. We've learned from Newton's first law of physics that all things remain inert, at rest, or in uniform motion (in a straight line) unless compelled to change their state. Newton's law goes on to say that only by the action of an external force can the state of inertia be broken or compelled toward a different trajectory of movement. But Newton had objects as his focus and not the mind, human behavior, or habit change. So what does inertia look like when it comes to human behavior? We could describe the human equivalent of inertia as living in a state of behavioral stasis and/or perceptual fuzziness—an absence of conscious awareness—in which we are being acted upon, whether by the outer conditions that shape and form our immediate context or by our habitual ways of perceiving, making sense of, and responding to our environment. As we seek to better understand how we can take greater responsibility for what is within our power to influence, let's look at how what we believe about change and our own role in that process influences our views of what's possible.

As is the case in Newton's first law, external forces can certainly be the cause for us to change behavioral trajectories. Sometimes we call these types of events crucible moments. When something extreme or even catastrophic comes to pass in our lives or those of our loved ones, it can create the impetus for us to break free from whatever behavioral inertia we may otherwise be experiencing. And while these sorts of external forces can set us on a new course, what happens thereafter often determines how short-lived or lasting the effects will be. We know from certain experiments in quantum physics that objects observed behave differently than objects not observed. Lest I open a can of worms that can't be put back in their subjective wormholes, "observed" in this example means subjected to invasive measurement by an apparatus, not necessarily by the experimenter simply opening her eyes in the lab. I bring this up not to stir pots—although I do enjoy a good pot stirring—but because the subject is germane and highly relevant to the idea that conscious awareness is the internal condition that gives us the capacity to behave and respond differently than when we are on autopilot and simply being acted upon. The two ways of moving through the world are not only qualitatively different but have the potential to yield profoundly different consequences.[1] As we'll see, the moment we introduce a conscious observer, in this case our own awareness, it opens up the possibility to shift seemingly immovable components within our lives.

As we saw in the Awareness Matrix and qualities and expressions of our mind, our awareness exists more as a continuum than as any singular way of being aware. We can be aware of, well, everything that comes into our conscious field of experience, even things we become aware of indirectly or by inference. We can think of this capacity to be aware as the cognizance aspect of our minds, a conscious, awake, and intentional awareness as distinct from a passive or neutral backdrop of awareness in which our brain is still processing various inputs while our conscious awareness has receded into the background, beneath the surface of what we are actively aware of. In that moment, we may experience our own awareness as more of a foggy, dull, or oblivious state of mind, which I sometimes liken to being on cruise control or autopilot. Our own awareness is arguably the one aspect of our own minds that is on-demand. Like an obedient dog, it will come if you call it—even in the dream state. Now, it may wander away again just as quickly, but it's always within mind's reach—so to say—poised and ready to perceive and be perceived. Our awareness gives us the ability to do what we do consciously and intentionally.

Given our stated objective to identify and take action on what we have direct influence over within ourselves, it stands to reason that we need to locate and activate the impetus to unseat our own inertia. And on top of that, we also need to isolate and repeat whatever it is that allows us to perpetuate and sustain our momentum toward the changes we want to make.[2] When we look at what within ourselves gives us the possibility to do that, what other than our own awareness, at a most fundamental level, gives us the wherewithal to act and to sustain the momentum of our conscious actions? Any experience when coupled with our conscious awareness behaves differently than when our awareness is passive or absent altogether.

We don't have to look very far for a relevant example. Let's take our autonomic nervous system. Barring a physiological malfunction or flaw, it runs reliably and smoothly to keep core functions up and running. If it were an employee, it would be the person who shows up without fail, rain or shine, someone we can count on. Whereas when it comes to functions that don't fall under its domain, our ability to perform those tasks can be highly variable and reliant upon if not our conscious awareness, then our habits. Habits are actions triggered in response to contextual cues (Gardner, Lally, & Wardle, 2012). So, as long as no one is rocking the boat and we have the cues and the context, the habit is good to go. If habits were an employee, they would be like a steady performer. As long as they're clear with expectations and instructions and they have the resources to do their job, they're self-sufficient. But in moments when there is a function in need of our conscious attention or awareness—like forming a new habit or breaking an old one—sadly, like the internet at my house, both are in high demand yet relatively short supply, not to mention behave a bit unpredictably. They are not like a steady employee but more like a general contractor, high-priced and hard to come by; good at what they do but incredibly unreliable—what my teacher sometimes terms "washy-wishy." When it comes to building a new habit or behavior or breaking an old one, our awareness and our agency of mind are necessary ingredients.

Awareness + Agency of Mind = Momentum

Awareness is the necessary internal condition, while our agency of mind is the internal force needed to break us loose from our own inertia. Both are essential to propel us toward our target and desired outcomes. While our awareness is easy to summon, it requires that we remember to do so, and even when we are successful at catching its attention, it's equally challenging to convince it to stick around. It requires our presence, or agency of mind, to keep us on point, which in turn necessitates we train in our own awareness in a dedicated and ongoing manner. As we know from experience, our perceptions have the capacity to catch us off-guard and knock us off-center, along with a host of other self-generated obstacles we've been exploring, which is why we need to be prepared to distinguish and act upon what we have influence over within ourselves to regain our footing and carry on. Together, this dynamic duo, awareness and agency of mind, are the primary inbuilt features we have to work with that give us the capacity to point our perceptual stance and trajectory in the direction of our aspirations.

Habits and Behavior: The Momentum of Many Moments

We often experience triumph or defeat retrospectively, as an event, outcome, or memory, when in reality our successes and losses unfold like individual moves on a chessboard. Behavior and habit change are the same. Both are concepts that allow us to talk about and conceptualize the outcome of a series of actions we undertake again and again. We use the word "habit" to refer to repetitive actions we take so many times we no longer give them much if any conscious thought while doing them, whereas "behavior" is a word we use to define how something, or someone, repetitively behaves or acts. Habits are the "what" and behavior is the "how." Both come about by virtue of actions we take until they become pervasive enough we say things like, "She has a bad habit of interrupting people," or "She is a better talker than she is listener." In other words, we've performed and repeated the same kinds of actions so many times we no longer think of habits or behaviors as having come about through repeated individual actions. Instead, we think of descriptive words to describe the person who embodies the habit or behavior. *Language and the words we use to communicate complex ideas predispose and shape our conceptual understanding and expectations not only of what they mean, but what it takes to achieve the meaning they are meant to convey.* When we use words like "habit" or "behavior" on their own, we risk losing track of the fact that they also convey a process. Put another way, these kinds of words don't in and of themselves convey they've come about as a result of a longer time horizon—short of combining them with other process or movement words, like "flow" or "process," or even a symbol that would serve to remind us this is the case.

Let me illustrate using the following analogy. When a magician performs a magic trick, we aren't necessarily focused on what took place before, during, or after the magician performed the magic trick to give the impression something indeed magical has occurred. We only notice the "magic" or end result of the trick, such as when a magician successfully saws an audience member in half. We don't see the "magic" of the trick for what it is, a series of actions undertaken in a particular kind of way to bring about an end result. All we see is a pair of legs with three-inch red high heels detached from the torso of the owner of these amazingly pointy shoes who is smiling and waving at us gregariously from the other end. We see the outcome, but cognitively we aren't connecting the dots on the factors that produced that result. When left to our own devices and unless we have explicitly trained otherwise, we aren't inclined to conceptualize cause and effect as it pertains to the "magic" underlying our own perception, let alone second- and third-order thinking, which invite us to ponder second- and third-order effects, or consequences of our own or others' actions. This is more than a bit ironic given our brains are constantly simulating a picture of reality that is both anticipatory and predictive by nature. I guess the natural talent we have in this arena and the metabolic resources needed to enact them, end up being channeled toward ensuring we meet our short-term or immediate needs and not so much on the potential downstream impacts.

The fact that we are bound by single words, like "habit" or "behavior," to describe something that comes about as a result of a process or series of actions performed doesn't help matters. To the extent our way of speaking about processes are held hostage to the conventions of language itself, the need for us to go the extra step of contemplating actions along with their potential consequences becomes more critical. In the meantime, our expectations about what it takes to move the needle on our habits and behaviors informs the level of effort we're often willing to invest. Only once we understand any shift in habits or behavior depends on creating the necessary causes and conditions within ourselves, not to mention our immediate environment, over a much longer, if not perpetual, time horizon can we attempt to gear our expectations and efforts accordingly. Otherwise, we won't be as inclined to give the undertaking the level of attention, priority, or time it merits and are more likely to become frustrated when we don't reach the end point of our goal.

All eventualities begin right now, in the present moment. Most of what we aim to develop by way of competencies, personal traits, or qualities unfortunately can't be achieved by checking off a box once and for all or by performing a single action, like reading an article or book, meditating once or twice, or signing up for an online course. If that's all it took, we would have met the minimum threshold of required action a long time ago. Yet somehow this is what we have naively come to expect. And if what we want to have happen doesn't happen quickly enough, we become impatient, jumping impetuously from one thing to the next. The conditions needed to bring about better versions of ourselves are a function of both our outer parameters and our inner propensity for change. In this way, the habits of mind we build for ourselves can either aid or hinder us on our journey to discovering how we ideally want to live our lives and the impact we want to have.

Cultivating anything in ourselves, whatever it may be, requires the momentum of many moments and is not a singular, one-time event. By expanding our knowledge base and our application of those concepts, the options we have available to us increase. The very process of learning and putting ourselves in different scenarios contributes to shaping and influencing not only how we perceive the world, but what we have available to choose from relative to how we consciously make sense of what we perceive and how we interpret what is valent and salient for us. The actions we consciously undertake assert themselves in each new moment, until those moments create a continuity of moments, and the continuity of individual moments builds enough momentum to give rise to new ways of being and new ways of behaving, and, in turn, new ways of showing up in the world. This is what is meant by the term "emergence" or "emergent." We're all in a constant state of flux, change, and emergence. Not only is our context constantly changing, we're constantly having to change relative to it. The tools you're being introduced to in this book not only allow you to have maximum say and agency in that process but allow you to change the way in which you perceive, make sense of, and respond to the fundamental condition of the temporary and impermanent nature of all experiences.

At some point, we acknowledge having developed a new habit or behavior. We've done it enough times to recognize it as something we just do now until it describes more of how we are than how we aren't. Equally important, others around us start to acknowledge these sustained moments of change as a new habit or behavior that inspires them to say things about us or to us that indicate we aren't the only ones who detect a shift worth noting, like "She has come a long way." Hopefully, they say that instead of, "You know, Michele, you're even bossier than you were before the pandemic." In this way, each moment is a proposition to be won or lost. We either inch in the direction of our aspirations or we take a step further away from what we want to become or to have happen. However, just because we acquire a new habit doesn't mean it will stay put forever—unless it is permanently anchored to a cue. I'm suggesting the primary cue be the one thing you always have with you, apart from your breath, which is your awareness. Let your own awareness be your cue, the common denominator within yourself that you cultivate and train in.

Unless we continue to take the actions both internally and externally to support what is required to maintain a habit, it will erode over time, giving way to and taking shape as whatever new actions we're investing our time in instead. That is why we each must create internal cues to remind us of how we would like to respond or behave. We can think of these as our internal supports we're prepared and trained to fall back on irrespective of other contextual factors. That is precisely what all of the models, practices, and frameworks you're being introduced to in this book are meant to do— to provide you with your own means. The VSM and Awareness Matrix help remind you where you have wherewithal and influence, while the qualities and expressions of awareness summarize what you have available at all times to shift your perspective and view. They summarize all the ways in which your own awareness affords you agency of mind and access to your conscious awareness. The 12 Self-Discoveries act as internal prompts, cues designed to remind you in the moment you can cognitively reframe or recategorize what you're feeling and your interpretation. Finally, the Mind-Body Map, which you'll be introduced to in the upcoming chapters, is a framework you can use to better understand your motivational drivers, behavioral preferences, needs, and expectations. It's meant to help you pinpoint and work with your underlying beliefs, mental models, and social influences and how each impact your overall MindBody alignment and your habits of mind. In short, it's a tool to help you figure out your perceptual and interpretative habits; specifically, how you perceive, interpret, and respond to your own perceptions.

Experiencing Emotion as Energy and Movement

As you practice keeping hold of your own nose rope, imagine your emotions to be what they are—temporary valence and salience, sensory signals and energy surging through you, a message from you to you by you. Let your awareness mingle with whatever sensations you may be feeling as you experience the path their charge and energy take within you. You may feel compelled to give voice to what you are experiencing or to name and describe it, which is what we do if we're using our interoceptive awareness along with words and concepts to recategorize how we're feeling, also a valid method. But in this particular practice, you're going to suspend your urge to conceptualize. Instead, just notice the quality and energy of the sensations themselves. See if you can observe and let the valence or salience of what you're experiencing run its natural course without the need to conceptually intervene or elaborate by trying to name or make sense of it.

What happens when you try to grasp the ungraspable? The moment you try to name or conceptualize what you're feeling, while you may be satisfying your brain's urge to assign meaning, you're also concretizing something that in and of itself is nonconceptual and temporary. The moment you try to name it, the mind also wants to understand it, make sense of it, which solidifies it. The act of interpretation changes its trajectory. The path the energy of the emotion takes along with its coordinates, valence and salience, determine its destination. Any meaning you assign this nonconceptual experience can become even more intense, or it can lessen and dampen what you're feeling by way of its sensations. If what you're feeling becomes more intense, instead of zeroing in on it or narrowing your attention, try circling it from above, opening your awareness back up. Orient your perspective to the spaciousness of your own awareness instead of the sensations themselves or your conceptualizations about them. Try taking slightly deeper breaths in and then out, imagining you're expanding the vast quality of your own mind as you do. Notice how expansive and open your awareness can become. When you let the spacious quality of your awareness expand, whatever else is present by way of thoughts, feelings, or sensations has greater space to resolve itself, to dissolve naturally. In fact, the more you turn your attention to observing the qualities of your own awareness in these moments, the more you are shifting the focus away from the specifics of whatever else is unfolding in your experience, such as any thoughts or feelings you may be having about the situation. Instead, turn your curiosity toward itself. Investigate the mind that wants to know and that perceives versus the objects it's drawn to investigate and make sense of. Observe the one experiencing and watching and see what happens.

While perhaps more difficult and abstract to do and certainly different than the practice of observing and naming your sensations and recategorizing whatever you're feeling using concepts, when you work with your own awareness and mind in this way, you are developing the dexterity of your own awareness, keying into your experience of its many natural qualities, nuances, and expressions. In this practice, instead of constructing emotion, giving it a level of precision and granularity, we're working with its antecedent, the mind that perceives the traces of emotion before it becomes a full-blown conceptualization or rendering of the physical sensations, affect, and meaning your brain would normally assign it. After all, it's the conceptual meaning we assign our sensations that earn it the title of being an emotion. Since we're always thinking, why not give it a rest? Mix things up a bit for yourself and try something new. Expand your repertoire of mental habits, and as you do journal about what is different about working with your emotions in this way and to what degree you have the presence of mind and wherewithal to work with your own awareness, particularly when you are faced with swells of sensations and feelings that appear to you as if out of nowhere.

9

Mantras, Metaphors, and Maps

Mantras

A mantra is a sacred utterance that has the capacity to move the mind. The word *mantra* in Sanskrit derives from the words "man" and "tra," which translate as "to think" and "vehicle," respectively. So, quite literally, mantra is a vehicle for thought. What is thinking? Thinking is the mind moving. In one sense, mantras can be thought of as that which evokes or moves the mind.

Remember the analogy of the lake and its waves in the context of the mirror-like aspect of our awareness? In this metaphor, the surface of the lake undisturbed is calm and reflective. When waves appear on its surface, the mind temporarily loses its reflective quality and bends in the direction of its movement. It becomes absorbed in and by its own movement irrespective of what moved it. Our awareness moves by virtue of the capacity quality of our minds, that is our mind's ability to move and shift itself. Words that hold meaning for us move our attention in their direction. If words do not have meaning for us, they may still catch or move our attention, but until we understand their meaning, they remain meaning-free. The mind moves with sound and the meaning it makes of that sound. Mantras have great importance and varying significance and contemplative use within many religious traditions, which is important to mention but whose full meaning and use within that context is out of the scope of our aims. Within the context of the 12 Self-Discoveries, however, mantra refers to a saying or a phrase that captures the essence of an insight, a cue that quickly jogs our memory of that insight and guides our actions and responses accordingly. It can be extremely helpful to generate phrases that hold personal meaning as a method of calling to mind something we are trying to remember; for instance, how we want to show up and respond in certain contexts or situations. An example of a mantra could be, "I don't have to believe everything I think." In fact, most of the 12 Self-Discoveries function as mantras, reminding you of what you're either going to try to adopt and start doing, or what you are going to refrain from and stop doing.

Metaphors

Metaphors stretch our minds like the concepts that give them meaning. Like personal mantras, metaphors are tools, methods that serve the purpose of encapsulating and portraying complex ideas in a way that helps us immediately relate to and understand the essence or meaning of what they describe. Throughout the book, I've purposely made use of metaphors to describe functions and processes of the mind that might otherwise be unapproachable and/or difficult to translate into something we can understand and apply. Using metaphors as a means of discovering what's operative for us relative to our habits of mind not only allows us to gain some perspective of what is normally too close for us to see but allows us to wrap our minds around abstract and complex ideas. Metaphors illuminate subtle interconnections and relationships, such as those between symbols and their meaning or our mental models and their effect on our response. Both are examples of making the intangible relatable. Metaphors allow us to shift our perspective to see through a different lens or from a different vantage point. Since metaphors are hypothetical, this allows us to relate more playfully with the subject matter at hand. By their nature, metaphors invoke the creative capacity of our minds to bend the rules and norms of association with the intent of conveying multiple layers of meaning at once.

Metaphors have a unique capacity to distill wisdom. They're often the impetus for us to gain insight, to make mental connections we hadn't yet made, or to see something we didn't see before even though it was right before our eyes, like the moment you notice the doughy letters floating in your alphabet soup have formed the word "soup" and you suddenly realize you're eating letter *soup*. There aren't many conventions or rules when it comes to metaphors, which is what gives them their capacity for novel combinations and formulations of thought, word, feeling, and meaning. When life gives us lemons, we'll give it a juicy metaphor.

Maps

We often live in our heads. We get busy, and we forget we have a body. Although our brain and our body are designed to provide us with important cues and signals, our capacity to key in and make sense of them is tied to our ability to notice them to begin with. As we increase our awareness of what is both valent and salient for us physically and psychologically, our bodies become a more reliable GPS system. They can help us detect and navigate the meaning we make of what we feel and what we do with it. The very act of tuning in and identifying how our emotions are showing up on a psychophysical level increases the odds of us having greater influence over which meaning and response sequence we set into motion. Our ability to interpret our body's signals accurately provides us with clues in advance of what is to come, thereby creating a window for a more consciously considered perspective and interpretation.

If you've never meditated before, the act of simply noticing and/or dropping any movement of mind by way of thoughts, sensations, feelings, or emotions can be very difficult. We may not notice when our awareness has deviated from its mission and instead has begun to engage with its own mental phenomena. However, with practice and over time, we detect when our awareness is pulled in the direction of its own movement. We begin to notice the gaps or space between two thoughts, for example, when before all movement within our mindstream blended together indistinguishably. Similarly, when we practice noticing the body's signals and sensations relative to their valence and salience, we learn to use these clues as our barometer. They provide us a preview of what is to come, while it's still unfolding, as well as a map back to our inner equilibrium.

Putting the 3M's into Practice

Perhaps you already use mantras in your life today, and if so, you may want to keep working with a mantra you already use—though you may have never referred to it as such—or you can come up with a new one. If none come to mind, think of something you want to put into practice in your life. Maybe it's a new response to a not-so-new set of circumstances, like how you behave when you bump up against an old tension or dynamic with someone in your life or even someone you actively dislike. Reflect on what your objective is for that relationship or for the interactions you have with that person. Now, think about how you'd like to show up in the relationship to achieve that aim. Jot down any thoughts you may have on the topic in your journal. Can you think of any specific behaviors or actions you'll need to take to be able to show up as you'd envisioned? Put another way, what conditions within yourself will you need to summon to have the kind of interaction with this person that will lend themselves well toward your aim? What might you say to yourself in the moment to remind yourself of what you've reflected upon and are committed to doing differently to make that happen? Write it down and experiment using it the next time you have an interaction with this person. Afterwards, reflect how it went and whether there is anything you might do differently next time, perhaps a different stance or perspective you'll take, not being shy to experiment with any of the many options available to you that you've been learning about, such as perceptual or cognitive reframing, orienting your perspective to one or more views available to you through your own awareness, or one or more of the 12 Self-Discoveries.

It may not have occurred to you to see your own life and the various aspects of who you are in terms of a metaphor. It can be a helpful lens to apply to gain access to a different view of yourself and the various aspects of who you are and/or the many hats you wear in your own life. Is there a metaphor you can think of now that mirrors or represents these different elements of who you are and your life? Sarah, one of our coaching certification graduates and now one of our faculty members, chose the sun as her life's metaphor. When she was initially asked to think about a metaphor that captured various elements of how she perceived her life, she immediately thought of her Airstream, named Sunny, which had carried her through a recent period in her life in which she had left her marriage and the life she had known to set out on a new and unknown path. To this day, the image of the sun serves as a reminder of the things that bring her joy and energy versus the things that are dragging her down and depleting her energy. For her, the sun's rays represent the energy she is putting out into the universe and the positive impact she can bring to others' lives. She ended up having a silver necklace crafted of the sun in which she placed the diamond from the wedding ring of her first marriage as a reminder of where she has been, and the importance of these experiences in her life's journey. She can often be seen wearing her necklace in her Airstream, which also doubles as her office. Another of our program graduates chose a skein of birds flying in a V formation to symbolize his commitment to delegate more often among his senior team, remembering to allow others to take the lead. For him, this was a potent and apt metaphor to remind him that being a leader doesn't always necessitate taking the visible lead. We can lead by being part of the group's collaborative efforts, allowing other team members to shine and take their turn navigating. These are just a couple of examples to give you an idea of how you can personalize and craft your own metaphor to remind you of what's important to you. Often there is a symbolic or visual component to the metaphor that lends toward its ability to function like a mental cue. Here are some helpful questions to consider as you reflect on what your life metaphor might be.

1. What is the highest purpose or aspiration I'd like to embody in this life?
2. What are my greatest gifts and strengths I have to offer in this regard?
3. Of the various roles I am playing in my life right now, which ones are helping me live in alignment with the direction of my highest purpose?
4. Are there any aspects of who I am or the various roles I am playing that need to be reprioritized or elevated in order for me to move in the direction of the aspirations I have imagined for myself and my life?
5. What, if anything, would I like to stay the same, shift, or change entirely relative to each of the above elements?

Once you've had a chance to reflect and journal on these questions, see if any metaphors or images come to mind. They can visually depict or symbolize various aspects of yourself, your life, or your habitual tendencies you're committed to shifting along with their symbolic equivalent. Periodically, revisit your metaphor to see how or if it has transformed or perhaps even morphed into another metaphor entirely.

Our MindBody Map

The second meaning of "map" refers to our MindBody Map, a framework designed to help us see those aspects about ourselves we either aren't normally aware of or may struggle to see. The MindBody Map outlines four spheres of influence, our Self-Identity, Self-Expression, Social Identity, and Relationships, and how each impacts our overall wellbeing. First, it helps us to uncover the mental models, or conceptual frameworks, we draw from, either intentionally and consciously or inadvertently and habitually to make sense of our perceptions. Second, the map highlights where in our lives we may or may not be living in alignment with what is most meaningful to us—our values, beliefs, motivational drivers, and behavioral preferences. Finally, we can use the MindBody Map to shed light on the root causes, contributing factors, and impacts of our habits and unconscious patterns of belief and mindset.

The concept of MindBody was initially inspired by a teacher of mine, Tokpa Tulku, who introduced me to a practice in which the objective is to keep our awareness in sync with our body. Our mind often wanders away from what our body is doing in the moment. When this happens, you might salt your drink instead of the food on your plate or put the cereal box in the refrigerator and the milk in the cabinet, for example. We go entire stretches of our lives disconnected from one or more aspects of ourselves. Thus, the point of this practice is to bring your awareness completely into sync with your body. Instead of thinking of your mind and your body as separate, in this practice they become one, MindBody. Similarly, we can train our awareness to become aware of itself, its contents, and its movement. In this practice, we are mingling our awareness with each action, each word, and each sensation. When you engage in mundane tasks like brushing your teeth, making food, drinking your morning beverage of choice, or whatever it is you're doing, keep your awareness in step with your body. Notice when your awareness deviates or drifts away from what your body is doing.

The moment you notice, your awareness is already back. Take note of your bodily sensations as they arise. This practice consists of both attention training, keeping your MindBody together as the focus, and developing greater awareness of your bodily sensations.

The MindBody Map has its origin in what is known as the Motivational Drivers & Behavioral Preferences (MDBP), an assessment I originally designed to help coaches and their clients discern what isn't immediately obvious yet central to what is operative relative to their habits of mind (see Figure 9.1). I've used numerous behavioral assessments and 360 instruments over the years as a coach and HR executive; however, none produced exactly what I wanted to know about the person I was coaching, nor what I hoped my clients would learn about themselves. So, I created one that would.

Contemplated within the design of the MDBP and MindBody Map is Maslow's hierarchy of needs, in which our needs and expectations relative to each of the map's domains highlight personal norms that define what optimal looks like for us within each of those contexts. The five areas depicted in the MindBody Map not only shape and inform who we have become and are still becoming but help us uncover the mental models we've used up to this point in our lives to make sense of our experience. We function

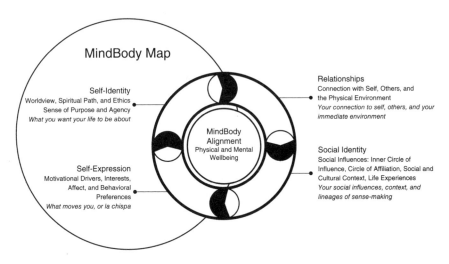

Figure 9.1   MindBody Map
Source: © Brain Capital LLC.

optimally when our MindBody needs are met, and the conditions to thrive are more consistently present. However, the idea that all of our needs would ever be fully or simultaneously met, or would permanently stay that way, is simply a myth. Like the term *syzygy*, which speaks to the alignment of one or more celestial bodies, such as the sun and the moon in conjunction (new moon) or opposition (full moon), balance is the temporary alignment of inner and outer conditions in the moment to produce a conducive playing field (Wikipedia, 2021). We are in constant flux with respect to everything in life, including our MindBody wellbeing, our mental outlook, and our perceptions, which means we have a lot of variables we have to learn how to juggle and navigate effectively for ourselves on an ongoing basis. *Our challenge and opportunity is to enact what we have direct influence over that will have the greatest incremental and positive impact relative to our context.*

Because our physiological needs often take precedence over all else and our brain is constantly making predictions and choices in favor of those needs, the more we engage in practices that promote our overall wellbeing, the more we set ourselves up for success across the board. In her book, Lisa Feldman Barrett makes a number of extremely helpful suggestions, like engaging in physical movement or changing one's context as a means of inviting a new set of parameters for our brain to navigate when the ones we're stuck in, emotionally or otherwise, aren't conducive (Barrett, 2017). She offers many specific suggestions, which I'll leave you to investigate first-hand.

As we saw earlier, we each have expectations we carry with us, irrespective of whether or not we are aware of them. Our ability to manage these expectations is dependent upon our awareness of them to begin with. The process of becoming aware of our expectations requires conscious examination of what they consist of. Many point back to our social influences while others are habitual, aligning in many cases to our own behavioral preferences. Even when our baseline needs are mostly met, if our expectations aren't, and we don't have the ability to discern or work with them constructively in that moment, they can easily become the loudest voice inside—and sometimes outside—of our heads.

The Five Domains of MindBody Alignment

The foundation of the MindBody Map is our wellbeing, what is referred to in neuroscience as our "body budget." We could say syzygy is a symbolic alignment between our mental and physical wellbeing and our capacity to act on this basis. Anyone who has ever been sick or suffered a serious medical or chronic health condition knows first-hand that everything we do is predicated upon our overall health and wellbeing. Similarly, if our mind is quite disturbed, we don't even feel our bodies. Thus, our MindBody wellbeing is visually depicted at the center, with each of the four domains either supporting or detracting from our capacity to act in alignment with our *ikigai*, a Japanese word for which there is no English equivalent that refers to our reason for being, our direction or purpose. We can't expect to receive anything back from something we don't regularly invest in. Even within a single day we move from having various of our needs met to having others only partially met, strained, or drained. When we are chronically taxed and depleted without frequent enough infusions of the opposite, we tend to burn out. The trouble is most of us don't have a personal baseline or framework to provide us with insight and a personalized map of the specific elements that factor into maintaining our psychological and physical wellbeing. One that factors in our behavioral drivers and preferences, for instance, or the mental models we habitually fall back on as a means to regulate our own and others' wellbeing. Each domain of our MindBody Map allows us to see where we may be depleted or operating at a deficit along with what it would take to replenish and bring us back into equilibrium, not just physically and mentally but existentially. How often do you consider your wellbeing and what's important to you from a variety of pertinent angles? While most of us would rather opt for the quick fix, we've only got one body and one mind. So, as long as that's the case, we're always going to need to keep our eye on the ball of doing our best to create and maintain optimal conditions for ourselves. That's if we're interested in being closer to the freshly lit end of the candle than the perpetually burnt-down one.

Our Relationships

The domain of Relationships speaks to the central role they play in meeting our fundamental need for connection and in shaping our overall MindBody wellbeing. We can think of our relationships in terms of ever-expanding layers of proximity, influence, and impact. These are relationships with loved ones with whom we enjoy close bonds as well as those with whom we regularly interact. But it also includes people we may have only met once or may never meet. While we may not think of the relationship we have to our immediate environment, such as where we live, our community, and the multitude of ecosystems of this earth, each carries profound implications for our lives. Finally, there is the most enduring relationship of all, the one we most frequently overlook, and that is the one we have with ourselves. Each and every relationship we have, whether seen or unseen, contemplated or not, has a profound effect on the very fabric of our being. We are constantly experiencing both the generative and life-giving elements of our relationships as well as the collateral damage we experience when they go awry, become difficult, or flat-out fail.

Let's say you get in a squabble with your pelvic affiliate over why they keep squeezing the toothpaste tube aggressively from the middle. But instead of committing to renew their efforts to work the toothpaste tube from the bottom up, they have the gall to change the topic to why you insist on loading the forks tine-side-up in the dishwasher such that they are poised and ready to stab the unloader. Or let's say that you politely ask your mate to stop texting the word "okay" as their only response to you if they care at all about conveying the affect of their meaning. Instead of just saying, of course, delighted to be clearer with how I actually feel, they lecture you on its sufficient meaning and that when they use it, it always means "good." Perhaps your teenager greets you by telling you they hate you and everything about pandemic life and suddenly refuse to conduct their lives mediated through Zoom, including their high school classes. Chances are even if you were looking forward to eating your bowl of oatmeal drowned with brown sugar, butter, and milk, it loses its appeal and sway over you in that moment. Instead, your mind and body may be flooded with mental impressions—that may or may not include expletives—not to mention sensory grime and residue left over from these unpalatable interactions, manifesting as sweaty palms, a flushed face and neck, or a tightened lump in the place where your heart normally beats freely in your chest. You might be preoccupied by your concern for your teenager's wellbeing and potential fallout from their impending Zoom strike or left wondering how you and your main squeeze never managed to cover the showstoppers before shacking up. In moments like these, or when things don't go as hoped in our relationships, nothing we do feels quite right—not even that first sip of coffee that normally brings with it inexplicable and unbearable joy. These kinds of exchanges and events happen many times throughout the day, each and every day. That's not even factoring in when things go seriously wrong in our relationships, which sadly also happens. We find out a colleague at work has been "con-kniving"—conspiring and conniving—behind our back, secretly sabotaging our efforts, while shamelessly taking credit for our work. Perhaps someone we love suddenly dies without us having a chance to say that last goodbye or tell them how much we love them. We all face these kinds of interpersonal dilemmas and predicaments, some less egregious, some more so, each moment we're alive. They add up. They end up taking their toll on us.

Conversely, when we experience moments of genuine caring and connection, the loving and unconditional acceptance and support of our friends and loved ones, they act as unguent for our easily bruised yet desperately in need of love selves. Each time we have a net positive exchange with someone, we are adding to the well of our overall being. Regardless of which kind of moment we find ourselves in, the invisible bean counter never stops tallying our gains and losses nor can we escape the ramifications of our wellbeing's rolling profit-and-loss statement. Since we're the ones who have been left in charge of our own MindBody operations, we're each responsible for figuring out how best we can find and capture value in the system, starting with the meaning we assign and derive from what happens to us. Once we figure out it takes a lot of practice and training in the various strategies we've been learning about to seize the moments we can do something about, we realize we better get on it. It takes as much untraining as it does intentional training to sort through and retool the conceptual constructs we rely upon to make the meaning we want our lives to have.

Identifying the beliefs and assumptions that no longer serve us and rallying around the voices that represent us better is the work we each have in front of us.

Our Social Identity

The domain of Social Identity speaks to the myriad experiences and social influences that have shaped, defined, and biased our perceptual tendencies and cognitive lenses. Like our relationships, our social influences impact us based on the relative proximity, weight, and value we assign them. Like inoculations, we receive doses of meaning intended to guide our actions based on the sense we make of topics ranging from how the universe came into being to how we came into being—God, the stork, the big bang, sex, or evolution—take your pick. This process of assimilation begins the moment we arrive—just after receiving our self-destructing mission details—you see, you already forgot. There is no stone left unturned relative to what we learn on topics as diverse as race, gender, culture, religion, ghosts, superstitions, the physical universe, you name it. We can liken each to the equivalent of basic military training, which in this context is more like boot camp for the brain. Our brain and our perceptions are shaped by our experiences, countless inputs from the moment we're born to when death do us part. From these myriad experiences, expectations, mental models, and biased narratives our habits of perception and interpretation are born. *We are the recipients and products of lineages of sense-making as much as we are expressions of our genetic birthright.* In one sense, the brain can be seen as a time capsule, a repository and keeper of ways of thinking, interpreting, and responding that reflect social norms and influences. From this, we receive a transmission of appropriate ways to respond and react relative to a variety of contexts based on what we have seen modeled by those around us—specific ways of thinking, interpreting, and responding to nearly every situation we can fathom.

It is from our social identity and our relationships that we receive the most consistent, direct, and indirect messages about the degree to which we pass muster, or whether we don't cut the mustard. It's hard to say exactly why some people are more inclined than others to feel a sense of duty to live up to the norms and expectations laid out for them, while others don't appear to give a flying duck or a rat's booty—expressions I've disguised to protect the innocent from expletives and butts. The existential weight one feels in this regard is thought to be a function of both our genetics and—you guessed it—our social influences, that is, our shared and nonshared environmental influences. For example, when we look at the genetic influence of the big five personality traits, as compared to how much they are thought to be an outcome of combined environment influences, openness comes in at the highest at 61%, with extraversion next at 53%, followed by conscientiousness at 44%, and neuroticism tied with agreeableness, each at 41%, which means that for at least these five discernible and extensively studied traits, our social influences are still thought to play a meaningful role in their presence or absence (Jang, Livesley, & Vemon, 1996).

Irrespective of how our desire to meet others' expectations of us may have cropped up in our psyche, in coaching people over the years, I've found there is often an inverse relationship—albeit an anecdotal one—between the extent to which people care about how they are viewed by others and their relative level of ease and contentment. The more one cares about how they are viewed, the less content and at ease they seem to be, though they are also often influenced by whether their motivational drivers are predominantly governed by intrinsic or extrinsic factors—as we explored briefly earlier. Irrespective of where you dangle on the scale of social ambition and/or conscientiousness—formal measurements in many assessments—it's hard to please oneself, let alone everyone else at the same time. Like Murphy's law, there must be some universal principle prohibiting both from happening at once. I've managed to explore and test that theory out, which is how I arrived at it. Trying to please everyone is a sure way to please no one—least of all yourself, although actively aiming to displease everyone can also be a nonstarter depending, of course, on one's goals—though decidedly easier to do.

Exploring the degree to which you are influenced by others' expectations and to what degree that has become a fixture in your own conscience is not only a worthwhile undertaking, but really important to do.

Only then will you discover the source of the voice you have in your head—the presiding judge—about what is right and wrong in this or that situation. That is also where you're likely to locate the other end of your nose rope. *Only when you make conscious the habits of mind leading you in circles around yourself but never fully to yourself do you begin to understand the difference. Only then can you make your way back to your rightful home.*

Self-Expression

The domain of Self-Expression speaks to how you naturally express yourself, both literally and figuratively, as well as where your chispa and joie de vivre like to hang out. You may recall from earlier discussions that chispa is the spark or flame that acts like a magnet or sorting hat for our interests, that which attracts or stirs our attention or that which repels or repulses us. When chispa's flame is kept alive, it can fuel our ikigai, our sense of purpose and fulfillment. Our self-expression also captures our behavioral preferences across a range of potentialities, with the understanding that our preferences are influenced not only by our habit but also by our context, and to varying degrees our genetic stenciling—for example, whether we tend toward faster or slower pacing, are more literal than we are figurative, or are less tolerant of ambiguity or change than we are of certainty or consistency, to name just a few, among many behavioral spectrums. We can also think of self-expression not only as how we show up, but what brings us unfettered enthusiasm relative to how we like to express ourselves.

Self-Identity

Finally, the domain of our self-identity speaks to those aspects of ourselves we hold as near and dear as our own lives, such as our values, our spiritual or religious beliefs, which may or may not be the ones we grew up with, along with our sense of purpose and agency. When our self-identity is in alignment with what we deem as most important and our needs and expectations are met, then we are optimally poised for self-actualization, or what I refer to in the context of coaching and personal transformation as capacity and emergence. When in sync, this trifecta is the ultimate syzygy, or alignment, of our potential.

As you've probably begun to see for yourself, doing the work to uncover your own meaning and belief structures is tantamount to you cracking the key to your own code, the mental constructs you've grown accustomed to parse your moment-by-moment meaning. By identifying the elements that make you tick and the degree to which you are or aren't living in resonance with yourself and what matters to you, the better poised you are to take action on what is within your direct influence. All of the actions you do or do not take add up to your life's results, which only you can configure to reflect and conspire toward your highest aims and inner compass. Otherwise, it's like shooting an arrow into the night sky; you never know where it's going to land.

10 | Cultivating Emotionally Intelligent Habits of Mind

When it comes to identifying and working with your existing habits, beliefs, and mental models, short of working with a coach who is trained to help you sort through and cull out what may or may not be serving you well, there are at least a few methods you'll be introduced to in this chapter that will be more than enough to get you started. The invitation is for you to continue refining from there, drawing on whichever methods speak to you and/or may best fit your situation. The first approach we'll explore highlights how you can use the MindBody Map to get to the bottom of what may be keeping you stuck in a particular habit or behavior as well as how you can create the inner and outer conditions needed to shift the habit. We'll then focus on how to surface our mental models, ones that are operative on both a conscious basis and subterranean level of what you're presently aware of. The first priority is to find a journal or notebook you'll use to capture your observations and insights as you work with these methods.

Be Vewy, Vewy Quiet, I'm Hunting Habits! He-e-e-e-e!

Start by identifying a habit you'd like to work with in this and the next several exercises. It can be any habit or set of interrelated habits you engage in on a daily basis, within the context of work or home or both. It could even be a habit of mind, something that is more a function of how you habitually perceive, interpret, and act upon your perceptions. Start by reflecting on why you've selected this particular habit or set of habits you'd like to work on. Why this habit? Why now? Next, write down as many reasons you can think of as to why you haven't retired this habit and what may be keeping you from doing so. What are the obstacles standing in your path? I'll take you through an example from my own life to give you an idea of what you're aiming for. Let's say somewhere along the way I have acquired a habit of working myself six feet underground. While by no means a new habit, it is like a ransom greater than its return.

Obstacles to changing this habit:

- I've led a start-up effort to launch a company for the past six years, which had no funding to speak of—I mean zero capital. Despite having to contend with some of the most inhospitable conditions one can imagine, mostly from unexpected sources, our small but mighty team managed to get the company and suite of products and services off the ground. The fact that we managed to take a business from literally nothing to something of this magnitude, not necessarily in size but positive impact, is remarkable.

- During this time, I've served in a number of capacities, many of which at the same time: co-founder, co-owner, CEO, business development and sales, subject-matter expert, client management and program delivery, chief education officer, programs design, content development, and faculty member, to name a few.

- Like many businesses, we had to trim back our team in response to business conditions and revenue streams shifting in the face of the pandemic and lost a few good team members along the way, resulting in a few lessons learned, one of them being that start-ups aren't for everyone.

- And I'm writing a book, which I've managed to do in seven months while being a CEO and a mom to four kids—two grown and two less grown. I am the sole breadwinner for my household.

- I play an active and integral role on four separate boards of directors for nonprofit organizations.
- At the moment, I am completing a global leadership training program with 144 leaders from around the world who were handpicked to participate, for which I am now also a facilitator.
- *I have what I'll term a Bodhisattva mindset, meaning I am willing to make significant sacrifices for the greater good and in order to benefit beings.*
- I have the belief (and experience) it takes work to do big things. No business—that is also financially viable—ever got built by sitting back and watching the clouds go by.
- *There is no doubt about it, I am a hard worker. While I don't wear it as a badge of honor, it is part of my self-identity. I come from a long line of hard workers, migrant farm laborers and bootstrappers. Were it not for their efforts, I wouldn't be who I am today, and I wouldn't hold the values I do today.*
- I spent 25 years working in corporate America, working twice as hard to make 75% as much money as my male counterparts, many of whom I was more qualified than in our respective fields.
- Lastly, I know that *busy people find a way to be busy regardless.*

Once you've written down all the challenges you can think of as to why you've not given up the particular habit, reflect on the following questions from the MindBody sphere of influence (see Figure 10.1).

My Responses to MindBody Questions

- Self-Expression: This habit manifests as working too much and taking on too much at once; not having enough downtime to replenish, to sleep, or to properly take care of my body and my mind. My inner

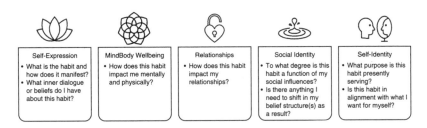

Figure 10.1   MindBody Map of Our Habits
Source: © Brain Capital LLC.

dialogue on the matter sounds like this: *To whom much is given, much is expected. I have taken a vow to work toward my own enlightenment and the commitment not to forsake or leave behind a single sentient being. My problems are luxury problems by and large. If I don't do this work, who will? Then again, if I kill myself in the process by overworking, I won't live as long.* Intellectually, I know this. I know when I deplete myself without replenishing myself, I can't be at my best. *If I destroy the mothership, what will I have left to give?* My grandfather died of a massive heart attack at age 59. He too was a very hard worker.

- MindBody Alignment: This habit impacts my physical wellbeing the most. I've gained a significant amount of weight over the past five years and had to have spinal surgery last year to remove one of three herniated discs in my cervical spine. I'm positive it was related to how hard I had been pushing myself, not just these past years but for most of my adult life. Cumulatively, I've just not slept nearly enough. That said, the work I'm doing makes me happy and brings me a deep sense of fulfillment and joy.

- Relationships: My work has at times negatively impacted my relationships, mostly with my loved ones but also with colleagues and team members who regularly need my time but are often unable to get enough of it because there simply isn't enough of it or me to go around.

- Social Identity: It's a bit of a conundrum because I end up working a lot in order to benefit others, yet when I work too much, I let others down. I have rightly received feedback from my team for working too much. It's the classic cobbler's children who want their cake, their cobbler, and their shoes—pretty sure that's not actually how the saying goes. Knowing the science of burnout and depletion intimately and then overworking myself ends up making for strange if not incompatible bedfellows. Without a doubt this is easily the most difficult job I've ever had, and I've had many big jobs. We've achieved huge aims with remarkably little means.

- Self-Identity: Ultimately, the purpose this habit is serving me is to be able to serve others at the level I am capable of. The remarkable work of our small team has enabled upwards of 22,000 people to go through emotional intelligence training in the three years since we launched our programs and roughly 200 people from across the globe to get certified as EI coaches and meta-coaches. As part of the coaching certification program, we offered upwards of 300 individuals the opportunity to get coached and gave free access to resilience training to 25,000 people and counting during the pandemic. We sponsored 15 coaches to complete their coaching certification with us on a work-study-internship basis. We're now leading our second cohort of 30 physicians through a six-month leader-level EI training certification program. I had the honor and privilege to speak at the United Nations to upwards of 6,000 people across the globe about the role of EI and personal agency as a means of igniting global impact to reach the Sustainable Development Goals. We launched our company in conjunction with a speaking engagement at the World Economic Forum in conjunction with Digital Intelligence (DQ) Day. I was invited by BBC Radio to give a talk on the role of EI in AI and recently had the honor of being invited by the vice president of Colombia to speak at an international event they sponsored exclusively for women, which drew a total of 12,000 participants. Our company's mission is, after all, to democratize and make accessible the application and embodiment of EI, which I feel confident in saying we've given it all we've got to do that.

- How is it serving me? I love this work. I love sharing it with others, and I also enjoy applying it in my own life. There is no question I'm doing work I love, and I'm living in alignment with my spiritual path and what is most important to me.

Now It's Your Turn

Once you've had a chance to reflect on what you've just written down, look at the list of obstacles you initially identified, the things you noted may be getting in the way of you changing this habit. Then, look at your responses to the MindBody questions. Does any of what you wrote relative to each shed any light on why this habit may be difficult for you to change? Do any of the obstacles you identified overlap with what you wrote in response to the MindBody questions? See if you can start to spot any beliefs or mental models you may have surfaced in this process. If you think you spot one, circle or highlight it in some way, given that you'll have a chance to come back to it in the next chapter when we explore the topic of mental models in greater depth. I've italicized these elements in my own reflections on my habit of overworking myself.

After using these tools to work through one of your own habits, what if any insights or ideas do you now have about what you may need to shift or come to terms with if you want to change this habit? What are the things you're going to need to change inside yourself, and what are the things you're going to need to change outside of yourself? This may be all you decide you want to do for the moment by way of reflecting on this particular habit or set of habits. If so, you can pick up here next time, or you can keep working with this habit in the next section, which will take you through the second part of this exercise, in which you look at the ideal conditions needed to change a habit.

Creating the Ideal Inner and Outer Conditions for Habit Change

Often, when we're working to shift a behavior or a habit, we don't pay attention to all of the conditions that are coming together in our external environment and our internal landscape to create circumstances ripe for allowing a habit to persist. As a result, the aspects you've not addressed will continue to give rise to the conditions for that habit to thrive. Eventually, we may give up trying to change the habit because we don't know what more to do relative to all of the factors that seem to be conspiring against us. In this next section, you'll learn how to spot which obstacles you're being held up by relative to your external and your internal environments along with some strategies to work with both types of obstacles.

Get your journal out, the one you've been using up to this point, and draw a line down the center of the page you're about to take notes on. On the left side, write "Outer Conditions" or "External Environment" at the top of the page. On the right side of the dividing line, write "Inner Conditions" or "Internal Environment." Now, reviewing the various obstacles you identified in the previous section relative to the habit you're presently working with, write down the obstacles that seem to be tied or related to outer conditions, that is, your external environment. Of the obstacles remaining, write down the ones you think may be related to internal conditions, that is, the landscape of your thoughts, feelings, emotions, expectations, beliefs, and so on. Do your best to separate the obstacles into these two types of conditions, external and internal.

Going back to our example—my own in this case—here is a quick summary of what I came up with, relative to the outer conditions and external environment:

- There is simply too much work to be done by one person with all I have going on in my life. I'm involved with too much.
- Outer circumstances are in fact challenging. We have a relatively small team and are attempting to grow revenue streams difficult for even big businesses with means to achieve. Finally, we are trying to maximize benefit across the globe without having an ideal organizational structure, financing, or size of team to do so.
- I do very much have my own personal financial pressures, just like everyone else does, which weigh quite onerously on me.

By way of inner conditions and internal landscape:

- A big part of my self-identity, as well as my social identity, is such that I believe I have contributions I must make within my lifetime and am equipped and motivated to do so.
- I respect the lineages on both sides of my family greatly and understand the hardships they went through in their lives. I feel I cannot let their efforts come to naught. I hold the weight of all their hopes and dreams, especially the ones that went unfulfilled.
- My spiritual beliefs inform and guide my actions. By virtue of my Bodhisattva vow, I have not only vowed to work toward my own liberation, I've committed to do so with the aim and aspiration of not forsaking or leaving behind a single being. That's a big job, especially while I'm still under the sway of confusion myself.
- I am of the mindset that hard work isn't negative but in fact necessary. What is our purpose if not to work for the betterment of ourselves and of this planet? What good is it to have this body and this mind if they aren't being put to good use to benefit all beings? What a waste to have been given the wherewithal and circumstances, all of the conditions one could ever hope to gather in a single lifetime, only to let them dissipate without consequence, without the feeling I laid it all out on the line and made a respectable run at it. Who knows what had to come together in order for me to have been given the opportunities I have been given? Who knows when I will have these circumstances again?

- *While we each have vast potential, we manifest and live into that potential in a limited and finite way according to how we perceive the purpose of our time on this earth, and how we respond to our circumstances.* Who would have guessed Harriett was right? While our potential is limitless, we each only have so much potential we will realize and bring to fruition in this lifetime, and that's it.

- Thankfully, I also know without our health and the basis of mental and physical wellbeing, we simply can't be at our best. Our best is limited to the extent our wellbeing, beliefs, and mindset are or aren't in mutual alignment and support. Therefore, I need to increase my priority over ensuring this vehicle I have on loan will perform optimally for as long as possible.

My Own Insights and Takeaways

- The greatest leverage I have with myself on this particular habit is to remind myself I can't benefit beings (or myself) if I'm dead or dead tired.

- I'll sum things up with an Indian saying I recently heard for the first time from a friend of mine: "If the water catches fire, what will you douse it with?" If the remedy loses its efficacy, then what?

Who knew a single habit could be so jam-packed? Now, hopefully, you see why changing our habits and behavior is more complex than simply one-dimensional. Imagine if someone were to hold the point of view that all it took to change a habit was to change what's happening in our lives on the outside. They might quickly fall into the trap of trying to rearrange the furniture in a burning house, to borrow the words of another good friend. If we can spend as much time familiarizing ourselves with the inner conditions of our own mind that give rise to our perceptions and, in turn, our interpretations and responses, then we can come to know and work with the whole story and not just a fraction of what is begging our full attention.

As you complete this exercise for yourself, you can do as I did, which is to sum up or reflect on the outer and inner conditions as you perceive them, or you can do so after the fact as you journal about any insights you gained. Once you've done this, look back over everything you've written, starting with the obstacles you identified to changing your habits relative to each MindBody sphere as well as this last exercise of identifying the inner and outer conditions present. See if you notice any patterns in your thoughts, beliefs, mindset, or mental models that tie back to or resemble one or more of the12 Self-Discoveries, either when they're helping or hindering. Feel free to use my example to start with, if you wish. It is often easier to see something about someone else's life. If you go through this process enough times, practicing with your own habits, soon you'll start see where in your life you're a dead giveaway. We always say what we mean, and in order to hear what is meant, we need simply to put on the right lens and listen for what wants to be heard. It may not always be communicated directly but is more like the concept and Japanese word *komorebi*, which means seeing the scattered light filtered through the trees. I'm not sure there is a term that conveys the same sentiment about our ability to see our own meaning filtered through various aspects of who we are, like our thoughts, our mindset, or our beliefs, but this is exactly what we need to train in learning how to listen and see. When we do this, we're training in igniting our inner coach—which is really just another way of saying our inner wisdom. Have fun exploring! I'm certain you won't run out of content to consider and to contemplate as you seek to understand the richness of meaning underlying your results.

Dealing with Outer Obstacles

As I mentioned early on in the book, there are many excellent resources and books that offer strategies for arranging one's external environment to break bad habits, like the ones James Clear offers in his book *Atomic Habits*, in which readers learn about the habit loop, whereby we break down the cues that precede our mostly unconscious cravings and habitual responses to our habits, and the feeling of gratification and reward when we do (Clear, 2018, p. 49). Clear does not disappoint, providing readers with a very clear means of creating new habits and breaking old ones according to the four laws of behavior change. By all means, delve into each of these resources, this being one of them, if you haven't already. I too will offer a few suggestions for working with your external environment and what you can do to create conducive conditions for habit change. But please don't lose sight of the fact that anything you attempt to fix by rearranging your environment to prime for desired responses to cues is always dependent on your inner capacity to carry those activities out not just once or twice but to stick to them, which is a function of your own awareness. That is, until whatever you're consciously working toward itself becomes a habit, which by definition of being a habit requires your minimum viable attention (MVA). We mostly acquire habits on an unconscious basis in response to cues in our environment unless we bring a level of conscious awareness to the cues themselves, which is why when we try to establish an intentional habit or break a bad one, the prerequisite is always our own awareness. Clear indicates as much when he writes about this phenomenon in his book: "Our responses to these cues are so deeply encoded that it may feel like the urge to act comes from nowhere. For this reason, we must begin the process of behavior change with awareness" (Clear, 2018, p. 62). This is precisely why this book has as its focus not just the seen, but mostly the unseen cues of perception itself and the sense-making and action sequences our brain sets into motion in response to both our outer and inner conditions.

Remarkably, it's not just a matter of removing the Modelo Especial from the fridge that doubles as our nightstand or the Doritos and taffy we've placed in a ring around our bed, it's about something more fundamental than that even—though for sure that helps if your goal is to cut down on alcohol and yummy junk food while you're watching late night television. It's about recognizing where we get hooked with regard to even more subtle mental cues, such as the valence and salience of emotions, in this case, our inner cravings and urge to fast-track to the reward phase. Yet, even when we get to what we think is the root cause or contributing factors of a habit, we are always in a position of having to spot the cues, be they external or internal ones. *Our conscious awareness is the necessary condition of what is required to unseat our habitual responses to cues—not just once and for all but on an ongoing basis.* We need to be strategic and intentional as we plant mental cues that tee up a desired response sequence. Since our brain is constantly predicting and appraising our ever-shifting context, setting into motion sense-making and action sequences relative to the cues in both our external and internal environments, we've simply got to be on our toes. For that we need to train in our awareness of the cues emerging from each domain, which are never static.

Lean In

By way of strategies to work with both our external and internal conditions that lend themselves toward predisposing a particular outcome, Lean management principles can be excellent methods. However, we often don't think to use them to discover or work with the value inherent in our mental processes whose outcome is shifting our own behavior and habits. But they absolutely can be used for this purpose. As we saw earlier, using a value stream map can be a brilliant way to see something you're struggling to see clearly or gain constructive perspective of. You could employ the value stream map, for instance, to get to a more objective perspective of the outer and inner life of a habit. Starting on the right-hand side of either a size A14 sheet of paper or any paper you like, draw yourself. Then, walk through each of the steps that occur up to the point of the habit you're following the path of, noting and drawing each step as you go along with the inner dialogue you may be aware of having along the way.

The five whys and root cause countermeasure (RCCM) methods, also tools that come from Lean, are brilliant at uncovering the heart of one or more aspects of a habit, like what purpose(s) it serves or its root causes. In the five whys process, we ask ourselves a question we'd like to know the answer to—presumably one that helps you discern the source or root cause of why something is occurring or behaving the way it is. For instance, Q1: Why do I overwork myself? A1: I overwork myself because I have too much on my plate. From our answer to the first question, we form the second question, Q2: Why do I have too much on my plate? A2: I have too much on my plate because I'm overcommitted. We then turn that response into our next question. Q3: Why am I overcommitted? A3: I'm overcommitted because I believe to whom much has been given, much is expected. In this example, we got to one belief among many that, as we saw before using the MindBody map, is at the heart of what is keeping this habit in place for me. We can go through up to five cycles of questions and answers until we get to what we call a "root cause." As we saw with my own example of why I chronically overwork myself, there can be, and often is, more than one root cause as well as likely contributing factors. Once we feel the root cause(s) we came up with are valid, and not simply symptoms, we complete the remaining steps of the RCCM process:

> Step 1: Are any of the reasons or potential root causes in fact symptoms and/or the result of a process or bigger ecosystem? If you try to fix a symptom, you'll likely not address the root cause, which is why it's important to discern the difference.
> Step 2: Can any of the root causes be eliminated on the basis of either not being a true cause or unactionable?
> Step 3: Of the root causes or contributing factors you've identified that are actionable, do any require further analysis on feasibility? If so, determine their relative feasibility before moving onto the last step.
> Step 4: For those for which countermeasures are both feasible and actionable, articulate the specific steps you'll take and how you'll know whether those measures have helped. Traditionally, SMART goals (specific, measurable, actionable/achievable, relevant, and time-bound) are developed at this point.

If we were to go through the RCCM process using my example, it would likely be a quick analysis. Unless I'm willing to change or give up the belief identified in the five whys analysis, as well as all the other beliefs keeping me locked into a habit that is ultimately self-destructive, then the discussion is done. Why? Because unless I'm willing to transform or work on this belief I have, there is nothing more to take action on. That is, unless you consider removing my computer, phone, and internet access an option. It would be a temporary solution to a symptom, however, and not a means to an end. If I were to do this, it would create a tremendous backlog of work I'd never see the light of day from. The other option would be to whittle down the activities I'm involved with, but again this is a temporary solution to a more pervasive root cause—in this case my belief that it's my duty to be involved and to contribute in ways that are commensurate with my capacity. You see, it's not an outer environment problem—though undoubtedly, it can be made worse by cues in my environment. At the core, it's an inner environment conundrum.

However, if I'm willing to acknowledge this and am willing to use other beliefs to counteract or offset the strength and potency of the hindering side effects of my well-intentioned beliefs, then it's worth giving it a go.

If I were to choose to do that, then my RCCM might identify a specific belief I have—in this case, my training in the science of depletion and the imperative for renewal—to counteract the various hindering beliefs I hold, then I can craft a SMART goal that might involve use of a mantra, a metaphor, or one or more of the 12 Self-Discoveries along with the various perceptual stances I can take relative to my own awareness when I catch myself falling prey to one or more of my own beliefs and/or unhelpful responses to cues in my environment. A final option here might be to reverse-engineer the feeling of reward without the associated path of pain to get there; again, something the VSM can be useful for.

What I like in particular about the use of the VSM, the five whys, and the RCCM along with the next Lean practice I'll introduce to you is that when used in combination, they are powerful methods to help us gain insight into a habitual tendency we're having difficulty gaining enough distance from or perspective about that we're not able to make heads or tails of why it keeps happening or how to upend it. You can easily swap out exploration of your habits with exploration of specific mental models, beliefs, or expectations you have. The only thing you risk in the process is gaining greater clarity and insight into what makes you tick in order to undermine what makes you stick.

Poke Yoke

There is one more method from Lean process management I'd like to introduce you to, referred to as poke yoke, a Japanese term that means "to foolproof." Remember in the 1980s when microwave ovens used to keep running even when the door had been opened? At some point, someone somewhere thought, "Yikes, that's dangerous!" An edict was issued: "Never shall a microwave oven in operation keep heating once its door has been opened," enacting a "foolproof" strategy and setting a new standard for microwave oven performance and excellence across the globe. Now back to the habit part. What might you do to poke yoke a habit or behavior you're trying to change? That or one or more of the outer or inner obstacles contributing to it? I'll give you an example of something I did to poke yoke one of my own habits, though admittedly it's an example of manipulating the outer environment to short-circuit a mostly unconscious habit I have that isn't all that complex or intractable. Nonetheless, I'll share it mostly for ease of illustration. I have a habit of reaching for my phone when I wake up in the middle of the night (my phone charges on the nightstand right next to my bed). What's more, when I wake up in the morning, I often reach for my phone first thing to check my email and WhatsApp to see what the rest of the world has been up to and may want or need from me while I've been asleep. I don't particularly like that I do this. I think it means the people who designed the phones to be uber addictive win when I do this. So, I made the decision to charge my phone outside of my bedroom at night. This is an example of how to poke yoke a habit. It's follows the same general principle Clear outlines in his book relative to short-circuiting a bad habit and creating a new one using what he terms the four laws of behavior change in which he takes readers through a brilliant methodology of working with the four components of a habit loop (Clear, 2018, p. 53). Looking at the habits you've chosen to work with, are there any you might be able to poke yoke? The ultimate poke yoke we have available to us, including working with our emotions, is our own awareness. When we position our awareness in such a way it apprehends only itself, it undoes the proverbial Gordian knot to whatever else we happen to be perceiving in the moment. Why? Because awareness itself is nonconceptual. When you position the non-conceptual towards the nonconceptual, all that's left is its natural qualities. Irrespective of how brief those moments may be, we are no longer operating in a conceptual mode or frame of reference. Instead we could say we're training in the nonconceptual aspect of mind. It's our mental elaborations, commentary, and sense-making that render the nonconceptual, conceptual. That's the playground we're most familiar with and generally most comfortable with.

These methods I'm sharing with you to examine and work with your habits and behaviors can help you spot what's at their core, what's at stake, and what impact the habit is having on you and others. Only after examining what's at the root of its purpose(s) does it become clearer what you're up against, and if you're motivated enough to want to change it. We often continue doing what we've been doing either because the stakes to change said habit aren't perceived as great enough or have yet to be fully conceptualized. That, or the purpose the habit serves for us outweighs our interest in its alternatives. It's often easier to keep doing what we've been doing rather than investing the time needed to outwit and unseat the conditions keeping it in place. In the process, we may neglect critical data that just might be the factor either on its own or in combination with other drivers that motivates us to want something different for ourselves. This is where getting a handle on what motivates and drives us can be elucidating. Let's not forget these tools are not just about changing your habits, they are about understanding how your perception of reality is responsible for all of your outcomes, including your mental states. You don't need to have a habit you want to change in order to use these methods. However, you still have to have a taste for wanting to lead a more conscious and intentional life, or none of this will interest you enough to actually do it. If you've made it this far in the book, I'd say you're interested enough—in fact, you're well on your way!

Working with Inner Obstacles

As we saw earlier in working with one of my own examples, one of the best ways to work with inner obstacles is to trace what story or belief you presently hold about it as well as how it may relate to a need, an expectation, a value, or an ideal. As with all habits and behaviors, what we do generally serves some purpose, and sometimes that purpose is counterproductive or actively harmful to yourself or others. That's our clue it's time to do something about it. Either way, we must first understand the conditions allowing this habit or behavior to languish and persist. Now that you've learned some methods for identifying where you stand relative to assessing the role outer and inner conditions play in habit and behavior change, let's turn our focus to some additional methods you can use within the framework of the MindBody Map.

Discovering Our Mental Models

Now, we'll explore several ways we can use the MindBody Map to uncover specific patterns of thought, beliefs, attitudes, or mental models that may pose obstacles. Let's first define what is meant by the term "mental model."

A mental model is a conceptual framework, a set of beliefs, or concepts we employ preconsciously, unconsciously, and sometimes consciously to make sense of our perceptions. As we've discussed throughout the book, we need to be able to respond physically and mentally to the endless variety of situations we encounter and take action accordingly. At the level of preconscious sense-making, our brain takes actions commensurate with getting our needs best met based on our specific context, by predicting and interpreting what and how it will need to take action. For better or worse, we don't have much say in that process. However, what we then do with our perceptions is what we can consciously take action on. You have now been introduced to at least four different ways to remember what you have influence over: the value stream map (VSM) of Perception, the Self-Discovery of Perception + Interpretation = Your Reality, the Self-Discovery of What You Have Influence Over, and the Awareness Matrix. If we leave it up to chance or habit, the path of least resistance, our mental models will continue to unconsciously bias and assert themselves in how we interpret and make sense of our experience. If we are motivated to exercise our influence, then we not only need to uncover our mental models, we need to decide whether they are worth keeping around or are in need of a makeover.

A mental model can consist of several beliefs or few and is often tied to or associated with other beliefs we have, either categories of concepts or a constellation of interrelated beliefs. That said, our mental models can be and often are to varying degrees at odds with each other. At times, they may be inconsistent and create tensions for us. The mental models we employ are shaped not only by our prior experiences, but in ways we've learned to react in similar situations. This process doesn't happen in a vacuum. We respond based on a specific set of circumstances and the context we find ourselves in. Even though some of our beliefs are absolute positions we hold, the context we're in may lead to their inconsistent application or absence of use entirely. For example, I have an absolute belief in the unfailing law of cause and effect. But if we take a specific context in which I have to decide between hitting a deer that suddenly appears in my path while I'm driving and swerving off the road or risk having a head-on collision with an approaching vehicle, I'll likely choose to hit the deer—despite my belief in karma and my stance of not wanting to harm other beings. That's simply to illustrate that our beliefs, like our values, may represent our philosophical or ethical stance but remain aspirational or hypothetical until we're in a situation or context in which we either do or do not choose to apply them. That, or our autonomic response system kicks in ahead of our conscious and intentional response.

As we've seen, what we believe is to a very large extent shaped by our social influences and our experiences that unconsciously reinforce those mental models. We tend to fall back on what we've been taught and have observed others around us doing. Our mental models often represent what we believe to be true, right, and accurate. Moreover, each time we employ them it serves to reinforce them, like how we relate to our reoccurring thoughts, feelings, and sensations and the meaning we assign them. Yet from another standpoint, our beliefs are nothing more than thoughts, concepts we've learned we have the wherewithal to place credence in or not. Similarly, it's our decision to continue believing what we already believe or to shift the beliefs we've outgrown or that no longer best serve our aims. *Until we make conscious what it is we believe, our beliefs remain hidden to us, like the presence of our own awareness.* Instead of being a conscious force for good, our beliefs and mental models act upon us inadvertently without our conscious consent or even knowledge. We just take for granted that this is how things are and we're unable to assume a different vantage point relative to what we believe to be true. As long as we remain under the sway of our unconscious beliefs, there is little to no chance for us to see there are other ways of being and interpreting our perceptions, which may serve us, everyone else, and the planet better.

In these instances, we could say we're stuck in our own view. There is a rigidity or fixed quality to our perspective. In the same way there is no room for additional knowledge in the mind of an expert or someone who thinks they know it all, there are no alternatives in a mind that remains fixed or closed. Allowing our beliefs to go unexamined or unexplored amounts to giving up our own agency. We can't control what we aren't aware of, not consciously anyway. As we learned relative to the Awareness Matrix, there is much that falls below the threshold of what we are consciously aware of. So while it's true we can do many things and perform many important functions without being consciously aware of them, we can't do anything intentionally without the aim or thought to do so. While it does take practice to remember in the moment we can employ our own agency of mind to shift our perspective, the value in doing so makes the proposition of having to familiarize ourselves with our own mind well worth our time and effort.

In the same way increasing our emotional granularity allows us to pinpoint and articulate what we are feeling with greater precision, uncovering our mental models helps us see how we habitually make sense of our perceptions, and, in turn, how we are likely to respond. So now that I've given you the broad strokes as to why it behooves you to gain familiarity with your beliefs and mental models, let's give it a go.

Don't Try to Cover the Sun with One Finger

Uncovering our mental models starts with uncovering the answers to the questions wanting to be asked. But because we don't know what we don't know and may not have someone to process our insights with, I've given you a set of questions to ponder related to each sphere of the MindBody Map, starting with your Social Identity. Highlight what stands out to you by way of mental models or beliefs you want to keep exploring using the methods you've been introduced to as well as the practices that follow. As you reflect on these questions, journal your responses:

Inner Circle of Influence
- How are your beliefs similar to or different from what those in your inner circle believe? What motto or metaphor best characterizes or describes those beliefs?

Circle of Affiliation
- Identify the circles of affiliation or "tribes" you identify with most closely. Have you chosen them intentionally? Why or why not? To what extent are they conducive or not and what makes them so?

Social and Cultural Context
- What are the main lineages of thought, mindset, and belief you've inherited? To what degree and in what ways do these traditions of sense-making still influence you? To what extent do they reflect spoken or unspoken norms or rules?

Life Experiences
- Reflect on the key experiences you've had up to this point in your life. What are they and what did you learn from each? To what degree have

these experiences defined you? How have they impacted your self-perception? How about your reputation, or how others perceive you?

Relationships

Now, consider the impact of your relationships and to what degree they are conducive or may detract from your overall MindBody alignment and wellbeing:

Connection to Ourselves
- How would you describe the relationship you have with yourself? On a scale of optimal to suboptimal, where would it fall? To what degree are you last on your list?

Connection to Each Other
- How would you describe your relationship with those you are closest to? What are the points of resonance or dissonance between you? To what degree do you consider the wellbeing of those you don't know?

Connection to Our Surroundings
- How would you describe or characterize your relationship with your immediate environment? On a scale of conducive to not conducive, where do you stand in relationship to the conditions you've surrounded yourself by and the company you keep?

Connection to the Earth
- To what extent do you consider your relationship to the earth and the many ways it supports your capacity to live with ease, health, and abundance? What actions are you committed to take to ensure we can continue to enjoy optimal conditions without destroying the earth?

Self-Identity

Your self-identity consists of the beliefs, ideals, and values that matter to you most and are usually a result of what you've consciously chosen for yourself as well as a result of your social influences. As you consider the following questions try to assess to what degree you're presently living in alignment with each:

Worldview

- If you had to sum up your worldview in a sentence or two, how would it explain what it is you believe and your outlook on life?

Spiritual Path

- Do you have a religious, spiritual, or philosophical stance that guides your beliefs and actions? If so, what are the main tenets or principles, and how do you translate them in your day-to-day life?

Sense of Purpose and Agency

- Have you identified your life's purpose, your heart's greatest desire, or the legacy you want to leave behind you? If so, describe them. Do you believe you have agency over your own life and outcomes? If so, explain. If not, what do you believe is responsible for your outcomes?

Values and Ethics

- What values do you hold near and dear? Now, try narrowing the list down to your top five, making sure to define what you mean by them. Similarly, what are three primary ethical stances or principles you try to live by and why?

Self-Expression

Your Self-Expression is how you embody the most consistent expression of who you are. Epitomized by how you perceive yourself as well as how others perceive you, or your reputation:

Motivational Drivers

- What makes you tick? What is the reason you do what you do? What gets you out of bed every day and keeps you wanting to press forward? Try narrowing your list down to your top three motivational drivers.

Behavioral Tendencies

- Which of your behavioral tendencies do you feel are your greatest allies, strengths, or gifts? Which of your behavioral tendencies do you feel may be holding you back or not serving you as well? Could it be a situation of under- or overuse of your strengths or what comes naturally to you?

La Chispa

- What is the spark to your flame? What are you so passionate about you can't imagine your life without its presence? What are you doing to stoke the fire of what's meaningful and important to you?

Transience and Imperfection
- What does the embodiment or expression of who you are look like? What is it like to be around you? What do you like about being around you? In what ways are you authentically expressing who you are? What are you holding back and why?

MindBody Alignment

In the same way our self-identity and social identity are integrally linked and often inform and reinforce one another, there is a close connection between our self-identity and our self-expression. When we're able to express and embody what is most important to us, what gives us joy and meaning, it feeds our ikigai, our sense of purpose and wellbeing. Finally, when we can surround ourselves with people and conditions that are conducive, it helps us create the circumstances to show up in a way in which we are authentic, and there is an acceptance of our transience and imperfection, a worldview that is best summarized by the Japanese concept of wabi-sabi. So often we think we need to achieve this elusive state of perfection, when in reality if we could just show up with open awareness and a tender-hearted stance of holding what is both precious and heartbreaking all at once, it would be more than enough.

Using the answers to the questions you answered for yourself relative to each sphere of influence, let's now use them to piece together ways in which they may be enhancing or detracting from your overall mental and physical wellbeing. As you ponder the following questions, ask yourself to what degree each sphere of influence is helping you to create conducive conditions to thrive or hindering you from embodying your full potential.

Self-Identity
- Are you living in alignment with what you value most and what is most important to you?

Self-Expression
- Is your self-expression the highest expression of your self-identity?

Relationships
- Are your relationships with yourself, others, your surroundings, and the world fulfilling your need for connection and conducive to your wellbeing?

Social Identity
- Are your inner circles of influence and affiliation, social and cultural contexts, and life experiences enhancing or detracting from your wellbeing?

The Impact of Our Mental Models, Attitudes, and Beliefs

The last method we'll use the MindBody Map for is to explore the impact our mental models, attitudes, and beliefs have on each sphere of influence and our overall wellbeing in much the same way we used it to see what's operative for us relative to our habits. It's a method that allows us to explore any of our mental models, attitudes, or beliefs by asking ourselves the following series of questions below. You should feel free to add any questions you think are missing or that more closely suit your aims:

Self-Expression
- What is the mental model, attitude, or belief presently at work and how does it manifest?
- What inner dialogue, attitudes, stories, or behavioral tendencies do I have that fuel this mental model or belief?

MindBody Wellbeing
- How does this mental model, attitude, or belief impact me mentally and physically?

Relationships
- How does this mental model, attitude, or belief impact my relationships?

Social Identity
- In what ways does this mental model, attitude, or belief meet the expectations I have of myself or others, and, in turn, others' expectations of me?
- Does this mental model, attitude, or belief help or hinder me, others, or the planet?

Self-Identity
- What purpose is this mental model, attitude, or belief presently serving?
- Is this mental model, attitude, or belief in alignment with what I want for myself?

Using these questions as your guide, you can take almost any topic and put it through the lineup of MindBody questions. Our ability to understand the mechanisms we use to make sense of our reality is essential if we want to exercise our full potential and what we have influence over by way of how we choose to interpret our own perceptions. In the same way we can't wake someone pretending to be asleep, we have to want to wake up. It won't happen on its own.

11 | Reimagining Emotional Intelligence

Reimagining emotional intelligence (EI) would first mean arriving at a definition of what it is. Since we've established EI doesn't consist of just one thing, nor does it describe or point to a singular form of intelligence that can be pinpointed or tied to specific circuitry within the brain, we can say it consists of various capacities, skills, and means we can employ to detect, interpret, and respond to our own and other people's emotions in ways that improve our ability to make sense of and connect with how our own emotions make us and those around us feel. We can think of EI as a conceptual framework and set of methods that when consistently practiced and applied lead to "emotionally intelligent" habits, behaviors, and outcomes. To the extent our concept of what it means to be emotionally intelligent includes being able to respond with the same level of skill to other people's emotions as our own, which historically it has, then it requires we take a much broader stance relative to what will be required of us to do so. But, I suspect we will need to rely upon many of the same capacities, skills, and methods we've been introduced to in the book along with a host of new ones.

An Emergent View of Emotional Intelligence

What this amounts to is a paradigm shift that takes the exclusive spotlight off of our emotions and instead situates our experience of them within the broader context of the brain's mechanisms of perception and sense-making. In the same way self-awareness describes a particular stance we can take relative to our awareness, our emotions are a particular expression of the way in which we perceive and try to make sense of our own sensory cues and signals. While emotions are without a doubt a powerful feature of the human experience, they are but one among many leading indicators we have of perceiving and relating to our present moment experience. Thus, ideally, we would learn not just how to relate skillfully to our own and other people's emotions, but to our own and other people's perceptions. To do this we would need to understand more globally about perception itself and the mechanisms by which we each have the capacity and means to relate more skillfully to our own and others' perceptions. We're all in luck, because that's exactly what we've been learning about throughout the book. Let's recap.

To What End and with What Purpose in Mind?

In the same way I'm not particularly interested in definitions of EI that aren't actionable, I feel the same way about perception. Anything we're attempting to learn for the purpose of applying and embodying not only presumes we have the capacity to do so but that there will be some discernible set of outcomes when we do. This requires us to articulate what it is we are training in, how we train in it, and what it looks like when we do. Why train in familiarizing ourselves with our own awareness as our primary means of relating to our own and other people's perceptions? Here are the primary reasons; so, we can:

1. Operate from a place of conscious awareness and enact the various stances of our awareness beyond the mostly passive and unconscious ways we often move through our lives, oblivious of what we do and do not have influence over, responding habitually to cues.

2. Relate to and make sense of our experience going beyond our conventional self-other, subject-object perception of reality to access different qualities of knowing and being and adopt a perspective that is open, aware, flexible, and not exclusively bound by a handful of habitual stances we're accustomed to operating from.

3. Take action on what we have the capacity to influence within ourselves irrespective of context, using our own awareness and perceptual stance as the jumping-off point for how we interpret and act on our perceptions.

4. Cultivate the natural qualities and authentic expression of who we are in ways that bring benefit to ourselves and others, bringing skillfulness to our relationships and our ability to express, extend, and receive love, care, and acceptance.

5. Create the conditions for our own and others' wellbeing while living in alignment with the things that matter to us most.

While by no means an exhaustive list of why you might want to train in your own capacity for awareness, I can't think of too much else we would want that isn't addressed in one or more of these outcomes. Not that I am suggesting they are unreachable unless we formally engage in training. It's simply the case that the odds tip in our favor when we do, if for no other reason than we aren't leaving the variables up to chance or habit. When we train in what we have direct influence over in ourselves as a means of impacting our outcomes, we not only open up the possibility to reach our present-moment potential, but we also drastically improve our chances of tapping into the natural wisdom of our emergent capacity (see Figure 11.1), which is another way of saying the qualities of our awareness come into view.

Present-Moment Potential and Emergent Capacity

Since we are by and large the beneficiary of the perceptions our brain curates for us, our opportunity to influence occurs at the level of how we position our awareness, and how we consciously choose to interpret our perceptions. Having the wherewithal in the moment to shift our own

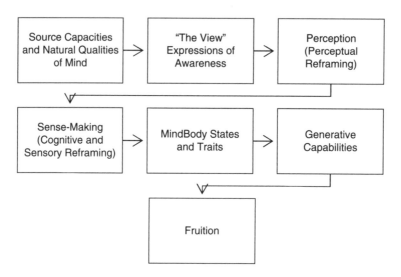

Figure 11.1   Present–Moment Potential and Emergent Capacity
Source: © Brain Capital LLC.

perspective, to reinterpret sensory signals and cues, and to be able to reframe how we make sense of our perceptions is where our power lies. Conscious sense–making and the methods we employ are the variables we have the possibility to influence. But to do so, we need to be able to access and maneuver our conscious awareness. Ideally, we need a habit of or practice in training our own awareness and the capacity to connect with its qualities and expressions in the present moment. A definition of this capacity might sound something like this: *"Our present-moment potential is the emergent capacity we each possess to bring into view our own awareness as the primary means to access our inherent qualities as a vehicle for the expression and agency of our own mind, irrespective of context."* The model I'm proposing is based first and foremost on how perception and emotion work relative to brain functioning and equally importantly on our ability to apply those insights in a manner that allows us access to what we have conscious influence over in the process. Let's recap what those elements are and the key components we can train in (see Figure 11.2).

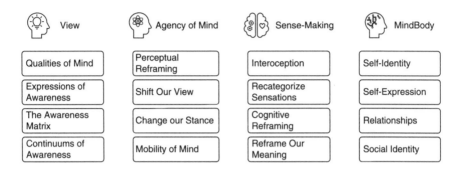

Figure 11.2 Our Means: Our Inner Coach
Source: © Brain Capital LLC.

Our Means: Our Inner Coach

We learned six ways to Sunday what we have the possibility of influencing within ourselves. We got our first peek of that in the value stream of perception and through the lens of two of the self-discoveries that identify where in that equation we have the greatest influence: "Perception + Interpretation = Your Reality" and "What You Have Influence Over." At the most fundamental level, our awareness gives us the potential to shift our perspective, our own view, relative to our context and gives us the capacity to reframe the meaning we assign our thoughts, feelings, and emotions. We have the ability to navigate our day-to-day experiences, which we do operating under varying levels of conscious awareness or lack thereof. Among them, we get to decide what kinds of experiences we expose ourselves to and how we make sense of them, as well as what we add to our mental Kanban, or storehouse of knowledge, by way of learning, application, and reflection. Finally, we were introduced to some ways to create the internal and external conditions to thrive. Let's review your inner coach's source of wisdom and wherewithal.

Our View, Our Awareness, and Agency of Mind

You learned what you do and do not have the capacity to be consciously aware of in the Awareness Matrix and how the variables of your experience behave differently when you're operating under the influence of what you have the capacity to be consciously aware of versus when you're not. You were shown new ways to become familiar with and practice trying on different stances of your own awareness, allowing you to shift or perceptually reframe the various ways in which you have the capacity to be aware. In so doing, you start to get a glimpse of the inherent qualities and expressions of your own mind even though you may not have never noticed them before—either because you didn't think to look or didn't know what you were looking for when you did. By learning to pay attention and practicing various ways you can be aware, you not only expand what you are consciously aware of, but you can also exercise different stances or views relative to what you perceive. *Our capacity to change our own minds is the most fundamental kind of agency we each have access to, independent of inner or outer conditions, context, or circumstances.* I can't think of a more empowering or inclusive message for us each than that.

By training in awareness, the smallest common denominator of what you have influence over within yourself, you gain access to your agency of mind. Your own awareness is the primary gateway to do anything consciously or well, including what's required to enact all other cognitive and sensory reframing techniques. In fact, there isn't anything we come by intentionally that isn't reliant on us engaging our conscious awareness. Even the statistical learning that takes place below the threshold of what we are consciously aware of still requires the inputs of our prior knowledge and experience. It just may have never occurred to you to think about the source of your own agency and what you have influence over in this way.

You were oriented to the natural qualities of your mind and its various expressions that allow you to shift your own view and perspective not only relative to mental and physical appearances but with respect to your own awareness. You learned your awareness can operate with and without mediation of you as the observer—the self-other, subject-object frame of reference through which you typically perceive reality. You were shown the many ways in which your awareness can adjust its own view, which can be articulated as expressions on a continuum, each possessing the four main qualities of the mind, recognizing they aren't actually separate from each other in our experience of them. Among its many qualities, our awareness has "capacity" or the ability to maneuver itself, which we have termed our "agency of mind." Our mind can calm and still itself, it can narrow its attention or it can become vast and spacious in its scope, or it can become fixated or preoccupied, which can take the form of perseveration or rumination. Our mind can also free itself by dropping or letting go of the object to which our attention is clinging.

Because of our habitual tendency to orient our awareness toward everything but itself, we remain at the mercy of what we anticipate perceiving next. Absent consciously directing our attention, we're only afforded the perspectives our brain anticipates and curates for us based on an ever-evolving set of outer and inner parameters and conditions. Even though everything still functions in this state, including how we're accustomed to perceiving reality, it isn't necessarily with conscious or intentional awareness—in fact I'd posit that most of the time it's not. But the moment we intentionally move from passively perceptive to consciously aware, we change our perceptual stance, thereby changing what's possible in the next moment. We alter the trajectory of our view and everything else that follows: the path of what can be seen, the meaning we make, and the subsequent actions we take.

Reframing Our Meaning

Our next best shot at altering our course of action is by changing how we relate to our perceptions, starting with how we interpret what we perceive. To do so, we can employ any number of cognitive and sensory reframing techniques that put the job of sense-making back in our own hands. Let's review the various methods we have at our disposal to reframe the meaning we make:

- The 12 Self-Discoveries, consisting of cognitive and sensory reframing cues and techniques that prompt us to remember the various ways we can relate to what we perceive, encouraging us to break out of our predictable habits of interpretation.
- Lean process management methods: value stream mapping, the five whys, root cause countermeasure (RCCM), and Poke Yoke.

- Recategorization of our bodily sensations using our interoceptive awareness; using specific language and emotion concepts to name and describe one's interoceptive experience in the moment.
- Using the MindBody Map to surface the variety of go-to mental models we unconsciously employ. By uncovering what may have previously been invisible or opaque to us, we can consciously shift how we make sense of what we perceive. We can choose meaning that evokes intentional ways of being as opposed to interpreting our experience exclusively through the lenses of our upbringing, social influences, and prior experiences.

By becoming aware of our beliefs, mindset, and underlying mental models, we not only increase our options to reframe our interpretation of whatever situation we're presently faced with, we increase our odds of being able to respond more skillfully when we do. *The questions we ask ourselves allow us to imagine new potentialities, which become our possible future.* Alternatively, we may choose to physically change or shift our context altogether, forcing the brain to engage its perceptual sense-making activity in accordance with its new context. But even when we do that, we're still going to be at the mercy of our perception and interpretation of the new context. Each of these methods relies on us being consciously and intentionally aware in the moment, as we saw in the Awareness Matrix—that is, until our consistent application of the various methods becomes closer to second nature, which like our habits then doesn't demand quite as much of our conscious effort in employing them. Bear in mind, however, that even our habits are adaptive to our context and not static. Thus, the methods we employ to work with them must also be.

Our Knowledge and Experience

We have the ability to change the contents of our mental Kanban, a metaphor for the brain's storehouse of residual knowledge and prior experiences. We can do this by learning new concepts, gaining new experiences, acquiring new ways of thinking, or deepening our proficiency relative to what's already in inventory, so to say. Each time we expand our knowledge and experience, we influence what our brain has to draw from with respect to the more unconscious elements involved in perceptual processes as well as what we have available by way of methods and mental models as we can use to work intentionally with our habits of mind.

Our Context and Wellbeing

Finally, depending on a variety of outer and inner conditions and the impetus to do so, we can change our context in any number of important ways. The MindBody Map provides us with many methods to be able to evaluate our current level of alignment and fulfillment relative to the meaning we want our lives and relationships to have. The map can be used to determine where we may be out of whack, and then provides us with methods to better see what's at stake if we don't make adjustments. Among the various methods you learned, here are the main ones:

- Surfacing your mental models relative to each of the MindBody spheres of influence and becoming mindful of where in your life you may be relying on outdated or unexamined ways of thinking and being.
- Exploring the potential root causes and impact our habits, attitudes, and beliefs have on our lives by MindBody domain.
- Understanding how our motivational drivers, needs, expectations, and behavioral preferences predispose and influence how we show up in relationship to ourselves and others.
- Determining which aspects of our lives may be out of sync or alignment and using the various methods mentioned previously to work with trouble spots to create the conditions to be able to come back into alignment—recognizing our wellbeing is always in flux and never set.

A New Paradigm of What It Means to Be Emotionally Intelligent

I'm proposing we start with what we have influence over in ourselves, placing an emphasis on what we need to develop within ourselves in order to truly embody what it means to be emotionally intelligent. If we start by giving rise to the causes and conditions to become aware of our innate qualities and expressions of mind, then we can rely on what we have access to in the moment to be wise and skillful based on the circumstances. If we can enact what we have agency over in ourselves, then whether we name its outcome "teamwork" or "inspirational leadership" or any of the other competencies of emotional intelligence that have to do with relating skillfully to other people matters less than the fact that we're ready to show up to each new situation able to discern and act skillfully based on what's needed. For instance, we can infuse loving kindness, care, compassion, and concern for others' wellbeing into our interactions, and because we are aware and can rely upon the ability to change our stance, our perspective, and the meaning we make, we can choose which mental disposition and view might best fit any situation.

The key is that we make a commitment to train in what will make the difference for us in real terms versus laying stake or claim to the result before we've established sufficient means within ourselves to get there. We like to do that as humans though, don't we? We get very wrapped up in how things will be, how we will be, and how wonderful everything will be. We don't have much experience being present-moment focused. We like to make plans, get everything sorted, and arrange things to make ourselves feel better. We think, if I just do this, or if only the situation were like that, I will finally feel happy, safe, and at ease. But that is just a myth. If we haven't practiced working with our own mental states, particularly the gritty, tough, or stubborn and untenable ones and gained some skill in conscious sense-making, when do we expect these magnificent changes within ourselves to take place? Let's start with being nice now. Being a good friend now. Being a good listener now. Not being stingy. Not being an egocentric asshole. Let's keep it simple, shall we? When we become obsessed with the outcome without having done our inner work or having the skill to create the conditions within ourselves in each new moment, which is the only place our opportunity exists, then it's easy to become overly focused on reaching a certain set of outcomes and what we call it while missing the main point. We crystallize the outcome instead of showing up with whatever the situation and interpersonal dynamics may ask of us.

Of course, I'm not saying not to have aspirations or a rough plan of what you think it will take to get there, but until you can deal with your own mind and your interpretation of what's happening in each new moment, whatever you outline for yourself remains purely theoretical and aspirational.

At the most fundamental level, we each only have access to what we have developed by way of habits of conscious awareness and dexterity from within our awareness to shift our perceptual stance. Having made that our primary focus, in any situation we find ourselves in, we can turn to that aspect of ourselves, our capacity to be awake and aware, to be observant of what's taking place right now, and how best to relate to whatever is unfolding. We each have what we need if only we would stop to notice what we already have. We don't have to shop around or compare or contrast EI models—adopting a mine-is-better-than-yours mentality. We already have all the resources we need to guide and inform our actions; we just need to train in accessing and gaining dexterity and skill in their embodiment. The qualities of our own mind are not different than our generative capacities or our receptive and conducive MindBody states. They are simply expressions of them. What I'm terming our "present-moment potential and emergent capacity" is a fancy way of saying that right now is the only moment you have the capacity to influence, to allow your awareness to come into view as a vehicle for how you can express your qualities and highest potential. Within yourself right now you can summon your own awareness. Your own awareness, which you may normally think nothing of, is your inner teacher, your inner coach, that has the capacity to offer you real-time wise counsel in how you view, make sense of, and respond to your own and others' perceptions. It is by virtue of your own awareness that you have immediate access to and the possibility of agency within yourself. This is the first step to doing anything consciously or well.

Generative Capacities and Receptive MindBody States

If we look at a handful of the generative and receptive MindBody states that naturally emerge from our qualities of mind and expressions of awareness, we can see the various conducive ways we can be with ourselves and others (see Figure 11.3). When we practice the full breadth of perceptual stances available to us, it inevitably predisposes and guides our sensory and cognitive interpretation of whatever is unfolding, setting into motion a different

Spacious	Cognizance	Presence	Capacity
Open-Minded	Discerning	Reflective	At Ease
Comprehensive	Capacity to Know	Clear-Minded	Calm
Big Picture	Aware	Awake	Introspective
Long View	Perceptive	Conscious	Inner Directed
Receptive and Inclusive	Intuitive	Fully Present	Nongrasping
Accommodating	Intelligent	Illuminated	Adaptive
No Observer Effect	Sensitive to Context	Resonant	

Figure 11.3   Generative Capacities and Receptive MindBody States
Source: © Brain Capital LLC.

set of outcomes than if we arrive with their opposites, which come more naturally to us by virtue of ego's narrow stance. In so doing, we also afford ourselves a different kind of knowing that isn't necessarily bound or limited by the self-other, subject-object stance we default to out of habit and by virtue of our functional design.

Resultant and Context-Specific Stances

Similarly, there are a variety of context-specific stances we can take with our awareness that yield certain outcomes or results (see Figure 11.4). We know all too well what can happen when we become extreme or stuck in any of these stances or when our awareness falls below the threshold of being consciously present, awake, and aware. These are just a smattering of perspectives we're already well versed in by virtue of habit. Some of these perspectives may very well be what the situation calls for but can also be the cause for us missing other vantage points that fall outside of our normal self-other, subject-object stance.

In sum, our own qualities of mind create all manners and possible ways in which we can be aware and the various perceptual stances and expressions our awareness can embody. The essential point is that we take every

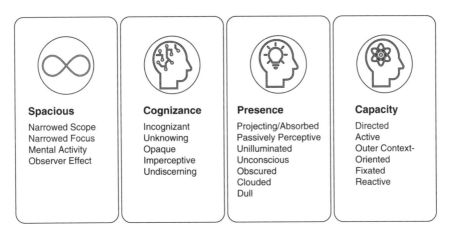

Spacious

Narrowed Scope
Narrowed Focus
Mental Activity
Observer Effect

Cognizance

Incognizant
Unknowing
Opaque
Imperceptive
Undiscerning

Presence

Projecting/Absorbed
Passively Perceptive
Unilluminated
Unconscious
Obscured
Clouded
Dull

Capacity

Directed
Active
Outer Context-
Oriented
Fixated
Reactive

Figure 11.4   Resultant and Context-Specific Stances
Source: © Brain Capital LLC.

naturally existing opportunity in our daily lives to gain familiarity with the various perspectives our awareness affords us and learn how to shift nimbly between them in the moment, which only happens by virtue of practice and training. Gaining dexterity and access to our conscious awareness is the necessary condition, the jumping-off point for all other practices and strategies we've been introduced to not only in this book, but in all other methods whose aim is to make us more skillful or to help us show up in alignment with our values.

Is the Observer an Illusion?

Most of us toggle between a state of being passively perceptive to having the perception that we are both the observer and so-called "owner" of this mansion we call a self, consisting of a mind and body, which is really more of a temporary house-sitting gig. We now have some idea of how much time we spend engaged in activities that only call for our passive perception, and the myriad functions and processes we are completely oblivious to when it comes to taking care of the house we've been left in charge of. Our perception of being the observer, who is cognizant and aware and able to shift our view, could very well turn out to be, like our perception of agency, an illusion whose purpose is just that—a seamless and well-orchestrated facade, albeit an important one insomuch as ego acts as a cohesive interface between the complexity of what our brain must do to keep us alive and our impression there is someone in control, not to mention someone on whose behalf we are acting.

If we didn't have the facade and hadn't yet fully realized how to rest unwaveringly in nondual awareness, the question remains, how would we have the conditions to wake up? It is by virtue of our temporary yet functional appearance as an embodied self that we have the necessary conditions to come to know ourselves and each other. It is in this state of being we share both a profound and mysterious sense of the beauty of the universe while experiencing an at times unbearable brokenheartedness arising out of our awareness of our own and others' suffering. Learning how to embrace each new moment with a stance of open awareness and a tender-hearted care for ourselves and each other slowly undermines and erodes our habitual stance of self and other. Right now, this thing we call and identify with as a "self" serves as our vehicle; it's what we presently have available to us to experience what it means to embody our own awareness and its natural qualities.

As a practicing Buddhist, I've often wondered on what basis I, or anyone else for that matter, would be able to gather the conditions and clear away our obscurations if there weren't other beings whose presence allowed us the grace and opportunity to do so. It seems only in relation to one another in an embodied form do we have the potential to clear up confusion and work for the benefit of ourselves and others as our primary means of being able to connect with the perfection of our capacity for cognizance. Not to be confused with becoming perfect—which is an ego-based and futile endeavor—but rather finding the inherent perfection, raw beauty, and transience of what it means to be a *sentient* being. And with that, we arrive at where we began, back at our mission of finding our way toward ourselves and toward each other. Despite feeling as though our heart may burst wide open as we witness and experience both the temporal joy and suffering of being disconnected with our own true nature, it's when we allow ourselves to embody the qualities of our own awareness we arrive at unconditional love of ourselves and others.

If true, and there is no observer or self performing the magic behind the pervasive hallucination, it would no doubt provide an evolutionary advantage worth covering up, at least until we are each ready to experience who we are unmediated by an observer or a self. Whatever we choose to believe about this experiment we call life and our mission in it, it's what we have to work with. Illusion or not, it's what we've got. Irrespective of who this observer is or whether there is an observer or not, the construct still functions. Even though it may very well be limited, we can still work with it. After all, what other option is there? So, unless my assessment of our capacity for agency of mind and conscious awareness is completely off base, that's my story, and I'm sticking to it. If we want to have full access to our agency of mind, it requires us to gain enough familiarity and practice with each of the ways in which we can be aware and come to rest fully in our natural state. When we use our own awareness to shift our perspective, our relationship to what we perceive shifts the trajectory of meaning we make and the actions we take, which is why it's so important for us to come to realize our full potential, by which I mean our present-moment potential for awareness itself.

All's Well That Ends Well

No good story should end without paying homage to a Shakespeare play with a quote thrown in for good measure: "There is nothing either good or bad, but thinking makes it so." It is my sincere hope and wish that as you are finishing reading this book, you've managed to take away at least one or two nuggets of wisdom in the form of your own insight that you can continue to ponder and apply in the context of your own life. If by no other means than repetition alone, hopefully, you're also walking away with knowledge of where you have the possibility, the capacity, to influence your own outcomes and the role your awareness plays in the process. As far as what is to become of emotional intelligence, I believe it will remain relevant and valuable. The journey I have been on these past years has convinced me we can all benefit from bringing along its theories and models to match our understanding of the neuroscience of emotion and the specific practices we can each employ to embody its timeless wisdom. I feel it is also important to adjust our perceptual stance of what it means to be emotionally intelligent to include where our emotions fit within the broader equation of perception itself. From my side, I hope to have given you each a small glimpse of what that might look like. Until we meet again, I'll leave you with these two profound quotes, the first by the Buddha found in the Dhammapada, as captured by Alan Wallace in his book *Fathoming the Mind*: "All phenomena are preceded by the mind, issue forth from the mind, and consist of the mind," (Wallace, p. 12). The second quote is from Yeshé Tsogyal (757–817 CE), considered a pre-eminent master in her own right, a terma, or treasure, revealer, who attained complete enlightenment within her lifetime: "When you look within to discover yourself, you will see there is nothing to see. The very recognition of this 'seeing' is what we refer to as the 'View.'"

Notes

Preface

1. Minding refers to how we perceive and pay attention, using our mind's own awareness and powers of observation.

Chapter 1

1. The 12 competencies are grouped under the four specific domains as follows: Within Self-Awareness is the competency emotional self-awareness. Within the domain of Self-Management are the competencies emotional balance, adaptability, achievement orientation, and positive outlook. Within the domain of Social Awareness are the competencies empathy and organizational awareness. Finally, within the domain of Relationship Management are the competencies influence, coach and mentor, teamwork, conflict management, and inspirational leadership.
2. Dr. Richard Davidson goes by the name Richie.
3. Richie Davidson is quoted in an article in *Mindful* regarding the measurable impact of contemplative practice on the brain, "We've shown in the laboratory that meditating for a half hour a day for two weeks is enough to produce changes in the brain" (Delehanty, 2017).
4. Lisa Feldman Barrett speaks to the origin of the triune model of the brain, what she terms "one of the most successful misconceptions in human biology," which she explains begins with a model of the human brain consisting of layers: the innermost geared toward our survival, our alleged emotion system known as the "limbic system" sitting atop that, and finally our allegedly rational and uniquely human cortex wrapped around that (Barrett, 2017).

Chapter 2

1. For some time now, I've been referring to the valence and salience of our emotions because it made sense to me to think of the energy of our emotions in these terms. When I investigated to see if there was any scientific research on the topic, lo and behold I found there was—lots of it. Here is the upshot of what I discovered on the topic in scientific literature: "Dimensional models suggest that emotion is best understood as occurring within a dimensional space, most commonly a two-dimensional space spanning valence and arousal. Emotional valence describes the extent to which an emotion is positive or negative, whereas arousal refers to its intensity, i.e., the strength of the associated emotional state (Feldman Barrett & Russell, 1999; Lang, Bradley, & Cuthbert, 1997; Russell, 2003, all cited in Citron et al., 2014)." To that I added the dimension of speed and duration based on Richie Davidson's work on resilience in which he talks about the rapidity with which we recover from a setback as well as how quickly or easily we go down the rabbit hole to begin with—my wording, not his.

2. I wasn't aware until reading the last chapter of *How Emotions Are Made* that this phenomenon is referred to in scientific circles as "affective realism" (Barrett, 2017).

3. "Your affective niche includes everything that has any relevance to your body budget in the present moment" (Barrett, 2017).

Chapter 3

1. "The amazing fact is that through mental activity alone we can intentionally change our own brains" (Richard Davidson).

2. A metaphor my teacher, Chokyi Nyima Rinpoche, often gives of what happens when studying the Dharma yet never practicing or applying it.

3. The terms "red pill" and "blue pill" refer to a choice between the willingness to learn a potentially unsettling or life-changing truth by taking the red pill or remaining in contented ignorance with the blue pill. The terms refers to a scene in the 1999 film *The Matrix*.

4. A phrase that has become somewhat commonplace inspired by the title of a poem originally written in French by Violet Fane, "Tout Vient a Qui Sait Attendre."

Chapter 4

1. Everett's many worlds theory goes on to posit there are also other versions of ourselves that, in turn, experience other versions of reality. I want to thank William Wootters, Williams College Professor in Physics, for talking with me on the topic and pointing me in the direction of work I would have otherwise been unfamiliar with.

Chapter 5

1. The term "emotion concept" comes from Lisa Feldman Barrett's work and describes the specific words and concepts we use to ascribe meaning to what we feel, lending toward what she terms increased "emotional granularity" (Barrett, 2017, p. 105).

Chapter 6

1. Even though I've chosen in this context to use the words "mind" and "awareness" and "consciousness" synonymously, please know that they have nuanced yet very important distinctions within Buddhist philosophy. For example, "sem," the word for mind in Tibetan, typically refers to confused mind. However, in English, the word has no such distinction.

Chapter 7

1. "Hit the Road, Jack" is a song written by the rhythm and blues artist Percy Mayfield and first recorded in 1960 as an a cappella demo sent to Art Rupe. It became famous after it was recorded by the singer-songwriter-pianist Ray Charles with The Raelettes' vocalist Margie Hendrix (https://en.wikipedia. org/wiki/Hit_the_Road_Jack).

Chapter 8

1. I say "potentially" here because our habits depend on our inner state and the outer supports we give them.
2. Newton's three laws of motion: (1) Objects in motion (or at rest) remain in motion (or at rest) unless an external force imposes change. (2) Force is equal to the change in momentum per change of time. For a constant mass, force equals mass times acceleration. (3) For every action, there is an equal and opposite reaction (Howell, 2017).

References

Ades, K. (2019). *What you focus on grows: Stories for your Frame of Mind.* https://www.amazon.com/What-You-Focus-Grows-Stories-ebook/dp/B07SFZ83WL

Bargh, J. A., & Morsella, E. (2008, June). *The unconscious mind.* US National Library of Medicine. Retrieved from https://www.ncbi.nlm.nih.gov/pmc/articles/PMC2440575/

Barrett, L. F. (2017). *How emotions are made: The secret life of the brain.* Boston and New York: Mariner Books.

Berkovic, E. (2017, February 8). *Why does your brain love negativity? The negativity bias.* Marbella International University Centre. Retrieved from https://miuc.org/brain-love-negativity-negativity-bias/#:~:text=Much%20research%20has%20been%20done,known%20to%20cause%20neu-tral%20feelings

Brown, B. (2021, March 1). *Brené with Dr. Susan David on the dangers of toxic positivity, Part 1 of 2.* https://brenebrown.com/podcast/brene-with-dr-susan-david-on-the-dangers-of-toxic-positivity-part-1-of-2/#close-popup

Cave, S. (2016, June). There's no such thing as free will. *The Atlantic.* Retrieved from https://www.theatlantic.com/magazine/archive/2016/06/theres-no-such-thing-as-free-will/480750/

Citron, F. M. M., Gray, M. A., Critchley, H. D., Weekes, B. S., & Fersti, E. C. (2014). Emotional valence and arousal affect reading in an interactive way: Neuroimaging evidence for an approach-withdrawal framework. *Neuropsychologia, 56*(100), 79–89. Retrieved from https://www.ncbi.nlm.nih.gov/pmc/articles/PMC4098114/

Clear, J. (2018). *Atomic habits*. New York: Avery.

Davidson, R. J., & Begley, S. (2012). *The emotional life of your brain*. London: Hodder & Stoughton.

Delehanty, Hugh. (2017, December 13). The science of meditation. *Mindful*, https://www.mindful.org/meditators-under-the-microscope/

Filevich, E., Kühn, S., & Haggard, P. (2013). There is no free won't: Antecedent brain activity predicts decisions to inhibit. *PLoS ONE*, https://www.ncbi.nlm.nih.gov/pmc/articles/PMC3572111/

Frankenfield, J. (2020, August 28). *Artificial neural network (ANN)*. Investopedia. Retrieved from https://www.investopedia.com/terms/a/artificial-neural-networks-ann.asp

Gardner, B., Lally, P., & Wardle, J. (2012, December). Making health habitual: The psychology of "habit-formation" and general practice. *British Journal of General Practice*. Retrieved from https://www.ncbi.nlm.nih.gov/pmc/articles/PMC3505409/

Goleman, D. (1998). What makes a leader. *Harvard Business Review*, November-December, 94.

Goleman, D., & Davidson, R. J. (2017). *Altered traits: Science reveals how meditation changes your mind, brain, and body*. New York: Avery.

Howell, E. (2017, March 30). Einstein's theory of special relativity. Space.com. https://www.space.com/36273-theory-special-relativity.html

Jang, K. L., Livesley, W. J., & Vemon, P. A. (1996, September). Heritability of the big five personality dimensions and their facets: A twin study. *Journal of Personality*. Retrieved from https://onlinelibrary.wiley.com/doi/abs/10.1111/j.1467-6494.1996.tb00522.x

Katie, B. (2008). *Who would you be without your story?* (C. Williams, Ed.). Carlsbad, CA: Hay House.

Mlodinow, L. (2018). *Elastic: Flexible thinking in a time of change*. New York: Pantheon Books.

Moore, J. W. (2016, August 29). What is the sense of agency and why does it matter? *Frontiers in Psychology*, p. 1272. https://www.ncbi.nlm.nih.gov/pmc/articles/PMC5002400/.

Rangjung Yeshe Wiki - Dharma Dictionary. (2003). Dran pa. Retrieved from http://rywiki.tsadra.org/index.php/dran_pa

Thaye, J. K. (1998). *Calling the guru from afar.* (E. P. Kunsang, trans.) Kathmandu, Nepal: Rangjung Yeshe Translations & Publications.

Wallace, B. A. (trans.). (2018). *Fathoming the mind: Inquiry and insight in Düdjom Lingpa's* Vajra Essence. Somerville, MA: Wisdom Publications.

Wikipedia. (2021, March 28). Syzygy (astronomy). Retrieved from https:// en.wikipedia.org/wiki/Syzygy_(astronomy)#cite_note-5

Acknowledgments

I've been blessed with a journey full of strong women as my examples. My mom was one of very few women working as an engineer in her field of expertise in the 1970s, who after being widowed at age 19 with a baby, went on to raise me and complete all but her thesis toward two PhDs, one in engineering and the other in industrial organizational psychology. Thank you for your immense generosity and support to me and my family over the years. To you I owe my chance at the life I'm blessed to be living. My Grandma Grace, who modeled both an untiring and relentless work ethic and unparalleled love and generosity, was the epitome of a Catholic Bodhisattva if there ever was one. Grace was my connection to my father, whom I lost as a baby, and was in her own right very much a second mom to me and to my daughter Sonya. Grace may very well be a contender for having made the greatest number of flour tortillas by hand of any single person over a lifetime—top 10 at least. I was at Grace's bedside along with my two aunts Dianna and Norma when she took her last breath. She left this world as gracefully as the meaning of her name, which mirrored how she lived her life. My friend Jane, who was the one person who truly saw me and understood both the complexity and simplicity of my being, thank you for seeing me. And last but not least among the women who have been my bedrock, my daughter, Sonya, the fourth in a long line of whipsmart and purpose-driven women who with her sheer brilliance and love will nudge humanity in the direction of new ways of living so as not to destroy the planet. And to my three sons, Daniel, David, and Dylan, may you each live unencumbered by the narratives the men of this earth have inherited and instead find your true and authentic identity, the natural face of your own awareness. To my beloveds, directly named or not, you know who you are and the steps of the dance we've taken together in this life. To each, I owe my heartfelt gratitude and aspiration to awaken and embody an unselfish, patient, and kind love. Thank you, Peter, for being my love and my rock.

Though I've not had many mentors to speak of apart from life itself and fellow travelers with whom I've briefly brushed paths, I have had one enduring teacher-student relationship since I was 20 years old. To my teacher, I owe much. Thank you, dearest Rinpoche, you have made this life worth showing up for. There's no greater gift than the one you've given me—introducing me to the one thing that makes all the difference, the natural face of my own awareness. May I and all beings recognize and gain stability in the wisdom of who we really are. It is with a deep sense of gratitude I thank my fellow sangha members, colleagues, family, and friends, whose kindnesses have provided sustenance along the way. Thank you for leaving me breadcrumb clues as I navigate my way through the scary and confusing bits to be greeted by the hugs of support and friendship awaiting me at the other end. Like the squishiest, most tender marshmallows one can imagine, you've cushioned me from life's blows, offering me both a softer and more loving landing. To you each, I offer a cozy spot at the hearth of my unconditional love and acceptance.

About the Author

S. Michele Nevarez is a native of Wyoming and grew up in Montana and Colorado. Her fondest childhood memories were spent standing on her head listening to KC and the Sunshine Band, flying with her Grandpa Billy Goat—as she affectionately nicknamed him—in his twin-engine plane across the wide-open skies of the Big Horn Basin, and eating delicious flour tortillas with her Grandma Grace and Grandpa Felix while discussing the origins and meaning of life, which is when she first learned there is a Lady named Luck.

Michele studied and lived in Spain and France before setting off at age 20 on her life's greatest and most important journey to Bodh Gaya, India, where she met her beloved teacher Chokyi Nyima Rinpoche and first began practicing Tibetan Buddhism. After graduating from Bryn Mawr College with a degree in religion, she moved to Boudhanath, Nepal, where she undertook further studies in Buddhist philosophy at Rangjung Yeshe Institute, a university she helped found.

While working in human resources and leadership roles across multiple industries which she did for nearly 25 years, Michele received her master's degree in Positive Organizational Development and Change from the Weatherhead School of Management. Thereafter, she co-founded and became the CEO of Beyond EI focused on helping businesses and those who lead them gain the knowledge and practical skills to become agents of world benefit through the practical application and embodiment of their own EI, namely, through applied coaching and training programs such as the Emotional Intelligence Coaching Certification (EICC) program.

She presently serves on the boards of two Buddhist meditation retreat centers, Gomde UK and Tara Mandala, as well as well as two nonprofit organizations, Shedrub Development Fund, supporting the monasteries, nunneries, and humanitarian projects of her teacher, and Dharma House International.

Michele has two stepsons, Daniel and David, who she has had the honor to watch grow into kind and honorable young men, and her daughter Sonya and son Dylan, both of whom she made from scratch and who are by far her greatest contribution and equally her heart's joy. While she remains a Wyoming girl at heart, she has made Western Massachusetts her home, surrounded by a mostly wild yet loving bunch: Louis, Tom, and Guru, the stray cats; Mr. Bo Jingles, the neighbor's cat with a collar that, you guessed it, jingles; an array of wildlife consisting of hummingbirds, deer, owls, a woodpecker, an occasional possum or skunk; her boyfriend, Peter; his kids Maya and Walker; her kids, Sonya and Dylan; and, most recently, a particularly friendly bear named Bernie, who has made several remote, live appearances on Zoom meetings from the back deck.

Index

NOTE: Page numbers in *italics* refer to figures.